FROM THE
Left Bank

FROM THE
Left Bank

*Reflections on the
Modern French Theater and Novel*

Tom Bishop

NEW YORK UNIVERSITY PRESS
New York and London

NEW YORK UNIVERSITY PRESS
New York and London

Copyright © 1997 by New York University
All rights reserved

Library of Congress Cataloging-in-Publication Data
Bishop, Tom.
From the Left Bank : reflections on the modern French theater and
novel / Tom Bishop.
p.   cm.
Includes bibliographical references and index.
ISBN 0-8147-1260-6 (clothbound : acid-free paper). — ISBN
1. French drama—20th century—History and criticism.   2. French
fiction—20th century—History and criticism.   3. Experimental
fiction, French—History and criticism.   I. Title.
PQ556.B57   1997
840.9'0091—dc21   96-45819
                                      CIP

New York University Press books are printed on acid-free paper,
and their binding materials are chosen for strength and durability

Manufactured in the United States of America
10 9 8 7 6 5 4 3 2 1

FOR THOSE WHO SHARED MY JOURNEY
AND THOSE WHO SHARE IT STILL

Contents

PREFACE   ix

BEGINNINGS   1

PART ONE: THEATER   11

  1   Changing Concepts of Avant-Garde in French Theater   15
  2   Two Decades of Theater in Paris: 1937–1957   25
  3   Pirandello and French Theater   41
  4   From Text to Performance: The Dialectics of
     Contemporary Theater   64

A. Introduction to Giraudoux, Cocteau, Anouilh   73
  5   About Jean Giraudoux   75
  6   Jean Cocteau Revisited   86
  7   Anouilh's *Antigone* in 1970   95

B. Introduction to Barrault   105
  8   Jean-Louis Barrault   107

C. Introduction to Ionesco   113
  9   Ionesco on Olympus   115

D. Introduction to Jean Genet   123
  10   Role Playing in Jean Genet's *The Maids*   125

E. Introduction to Tilly   131
  11   Interview with Tilly   133

F. Introduction to Sartre   139

   12   Sartre, A Life   141

   13   No Exit   146

   14   Becoming Sartre: The *War Diaries* of Jean-Paul Sartre   158

G. Introduction to Beckett   165

   15   On Samuel Beckett: 1906–1989   167

   16   "Heavenly Father, the Creature Was Bilingual": How
        Beckett Switched   177

   17   The Concept of Truth in Beckett's Discourse   185

   18   The Loneliest Monologues: Beckett's Theater in the
        1970s   194

   19   Camus and Beckett: Variations on an Absurd
        Landscape   212

PART TWO: THE NEW NOVEL   229

   20   The Image of Creation in the Works of Claude Simon   231

   21   *The Inquisitory* by Robert Pinget   240

   22   *The Park* by Philippe Sollers   243

H. Introduction to Robbe-Grillet   247

   23   *The Man Who Lies:* An Interview with
        Alain Robbe-Grillet   249

   24   Robbe-Grillet's Geography   264

   25   Conversation with Robbe-Grillet   277

NOTES   287

INDEX   295

All photographs appear as an insert following p. 138.

Preface

The pieces that make up this book were written in English or in French over the span of some thirty-five years for books and periodicals in the United States and in France. What they have in common is that they all deal with French culture, and especially with French theater and fiction. Intended for various audiences and dealing with subjects of considerable diversity, these pieces of criticism are different in tone. But they share a single authorial vantage point: I write on things French as an American looking at France, but as perhaps a special American, one who was not born in the United States, who learned French before he learned English, who feels almost an insider when speaking of France, and who has spent an entire professional life working on France. These pieces, then, are the views of an American Francophile, but not an uncritical one. In French literature, theater, and culture I have found remarkable nourishment for a lifetime of work but that does not mean that I approve of everything. Still, I tend to write on what I appreciate rather than what I dislike; accordingly *From the Left Bank* deals with some of what is best in French literary culture in the twentieth century.

Many of these texts are presented here relatively unchanged from their original publication; others are somewhat reworked; others still—those originally written in French—are translated and adapted by me. They are all quite faithful to the texts as first published. Since they stem from different moments of the past, the reader is requested to keep the date of composition in mind in order to understand why, for instance, a particular text on Robbe-Grillet fails to take into account those books not yet written at the time, or why in another, Jacques Chirac is described as the Mayor of Paris when he has since become the President of the French Republic.

ix

PREFACE

French works are referred to by their English titles except in a few cases where it seemed important to mention the French title also. For works not translated into English, the French title is given together with an equivalent English one. Quotations are in English, either from published English language translations or in my own translation (indicated in the notes).

I am deeply grateful to the Florence Gould Foundation for its support at various stages of the writing of this book. Its kind encouragement has been crucial for me.

I would also like to thank Margaret Parker and Christine Maillard for their assistance with the manuscript in various stages.

Beginnings

Paris, October 1982. Backstage at Jean-Louis Barrault's Théâtre du Rond Point, people were still rushing about frantically even though the play was about to begin. It was not that structured chaos which sometimes deceptively presages a smooth-running operation, that proverbial opening night panic which melts away when the curtain finally goes up. Theater professionals—actors, directors, managers, stage hands, makeup experts—are familiar with this last outburst of madness before the careful preparation of the rehearsal process asserts itself, the disparate elements fall into place, and confidence displaces anxiety.

Our problem was that we were not pros. There could be little assurance that in fact all the little pieces would come together and that it would "all" come out alright. Eugène Ionesco's flowing white beard had become loose and needed glue before he could go on as Lord Tennyson; sociologist Jean-Paul Aron was muttering elegant yet very annoyed epithets, in sharp contrast to the lovely, dignified gown he was wearing as Queen Victoria; Alain Robbe-Grillet, fully ready (his beard, being his own, did not need repairs), had enough time to make ironic comments on the frantic goings-on that managed to rattle director Simone Benmussa, who was in the last throes of a salvage operation to straighten out the wings that novelist Florence Delay was soon to wear as Ellen Terry modeling for her pompous painter-husband, played by drama critic Guy Dumur. Oblivious to all around him, Dumur was going over his lines yet again in preparation for his finding himself on the other side of the footlights for the first time. Joyce Mansour, the last of the surrealist poets, who had agreed to perform only on the condition that she could smoke a cigar on stage, was searching all over for a match needed to start up a Davidoff of truly epic proportions. The others contributed their share to the confusion. Tiny Rodika Ionesco, dressed as a saucy upstairs maid, was chasing after the makeup person to adjust her husband's beard. The fact that Catherine Robbe-Grillet and several others had nonspeaking walk-on roles gave them a greater detachment from the proceedings, but they were there, nevertheless, cluttering the stage that needed to be emptied to prepare for the raising of the curtain. Only Nathalie Sarraute, elegantly severe in a tuxedo, was a reassuring figure of Olympian calm. Not one to worry unnecessarily, she seemed serene and she knew her lines.

As for me, I knew my lines too, but I can't say that I knew absolutely that I knew them. But a little anguish is good for the creative process, and I felt reasonably confident. In my dressing room (my dressing room!), I had carefully put the final adjustments on my British naval lieutenant's uniform and fussed over the hairpiece that transformed me into the romantic lead, John Craig, who was about to woo and win the ravishing Ellen Terry. In the midst of all this (to me) strange effervescence, I was nervous and excited. In other words, I had a good case of stage fright. In a few minutes, the curtain would rise before a house packed with the who's who of Paris. For once, instead of being in the audience, I was to be on stage.

Of course, performing in Virginia Woolf's *Freshwater* was not the climax of my professional career as a university professor, but it was a wonderful moment for me to be playing (in French!) in this show, planned as a distraction, with a number of my friends who are among the most illustrious figures of the French cultural scene. We were to give eight performances, in Paris, New York, London, and Spoletto.

After one last once-over in front of the mirror, I left the dressing room, made-up, ready to go. I needed to get over my jitters and the somewhat disconcerting thought that, at age fifty, with my wig and beautiful chocolate soldier's uniform of a turn-of-the-century naval officer, I might seem slightly ludicrous in the role of the young leading man. Aside from Florence Delay and Guy Dumur, who had already been on the boards, the rest of us were rank amateurs. I wondered if they also had this strange feeling of being someone else. I had trouble believing that this character in disguise who was going to step forward on stage in a few minutes to speak his text was myself. And yet, this feeling was not unfamiliar to me; in fact, I knew it well. I had felt it every time I had been named to some function and every time I had been honored in some way, as if each title or each distinction awarded to me, pleasing though it was, designated some official public persona who was not quite myself, or rather with whom I could not completely identify. I was not sure whether this was due only to my personal history, or whether this interior distance (which is not always easy to handle—from time to time one would prefer simply to be one with oneself and ask fewer questions) is simply the intellectual's typical attitude.

We all managed to get through these last minutes as best we could. Dressed as a maid, Rodika Ionesco was still frantically looking for glue for Ionesco's beard that refused to hold in place. Robbe-Grillet, fully ready, was busy heckling Simone Benmussa, while Jean-Paul Aron, draped in a splendid cape, was bantering with my wife, Helen, who insisted on taking a photo of him. "A souvenir shot," she said. He accepted with a laugh, and just as Helen stepped back in order to frame him head-to-toe, he posed, leaning against a door, raised an arm with a grand, theatrical gesture, then pulled back his cape and, to general stupefaction, appeared in red underpants: "You must admit, a man is a beautiful thing," he said. Everyone laughed—except Simone. "Come now, Jean-Paul, hurry up," she said. "The curtain goes up in ten minutes." He went on to play Queen Victoria with remarkable aplomb. With his long, thin face and his precise and drawn-out elocution, his black bonnet and long dress, he offered a marvelous caricature of British majesty that brought down the house.

When the warning bell finally sounded, we were all ready to go. Ionesco's white beard was in place; Florence Delay's dress was finally adjusted; Guy Dumur put his text away as our glances crossed, Joyce Mansour lit up her gigantic cigar—the time had come. We were in our places on stage; we heard the three raps that announce the start of all French plays; the audience became silent; one spectator cleared his throat, another coughed; then finally, no more noise. The curtain went up.

If this evening has remained inscribed in my memory, it is certainly not for the brilliance of its acting. We all were and remained amateurs. The public knew this and in fact attended because of it, in order to see Ionesco play Tennyson stumbling through his text (even though he had it in front of him), to see Jean-Paul Aron in drag as Queen Victoria, to watch Nathalie Sarraute as a dignified butler. It was a merry romp; we all had a great time and we were a hit. For me, the

Freshwater evening somehow symbolized my affective links to France, which had their roots in my childhood, and to my lifelong passion for the theater.

I came to know France before ever setting foot in the United States and I learned to speak French before knowing a word of English. Early on, I was uprooted and have remained an outsider the rest of my life. Austrian born, educated in France for a while, I became and am happy to be an American who devoted his career as a university professor to making French language, literature, and civilization known in the United States and to a lesser degree, American culture in France. As an intermediary between two countries, between two cultures, I have found myself in a precarious yet always fascinating position, a bit like someone who tries to bring together his two dearest friends, hoping that they will get along like brothers, but aware of their differences, their faults, and their strong points, and concerned that they might not understand one another.

I was born in Vienna in 1929 to an Austrian father and a Hungarian mother. I spent the first nine years of my life there. Each year, I would be taken to Budapest for a holiday with my mother's family. Very early on—just about as far back as my recollections go—I was interested in politics. These were the 1930s, the rise of Nazism. In our circles—I came from a Jewish family—Hitler was at the time the principal subject of conversation and concern, and like my family, I lived with hatred for Germans. Imbued with nationalistic feelings for Austria that were as ardent as they were ephemeral, I wrote anti-German poems. These feelings were exacerbated in 1938, at the time of the Anschluss, when we were forced to leave our country. The memory of this annexation has never left me: the entrance of the German army in a Vienna decorated within the space of hours with enormous swastika flags (which certainly were prepared in advance!), Hitler, Göbbels, Göring, and other Nazi leaders haranguing a gigantic crowd of Viennese delirious in their enthusiasm and delighted to be a part now of the great German Reich. It was more than enough to overwhelm a nine-year-old Austrian nationalist for whom Germany was evil incarnate—and he was not mistaken.

Thanks to my father's uncanny ability to obtain a passport not stamped with the fateful letter "J," we left Nazi Austria for good, for Budapest. We then spent nine months at my grandmother's. With my brother, Emile, four years my elder, we secretly listened to Radio

Moscow, which we took to be the only "free" radio since Russia seemed to be the only voice opposed to Nazism. Finally, near the end of 1938, my father announced that we were going to settle down in Paris.

Paris! To my young mind, this charmed name evoked the most romantic scenes. Especially those of a novel which I have completely forgotten, including its name, except that it ended (the obligatory "happy end") with the reunion of a boy and a girl on the Champs-Élysées, where they embraced and kissed *in public,* with the Arc de Triomphe in the background. This picture-book image, if ever there was one for me, summed up at the time the irresistible attraction of the French capital. I really think that this image, born out of my secret readings, nourished me with dreams and hopes that I have kept within me and which helped me to deal with this loss of all sense of security that marked my childhood.

We arrived in Paris in December 1938. My Aunt Claire, who lived there, taught Emile and me the rudiments of French required for us to start school a few weeks later. I was not yet ten; the Germans had made me flee from what had been home; I thought that by taking refuge in France, we would find allies, people who would understand my situation. When I first set foot in a French school, the kids called me "boche." I couldn't imagine a worse insult. From that moment on, I was single-minded: to forget German, forget that mother tongue on account of which others identified me with the people I hated.

Three months after my arrival, I spoke French almost fluently. My greatest sense of pride during that year was to earn an excellent grade in French six months after starting school, 13 out of 20 on the French scale, something like a B+. Naturally I continued to speak German with my parents, but as soon as I closed behind me the door to our apartment, I only spoke French, even with my brother. To speak French meant not only to avoid that terrible misunderstanding of which I had been the victim but also to be admitted into this new world, integrated into it—or almost. I say "almost" because such an uprooting does leave deep scars, makes you look at life around you differently, and brings to your sense of identity a lasting doubt and fragility.

Moreover, this "new world" in which I began to feel comfortable threatened to fall apart; war was looming on the horizon. At first, our father had spoken of this exile in terms of a temporary measure: we needed to wait and see the turn events would take. But as the months went by, it became perfectly clear that we would not be able to return to Vienna. My father, a businessman, opened an office in Paris. Concerned about the ever more precarious future in Europe, he had applied for a visa to the United States. When it was granted, he decided to go, to look things over. He left for New York at the beginning of the summer of 1939. Two months later, the war broke out.

My mother sent my brother and me to spend the summer in a camp in Britanny, a few miles outside the town of Dinard. When war was declared, she decided to leave us there because children were being evacuated from Paris and other cities, on the theory I suppose that they would be more protected and better fed in the country.

In Dinard, my brother quickly made friends with young persons his age. I tried to follow along but that was not always possible: I was ten years old and they were fourteen or fifteen. I got in their way. The few friends I made lived in town, that is, too far for me to go by myself; as a result, I lived in almost complete isolation. As a foreigner—and what is even worse—an enemy alien (!)—my mother was not permitted to live near the coast; things were not easy and I saw her rarely. My father had requested visas to enable us to join him in New York as quickly as possible. Alone across the Atlantic, he was struggling to start a new professional life. During that time, my brother went to his first parties and found his first loves. As for me, I was living in anguish and desolation, and I realized that a new rupture awaited me.

It took me years before I could relive this era. Something resisted in my memory. Out of this haze an event stands out that I experienced as a veritable catastrophe: the signature of the Russo-German Pact. I am not very good on dates, even some which concern my personal life, but that one, August 1939, left a mark on me. My world crumbled on that day. I was ten years old and I couldn't stop crying. I remember that I was in a small woods, near Dinard, and I sobbed, hopeless, because the Russians, whom my brother and I had considered the last bastion of resistance to the Nazis, had yielded and had treacherously allied themselves with Hitler. This pact which shook the world, shook me up also: I felt personally betrayed and I wondered what was left to hang onto. My distress was total.

It was a period that did not deal in half measures: the good guys were on one side, the bad ones on the other. It was clear; I knew it; I felt it. And that was not limited to a child's viewpoint. Later, when I read Sartre, I found in his writings during and after the war the same manichean approach that I had perceived myself: between the good and the bad guys there was nothing, and those I had thought to be good had just gone over to the other side.

The months of the "phoney war" which followed were grey, solitary, and deeply sad. My brother and I spent all winter in the erstwhile summer camp near Dinard. In the spacious house crawling with children during the summer, we were the only six left. Emile and four other "big boys," and me. Perhaps, during these somber months, I lived through something akin to a depression; I don't know; I don't remember it clearly enough. It was school that helped me sublimate my loneliness. I studied well and earned my place among the best in my class. But two of my classmates were unbeatable; in a very competitive system where students were forever ranked, I had to content myself with third place. My mother encouraged me from afar and wrote us regularly. But the wait for visas continued, as the softness of the Breton spring replaced the long, cold nights.

At last, the visas arrived and our departure was scheduled for the end of May 1940. A few weeks before the departure, we came back to Paris where our mother met us. The capital was tense; they distributed gas masks and the blackout at night made the streets seem strangely suffocating and sinister. Belgium had been invaded; the Germans had swept around the supposedly invincible Maginot Line; the screaming of sirens announced nightly alerts. The phoney war was over; the battle had begun. In fact, it was the beginning of the collapse. On the train that took us to the Atlantic port of Saint-Nazaire (boats were no longer able to leave from Cherbourg or Le Havre, as in normal times), I remember seeing soldiers wounded in the invasion in the north. Two weeks later, Paris would be occupied.

It is hard for me to describe precisely my state of mind when I left France. Although I already had a fairly developed political consciousness (as did many children who lived through those years—politics was part of my everyday life) I was still only a child. Did I imagine that I would ever come back? I don't know. All I do know is that despite my painful experiences in this new country—the atmosphere of conflict, the fact that I had been slandered as "boche," the solitude of the last six months—I bore no grudge, neither against France nor the French. On the contrary, I had grown to love the country and its people. Most of all, I had quickly understood that I was in a land of liberty. I had found my true asylum in the French language which I now spoke fluently and without accent. I was enchanted by the physical beauty of Paris, by its gaiety which was obvious despite the troubled era. And finally, my mind was already elsewhere, turned toward the future. My father awaited us in New York; we were going to cross the Atlantic. Immense and magnificent, the *S.S. Champlain* was anchored in Saint-Nazaire.

I had the feeling I was living an unbelievable adventure, unimaginable even in my wildest dreams. I have said how much the departure for Paris had stirred my young imagination, what attraction and what romantic charm the French capital held out for me. Nevertheless, the idea of going to Paris had formed a part of things possible for me. On the other hand, to leave for New York struck me as completely incredible. Perhaps because, when I was a child in Vienna, I often played a game with my father we called "going to America." I liked this game as a child, the way children like to play with fantastic ideas, to lose themselves in their dreams, to believe in it while realizing that it is only a dream. But suddenly the dream was coming true. We *were* off to America, the real America. There would be no war there, no menace of Hitler; we would be able to stay there and finally to lead a normal life.

Of the crossing I have a mixed memory. There were many children on board. We played ping-pong, ran around on the decks, and took possession of the enormous and marvelous space of the great ocean liner. But we also lived in fear: the boat had to zigzag across the Atlantic in order to escape notice; the crossing took an interminable twelve days, and at night, all lights had to be out in order not to be seen by German submarines.

At last, New York came into view. The very sharp image that I retain of our arrival is dominated by the striking contrast between the obscurity of those many evenings and the countless dazzling lights that sparkled on the coast line. Now, all danger lay behind us: surely these lights were the sign of life, of liberty. A liberty which would have to wait a bit more—we arrived on a Friday evening; since the immigration service was closed until Monday morning, the *Champlain* had to remain anchored in the bay of New York for two days and three nights without unloading its passengers. The promised land was there and undoubtedly my father was waiting just beyond but we had to be patient, to play to while away the time which now seemed endless. From the deck, with the other children, I did not tire of watching the lights and the skyscrapers, the likes of which at the time did not exist at all in Europe, and which seemed to stand as if by a miracle.

Several days after leaving New York to return to France, the *Champlain,* the proud third-largest liner of the French Line, after the *Normandy* and the *Ile de France,* was torpedoed and sunk. It was the last boat to leave France for America.

In New York, the reception was very different from Paris. First of all, there were many foreign children, and then, the very notion of "foreign" is experienced very differently in the United States. Whereas in Paris, children had a spontaneous tendency to make fun of me (the foreigner being, in their eyes at that time, a somewhat bizarre, unsettling beast), I was enrolled in a public school in New York where I was surprised to go almost unnoticed. Spanish, German, Portuguese, Austrian, and Polish children of all ages mingled, speaking to each other in some rudimentary gobbledygook made up of many European languages, in a special class intended to teach them English and to acclimatize them to their new surroundings. As I recall now, this system invented to meet the needs of integrating many foreign children strikes me as having been efficient and intelligently devised. As children arrived, they spent their first weeks only in this class; then, as we began to understand English, we were sent for an hour or two at a time to a regular class in line with our age and level. Thus, after six months or at most one school year, the children were completely integrated into American classes.

As far as I was concerned, the transition went very quickly and I experienced none of the difficulties of adaptation that I had in France. But if I learned English very quickly, I did not forget French; with my brother, I kept on speaking this language that had opened for me the first horizons of liberty, that enabled me to escape from an identity which, at that time, was synonymous with suffering and persecution. Even now, so many years later, my brother and I speak French when we are together. As if, by speaking it (the first language to replace our mother tongue) we continue to share this crucial period of our lives.

As I grew up in New York, I began—and continue—to feel very much an American. But I remained attached to French culture as a precious heritage and I eventually decided to study and teach French literature. This led me to do a graduate year in Paris following my graduation from New York University, where I had been an undergraduate. I was twenty-one and this time really discovered Paris. The memory I had of the Paris of my childhood was fragmentary and mythical. Unlike my initial, difficult contact with France ten years earlier, I now spoke perfect French, came as an American not as an Austrian mistaken for a "boche," and was ready to appreciate what Paris had to offer. My studies at the Sorbonne were a revelation and confirmed me in my career choice. I went to the theater as often as I could and witnessed the beginnings of the renewal of French theater, the beginnings of the theater of the absurd. It marked me for life.

When my year was over, with a master's degree in hand, I set out to Berkeley, California, for four years to earn my doctorate in Romance languages and literatures. At the University of California, I read widely in modern theater and especially French theater—Sartre, Camus, Giraudoux, Cocteau, all the important playwrights of the interwar and postwar years, and the new authors who were just beginning to write for the stage: Ionesco, Beckett, Adamov, Genet. I wrote my dissertation on Pirandello and his influence on French theater and I have been permanently "hooked" on theater since then.

In 1956, I was hired as an instructor at New York University where I have remained for four decades. At NYU I have had the opportunity of meeting a multitude of writers, including all the representatives of the "New Novel" as it was becoming known. My attachment to experimentalism in fiction and in theater was reinforced by personal contact with its leading exponents. These contacts were amplified and led to close friendships, thanks to my increasingly frequent visits to France. For many years now, I have had "one foot" in Paris and in French cultural life—an ideal situation for someone who seeks to be an intermediary. I have assumed this role wholeheartedly, secure enough in my feeling sufficiently an outsider everywhere to be fully at home in New York and in Paris.

PART ONE

THEATER

If I have long had a passion for theater, it was never the sort of stagestruck passion of a kid who dreams of becoming a famous actor. In any case, my teenage fantasy was not to be on stage but to be a great jazz musician. Unfortunately, I did not turn out to be a good drummer or trombonist (the instruments I took it out on) and I soon gave up that notion. Since I grew up in New York, I had a chance to see plays occasionally. By the time I got to college (still in New York, at NYU), I went much more often and my taste developed. Those were heady years, with such works as *Death of a Salesman* and *A Streetcar Named Desire* on Broadway and the beginnings of what was to be known as off-Broadway where one could see Sartre, Camus, and other innovative playwrights. My fascination for theater was fueled by my classes in college: I took modern theater, Greek theater, Shakespeare, seventeenth-century French theater. (I nearly decided to specialize in Corneille, Racine, and Molière.) I thrilled to it all. These classes, marvelously taught, set me going for life. Later I became enthralled by questions of theatricality and staging, but in college, I became a theater buff through the text. I learned how to read a play, how to become my own "director" in the reading, imagining a staging as I read. It is

PART ONE: THEATER

an acquired skill. Soon, I was able to stage plays better in my mind than most productions I saw. Still, I never wanted to be a director or an actor. For a while, I *did* want to be a playwright and wrote a few scripts. But by then, I had come to know too much about theater and was too demanding not to realize that I was not a good playwright and likely would never become one. This was no great concession and it did not leave me a frustrated playwright. I found—and still find—writing *about* the theater very satisfying.

In graduate school, I continued taking as many courses on theater as were available and reading widely. During my master's year, in Paris, I saw many performances; I was very fortunate in that the academic year 1950–51 turned out to be a great year for theater in France. My horizons expanded with my first experiences of Ionesco, Beckett, and Genet and later as I devoured Pirandello for my doctoral dissertation. I did have a short career as an actor in Berkeley (where I did my Ph.D.): I performed in graduate-student productions of Molière and Giraudoux and toured the Bay Area with a staged reading of *No Exit.* I was a pretty good Garcin, in fact. Those were my only times on stage until my "triumph" so many years later in Virginia Woolf's *Freshwater* (see "Beginnings").

One of my most exciting and strangest evenings of theater occurred in 1960, when I had just published my first book, *Pirandello and the French Theater.* At the opening night, off-Broadway, of Tyrone Guthrie's magnificent production of *Six Characters in Search of an Author,* I was seized by a strange tingle of excitement; eventually I recognized that I was reacting as if I were the author. I felt so close to *Six Characters,* so possessive of it, that I had to control myself not to thank Tyrone Guthrie afterwards.

The theater has remained my greatest interest. I teach a number of courses on theater, not only French but the theater of many countries and theater as genre. For years, I wrote play reviews and reviewed for TV and radio. And of course, much of my spare time—and money—were spent on going to see plays. In the great years of the New York avant-garde, principally in the 1970s, I rarely missed a production of the Living Theater, the Open Theater, the Mabou Mines, Richard Foreman, Bob Wilson, and so forth, and I went to see the work of the great foreign directors such as Jerzy Grotowski, Peter Brook, and Tadeusz Kantor. My frequent trips to Paris always offer a multitude of choices for playgoing and I manage to take in many of the most interesting programs.

I confess to being a demanding theatergoer. If a play bores me, I would rather leave at intermission than continue suffering. Since I don't see plays in order to find out what is happening (I either know it or don't really care, since plot is not what I look for particularly), leaving before the end is not necessarily a great loss. I rarely walk out on a film (probably because my expectations are less), but when a play or a production lets me down, I feel betrayed. This is especially true for the work of well-known directors, from whom one expects even more. I recall once going with Julia Kristeva to see a production in Paris by the *enfant terrible* of directors that year—a production that had received abundant praise, especially for its opulent sets. Generally, I don't much care for opulence in the theater; when a staging has to win you over with gorgeous sets and/or costumes, I begin to worry about the play. Not that I go as far as Grotowski in demanding "a poor theater," but I prefer imagination and invention to be applied elsewhere. I had my doubts about what we were about to see, as did Kristeva. We agreed we would leave if we didn't like it. Before the start of the performance, the audience was dutifully filled with expectation, as if awaiting the ultimate revelation. After an interminable opening scene that took one hour (it felt like two) instead of the thirty minutes it should have taken, with each stage effect wildly applauded as if it were a stroke of genius, Kristeva and I looked at each other during the brief interval, nodded, grabbed our coats, and got up to leave. To extricate ourselves from our seats, we had to climb past some dozen spectators. Since it was obvious we were departing, people looked at us as if we were completely mad. I found myself whispering to one that my friend was not feeling well, as if required to give a credible explanation for this defection. But when I come across a truly great production, I can happily come back to see it several times.

If my scholarly and critical interests are not limited to theater, they are largely focused on it. I deal more with playwrights than with novelists and in the case of those writers who are both (for instance, Beckett and Sartre) I address myself more readily to their theater work. Most of the Beckett festivals I have organized have centered on productions of his plays.

I don't feel that the theater is better than the novel; I accept no such

PART ONE: THEATER

hierarchy and I have great passions for fiction—the New Novel, for instance, or Beckett's prose works. But if I have studied and taught theater more than anything else, it is surely because theater touches me more deeply—theater as literature, theater as performance, theater as pure imagination. My imagination, at least, finds its home there.

CHAPTER ONE

Changing Concepts of Avant-Garde in French Theater

It is difficult in contemporary times to speak of *the* theater of a Western country, because most of the time several forms of theater coexist: a theater of light entertainment, the serious theater of major authors, and the avant-garde. In France, since World War I, these distinctions are clearly evident. On the one hand is the boulevard theater which attracts a large public in search of entertainment with unpretentious comedies that still take delight in the eternal triangle situation. Dramatists such as Sacha Guitry, Marcel Achard, and Albert Husson were the uncontested masters of this often very amusing and well-written genre in years past; their successors are numerous and much performed. But the "real" theater with a more serious intent is found elsewhere: the "classical" or establishment theater, that is, a theater of dramatic and literary value with more lofty aims, written by the major authors of the period and intended for a sizable theatergoing audience. This is where one can situate Henry de Montherlant, Jean Giraudoux, Jean-Paul Sartre, Jean Anouilh, and, in later years, Jean-Claude Grumberg, Yasmina Reza, and Loleh Bellon. Finally, there is the experimental theater of a small group that reacts against established forms. Here we find Jean Cocteau, Guillaume Apollinaire,

15

Charles Vildrac in the interwar years, and, since 1950, Samuel Beckett, Eugène Ionesco, Jean Genet, Marguerite Duras, Fernando Arrabal, and others. More recently, this category would include Bernard-Marie Koltès, Philippe Minyana, Valère Novarina, Tilly, Michel Deutsch, and Hélène Cixous.

As in all forms of contemporary artistic expression, the avant-garde is omnipresent in the contemporary theater and notably in France—a country which has shown itself particularly hospitable to new forms of theatricality. The evolution of the French theater since the end of the nineteenth century is the history of avant-garde movements which provided the thrust for the renewal of the establishment theater.

So much has been written about the avant-garde that the very expression has become somewhat suspect. It is difficult to pin it down because a universal definition applicable to all art forms and to all eras seems impossible. For some, the idea of the avant-garde is limited to what is daring—even though today "daring" applies only to the work whereas, at the end of the nineteenth century, it applied also (and often principally) to the personal behavior of the artist who tried to shock the middle class. The avant-garde has been compared to fashion as if the spirit of the avant-garde were somehow linked to the psychology of the high fashion industry. In 1923, the great director Charles Dullin touched on an important aspect of the avant-garde when he stressed the nature of the audience: "In the theater, as in all the arts, there are those who can see and those who are born blind. The latter require an entire lifetime to get used to great things and it is only after having heard it said over and over for fifty years that something is beautiful that they yield to the judgment of others." [1]

How can one hope to find a global definition when it is not even easy to say what the avant-garde is at any one time in any one field? In 1959, theater people from around the world gathered in Helsinki to discuss the current state of the avant-garde theater. After four days of impassioned debate, the very definitions of the avant-garde remained contradictory. Eugène Ionesco spoke of it in terms of "opposition and rupture"—the work of a rebellious author who is a traitor to the established literary order. The East German delegate proposed six essential elements, including content, dramatic expression, the clarification of the essential interests of the people, and the entertainment value of a theater which needed to be both truthful and popular. Whereas the English critic Ossia Trilling spoke of John Osborne and the "angry young men," the American Francis Cowles Strickland admitted that he never considered setting Osborne "apart," that is among the writers of the avant-garde. Though recognized by all, the avant-garde phenomenon was approached in very different ways.[2]

It may be more fruitful to approach the problem negatively by considering that the essence of the avant-garde is opposed to the essence of what is currently accepted, to the establishment, to the spirit of classicism. Keeping in mind both the past and the present, the avant-garde—in theater, novel, or poetry; in ballet, music, or painting—represents above all a reaction against the established forms in each of these fields. These reactions take different shape in different eras and might have nothing more in common than their opposition to the established order. If for instance the current—and therefore already degenerating—mode of literary expression is realism, then the avant-garde will tend to be antirealistic. If, on the other hand, it is symbolism which, approaching its zenith, begins to lose contact with life and becomes exaggerated and arbitrary, then the avant-garde will be antisymbolist. Thus, the avant-garde artist is a revolutionary who wages a continuous minority struggle against the artistic forms generally appreciated by others. But these "others" are not the easily satisfied public of boulevard theater or of pulp fiction; rather, the avant-garde writer (to take that example) takes issue with literate writers who attract a large, literate public. For example, the theater of a Samuel Beckett or a Jean Genet does not stand in opposition to the light entertainments of an Achard but rather to the plays of Anouilh or Giraudoux. It is only in this manner that the military metaphor inherent in the expression *avant-garde* makes sense. The small advance guard of an army prepares the terrain for the main body of troops; similarly, avant-garde writers, when they are successful, show the way not for mere commercialism but for those serious writers who will later command a large public.

It was Ionesco who best described the avant-garde phenomenon:

While most writers, artists, and thinkers believe they belong to their time, the revolutionary playwright feels he is running counter to his time. As a matter of fact, thinkers, artists, and so on, after a certain time only make use of ossified forms; they feel they are becoming more and more firmly established in some ideological, artistic, or social order which to them seems up to date but which in fact is already tottering and yawning with unsuspected cracks. By the very force of circumstances any system, the moment it is established, is already outworn. As soon as a form of expression becomes recognized, it is already out of date. A thing once spoken is already dead, reality lies somewhere beyond it and the thought has become petrified, so to speak. A manner of speaking—and therefore a manner of being—once imposed, or simply accepted, is already unacceptable. An avant-garde man is like an enemy inside a city he is bent on destroying, against which he rebels; for like any system of government, an established form of expression is also a form of oppression. The avant-garde man is the opponent of an existing system. He is a critic of, and not an apologist for, what exists now. It is easy to criticize the past particularly when the prevailing regime is tolerant and encourages you to do it; but this is only to sanctify ossification and kowtow to tyranny or convention.[3]

What then happens to the avant-garde once it exists? It becomes necessarily subject to the laws of artistic evolution. An avant-garde can never long remain an avant-garde since it defines itself in relationship to the current establishment which, itself, changes constantly. Thus it is either rejected or absorbed. If an avant-garde fails (and that is the fate of most), it generally disappears without leaving any trace. But if it manages to impose itself, it eventually changes the current "classicism" or accepted forms. Its influence varies with circumstances: it might be limited to some new techniques or it might be far-reaching, as was the case for surrealism, for instance, which imposed a new esthetic with broad implications, even down to advertising.

The very expression *avant-garde* is restricted to relatively few writers or artists who, at least at first, have only a limited influence. It is a minority thrust that cannot enter the mainstream without ceasing to be experimental. When an avant-garde movement becomes fashionable, its revolutionary value is already spent. At that point, having attained its goal of reform, the avant-garde becomes part of the establishment; it will ultimately inspire new avant-gardes which will rise to oppose the "tyranny" that it has itself become, in a perpetual cyclical movement.

Generally speaking, an avant-garde is recognizable through its form (the most important aspect), its language, its content, and lastly its esthetic. Debussy was an avant-garde composer, having invented new forms and a new esthetic of music; in the case of Schönberg, his twelve-tone scale amounted to a change of musical language. In painting, Gauguin and Rousseau innovated through content while Picasso and Braque, as well as Kandinsky and Pollock, renewed esthetics through form and language. In fact, Picasso, who remained an avant-garde artist longer than perhaps anyone else thanks to his immense regenerative force, is an excellent example of an erstwhile experimentalist who became a classic for the intelligent public at large.

With respect to the novel, some writers innovated through language, such as Joyce, Proust, and Hemingway; others through form—the New Novel; others still through content, such as Sartre and Malraux. Most cases also involve a new general esthetic, for instance Joyce and the New Novel. Filmmakers such as Jean-Luc Godard, Alain Resnais, Ingmar Bergman, Michelangelo Antonioni, and Federico Fellini used approaches that constitute a renewal of the language of cinematography. The reinterpretation of classics on stage is also subject to the avant-garde; for instance, a director such as Roger Planchon applied a more or less Brechtian approach to redefine the esthetics of classic dramas.

The history of the French theater in the twentieth century can be understood only in terms of the various avant-garde movements that have continually promoted its evolution toward antinaturalism. Of the many innovating thrusts, only Antoine's Théâtre Libre was not aimed at least in part against excessive realism. Antoine, appearing somewhat earlier chronologically, rebelled *through* realism against the total lack of contact with life typical of the traditional theater of his time. It was Aurélien Lugné-Poe who, more than anyone else, launched the spirit of avant-garde in his country's drama—a spirit which was particularly important in two very fertile periods, roughly from the end of World War I to the end of the 1920s, and from 1950 to the end of the 1960s.

Lugné-Poe's early symbolist ventures proved not very successful, but they were an important initial sally against the slice-of-life play. His staging of *Ubu roi* in 1896 truly launched the massive assault to follow despite the fact that the production was short-lived. The celebrated "Merdre" ("Shitr") uttered by Ubu at the outset of Jarry's *King Ubu* is not only the beginning of the theatrical avant-garde whose lineage continues right down to Ionesco, it is also the beginning of the contemporary French theater. Nothing in *King Ubu* resembles reality: the characters are grotesque caricatures and the plot is, to put it mildly, lacking in verisimilitude. Jarry sought to scandalize with a

provocative work; he succeeded admirably and his lesson proved fruit-
ful, even if it took twenty years for the next play to be performed in
Paris with a verve and fantasy reminiscent of *King Ubu:* Apollinaire's
Breasts of Tiresias in 1917.

For the next four decades, Lugné-Poe and the other brilliant *met-
teurs-en-scène* of the Parisian stage helped orchestrate the avant-garde
movements. Experimentation in the theater is not solely a function of
the written text. The actor Jean Martin suggested quite correctly that
it is possible to create "new" theater by restaging *Phèdre*.[4] This concept is at the heart of the purifying influence exercised by Jacques
Copeau. His profound reformation of the esthetics of the French
theater is nothing less than a major milestone of the modern avant-
garde. Stanislavsky, Mayerhold, Craig, and others similarly were innovators without writing plays.

In France, the years following World War I proved extremely varied
in method and inspiration for the avant-garde theater. Typical of the
unbridled verve of the immediate postwar period are Cocteau's *Parade,* which for the first time blends theater with circus, music-hall,
and the ballet, and *Les Mariés de la Tour Eiffel,* a fanciful and often
amusing attempt to introduce a poetry of the theater—a poetry consisting not of cadenced lines but of a surrealist-like free rein given to
imagination. Others, such as Tristan Tzara, Raymond Roussel, and
Roger Vitrac, also strove to remove logic from the theater in order
to replace it with disconnected antirealism. The purely surrealistic
experiments, essentially unsuccessful in the theater, had no real effect
on the major dramatic forms of their time. However, Cocteau managed the transition from the experimental to the widely accepted:
Orpheus performed in a small theater in 1926 had been a revolutionary work thanks to its astonishing techniques and the innovation of
the modernization of an ancient myth; less than ten years later, *The
Infernal Machine,* a reworking of the Oedipus legend, reached a large
public in a major playhouse.

The early 1920s were also the time when Luigi Pirandello was
suddenly discovered and then "adopted" in Paris, where he became
the most widely performed playwright. His drastic dissection of the
human personality, his manner of dissolving the borderline between
reality and illusion, and his penetrating analysis of the very process of
artistic creation were very much in the realm of the avant-garde. After

initial experimentation with daring expressionistic forms, particularly by Simon Gantillon and Jean-Victor Pellerin, the Pirandellian reality-illusion dichotomy soon reached beyond the domain of the avant-garde in the plays of such "classical" authors as Giraudoux, Salacrou, and Anouilh. But Pirandello's exploration of the phenomenon of creation, couched in his highly original play-within-a-play process, still remains largely an avant-garde theme.

In contrast to the radical but generally unproductive experiments with form, other playwrights of the same period gave rise to another avant-garde, not so adventurous as to form but of almost immediate impact with respect to the subject matter and treatment of the theater. Jean Sarment, Charles Vildrac and Jean-Jacques Bernard introduced the "unspoken" to the French stage, while Henri-René Lenormand and Stève Passeur introduced Freudian psychology. It may seem quaint today to think of these writers as belonging to the avant-garde, but the subject matter of their plays, the use that, for instance, Sarment made of silence and Lenormand of the rapid *tableau* technique were great innovations in their day.

Copeau and the directors of the *Cartel* created a discriminating public swiftly conquered by these and other playwrights. Not long after that, their "respectability" became complete when they were performed at the national theaters, particularly the Odéon, rejuvenated and opened to modern trends by Firmin Gémier. The rapidity with which this erstwhile avant-garde became "classical" may be due in part to the dearth of literate non-avant-garde plays in the first two decades of the century. Writing in 1927, John Palmer claimed that the French theater, insular and resisting change before the war, had become the most revolutionary and contemporary theater in Europe.[5]

By approximately 1930, the great wave of experimentation, which had reached the theater after conquering every other means of artistic expression, came to a halt. (A similar decrease in the experimental approach was also noticeable in other genres.) Anouilh and Salacrou emerged as important dramatists, but the decade of the 1930s was dominated by the towering figure of Jean Giraudoux. Ionesco claimed that the theater returned then to outmoded forms, but in fact, if the revolution had ended, the "classical" authors, far from regressing, transformed the accepted and successful literate theater thanks to the influence of the previous decade's progress. Fantasy and total irreality—the most striking characteristics of Giraudoux's works—would not have been feasible without, for example, Cocteau. If it is proper to measure the success of an avant-garde movement by its lasting effect on the classicism it opposes, then the post-1918 generation of experimenters was successful in renovating the esthetic of the French theater in general for twenty years. A play such as Sartre's *Huis Clos* in 1944 might have been labeled avant-garde in the theater of most other nations; in France, only its existentialist philosophy was really new— its dramaturgy was fairly realistic and the theatrical convention of situating hell in a Second Empire drawing room was not startling to the French mainstream. And yet, that mainstream (which includes Sartre's other plays), if not given to a rigid realism, remained still relatively realist compared to the innovators.

A new explosion of avant-garde theater began around 1950—more powerful and farther reaching than that of the 1920s. The radical change had been anticipated by several striking works, notably Jean Genet's *The Maids* in 1947, as well as plays by Jacques Audiberti and Henri Pichette. But these were merely isolated events. Spearheaded by Ionesco's *The Bald Soprano* in 1950 and Beckett's *Waiting for Godot* in 1953, a veritable deluge of new theater swept Paris. This avant-garde can be divided into two principal tendencies: the more influential theater of the absurd or antitheater of Ionesco, Beckett, Adamov, Genet, Pinget, Arrabal, and so on; and the poetic avant-garde of playwrights such as Georges Schehadé, Jean Vauthier, Henri Pichette, and Jacques Audiberti, not principally concerned with the absurd. These dramatists did not form a school and made no attempt to work along common lines. There are as many differences among them as similarities: Adamov's arid language and Genet's verbal brilliance; Beckett's somber pessimism and Schehadé's gentle optimism, and so forth. They all shared a new revolt against realism by stressing the basic theatricality and irreality of the stage and many tended toward more primitive forms of nonliterary spectacle such as guignol, music-hall, ceremonial rite, farce, and ballet-pantomime.

Playing at first to very small audiences, this new theater quickly caught on, reached a larger public by the end of the 1950s and early 1960s, and then stormed the bastions of traditionalism, the great national theaters. By the start of the 1970s, its success had become so resounding and its public so considerable that the avant-garde label

CHANGING CONCEPTS OF AVANT-GARDE IN FRENCH THEATER

probably no longer applied. Meanwhile, the theater of the absurd spread throughout the Western world thanks to numerous close or distant disciples such as Edward Albee, Harold Pinter, Tom Stoppard, Israel Horowitz, Vaclav Havel, Max Frisch, Friedrich Dürenmatt, and Slowemir Mrozek.

The battle the French dramatists waged against all forms of realism was more far-reaching than that of their predecessors. In fact, their boldness was made possible by the advances initiated by those predecessors. Psychology, reason, and plot were devalued—a trend shared by avant-gardes in other genres: for example, the novels of Nathalie Sarraute, Alain Robbe-Grillet, and Michel Butor, and the films of François Truffaut, Alain Resnais, and Jean-Luc Godard.

The antecedents of the theater of the absurd can be found in a generation of French drama (in fact, one can go back to the *Ur*-absurd play, *King Ubu*). Salacrou and others had touched on the notion of the world's senselessness as long ago as the late 1920s. In the 1940s, Camus and Sartre described the absurd philosophically and in rational terms. Beckett, Ionesco, and all go one step further by *illustrating* absurdity through absurd processes. Their grotesque, contemporary vision of our world confronts the spectator directly, viscerally rather than intellectually, with a feeling for—not an understanding of—the irrational. Whereas in today's "classical" theater and even in much of yesterday's avant-garde, the play proceeds logically from one element to another, the antitheater—nonliterary in its downgrading of language—proceeds illogically through dehumanized characters, clichés, and inexplicable happenings. The spectator cannot identify with the characters and one rarely finds a "situation" in the Sartrian sense; one is finally confronted by the irrationality of one's own existence, of existence in general, of the human condition. The only realism for the spectator is a new, inner, metaphoric realism.

The foreign origins of so many dramatists of this new French wave were a striking fact: Ionesco was Rumanian; Adamov, Russian; Beckett, Irish; Schehadé, Lebanese; Arrabal, Spanish. Yet they all wrote in French, having spent at least long impressionable and formative years in France. Together with French-born authors such as Genet, Vauthier, and Pinget (who is actually Swiss), they formed a "School of Paris" as French as was the School of Paris in painting. The international aspect of this group is a tribute to the artistic and intellectual fertility of

Paris, especially in the 1950s. In that productive setting, this avant-garde theater triumphed in the Western world thanks to an indisputable authenticity, a prodigious inventiveness, and a new vision of the essence of theater.

Adapted from: the Introduction to *L'Avant-garde théâtrale: French Theatre since 1950* (New York: New York University Press, 1975), 1–10. Translation mine; and "Changing Concepts of Avant-Garde in 20th-Century Literature," *French Review* 38, 1 (October 1964): 34–41.

CHAPTER TWO

Two Decades of Theater in Paris: 1937–1957

One would have to go far back in time in order to find twenty years of theater that, by their sheer brilliance, their innovation, their production of great plays, can compare to the years 1937–1957 in Paris. The Elizabethan London of Shakespeare, Jonson, and Marlowe; the Spanish Golden Age of Calderon, Lope de Vega, Tirso de Molina; and also, of course, the Paris of Molière and Racine at the peak of their creativity. Ever since the seventeenth century, however, it would be hard to find two decades to match Paris from 1937 to 1957.

How much ground those twenty years of Parisian theater covered! With a masterpiece at each end: *Electra* by Giraudoux in 1937 and *Endgame* by Beckett in 1957, the plays inscribed within these boundaries touch upon nearly all the great moments of contemporary French theater since Jarry's *King Ubu* in 1896. The period between the two world wars, still so fertile in terms of invention, completely revolutionized theater in France. Later, the difficult years of World War II and the German occupation managed to produce a few great theatrical works; the postwar period also gave rise to a remarkable blossoming. The "new theater" of the 1950s, started in small Left Bank theaters by unknown playwrights named Samuel Beckett, Eugène Ionesco, and

TWO DECADES OF THEATER IN PARIS: 1937–1957

Arthur Adamov, would soon flood all of Europe as well as America. The Parisian "theater of the absurd" triumphed and became the prominent theatrical mode of the Western world in the second half of the twentieth century.

In a century in which painting shifted from cubism to surrealism then to abstract expressionism, theater in France follows a similar path; it moves farther and farther away from realism/naturalism inherited from the end of the nineteenth century. From 1896 to the mid-1970s, we witness a long reaction against the work of André Antoine who had established the theatrical norms of realism/naturalism in his Théâtre Libre. From *King Ubu* on, this reaction had major representatives: Apollinaire, whose *Breasts of Tiresias* constituted a true manifesto of antirealism; Cocteau, whose contribution is underestimated (the great shock of *Parade*, of *The Wedding on the Eiffel Tower*, and *Orpheus*, a key date in this attack against established forms); and great directors such as Lugné-Poe, Gémier, and Copeau especially; and then the four directors of the "Cartel" who were to dominate French theater between the wars, Jouvet, Dullin, Baty, and Pitoëff. Thanks to the achievement of these theater figures and of a few French dramatists (as well as a few foreigners: Pirandello, Shaw, O'Neill), the 1920s introduced a new aesthetic of theater thanks to a degree of experimentation up to that point unmatched in the "art theaters" of the French capital. Cocteau best expressed the burning desire of the new generation: "I try to substitute 'poetry of the theater' to 'poetry in the theater.' Poetry in the theater is a delicate lace impossible to see from afar. Poetry of the theater should be a thick lace; a lace made of ropes, a ship on the sea" (Preface to *The Wedding on the Eiffel Tower*, 1922).

Rather than materialize on stage the illusion of reality according to the fourth-wall convention dear to the realistic theater—that is to say, to invite the spectator to believe that what is going on on stage is "real," that there are "real" persons who discuss their problems in a "real" living room whose fourth wall has become miraculously invisible—young playwrights of the 1920s emphasized the *reality of illusion,* the frank acceptance of theater as a privileged locus for poetry, incantation, theatrical illusion.

Around 1930, this rich burst of the avant-garde diminished in French theater and yielded to the assimilation process which follows any important new movement. But the good "traditional" theater itself changed by absorbing certain innovations of the experimental theater. What had shocked in 1925 seemed familiar ten years later; the techniques that appeared so daring in the small workshop theaters became easily accessible to a large audience which, with time, had become used to them. Thus, the fantasy and the unreality of Giraudoux's theater no longer appeared as innovative and could be appreciated by countless spectators who, ten years earlier, would have been flabbergasted by his antirealistic esthetics. While the avant-garde thrusts of the 1920s were assimilated during the years preceding World War II thanks to major figures such as Giraudoux and Cocteau, other young playwrights heralded the preoccupations of the 1940s. Anouilh's and Salacrou's early works proved an introduction to the dark, cynical, grating universe which would soon dominate the French theatrical production.

1937–1940

The work of playwright Henri Bernstein, the vestige of an outmoded theater, was (still) being performed, and Viennese operetta continued to do quite well: at the Théâtre des Bouffes Parisiens, Yvonne Printemps and Pierre Fresnay triumphed in *Three Waltzes*. But at the Mathurins, Pitoëff staged a powerful and subtle work by the young Jean Anouilh, *Traveller without Luggage,* and L'Œuvre featured an antirealistic fantasy by Cocteau, *The Knights of the Round Table.* In it, the author reinvented medieval legend just as in *Orpheus* and in *The Infernal Machine,* he had manipulated and reinterpreted Greek myths.

But the theatrical event of 1937 (and indeed of the whole end of the decade) was undoubtedly Giraudoux's *Electra,* staged by Jouvet at the Athénée. The fruit of Giraudoux's maturity, *Electra* is the best example of the richest vein of the French theater between the wars: the modernization of Greek myths. While respecting the main lines of Euripides's *Electra,* Giraudoux wrote a thoroughly modern play. He invented new characters, particularly that of the Beggar (played by Jouvet) who replaced the Greek chorus and also became the author's mouthpiece; he scattered anachronisms throughout, which heightened the ironic tone, and he used a wholly modern, antirealistic theatricality. The Eumenides (who are seen growing up during the course of the play from little girls to young women) and the Gardener relate the events as if from a different sphere where everything has already happened and merely repeats itself. In his famous end-of-Act I monologue, the Gardener addresses the audience directly—a Pirandellian technique often used to create a link between the stage and the audience so as to assert the reality of illusion: "The play will go on without me. That's why I am free to come and tell you what the play cannot tell you itself."

The Electra-Aegisthus conflict is no longer simply that of a rebel against a tyrant; Giraudoux's characters are more finely shaded, less pure. To be sure, his Electra, like all Electras, seeks to avenge her father, yet her thirst for the absolute, her intransigence give her a fanatical side. Her antagonist, the ex-assassin Aegisthus, seems majestic at the end; he wants to save the city of Argos, threatened by destruction, but Electra will not allow him to survive, even if the entire city must perish. (Seven years later, Anouilh followed the same basic scenario in his *Antigone* by also shifting the emphasis from a manichean opposition of purity against corruption to that of two major protagonists, neither quite admirable nor entirely despicable.) "I have my conscience, I have Orestes, I have justice, I have it all," exclaims Electra at the moment the city collapses. Yet the play ends on a note of hope, on the evocation of dawn which might lead to renewal. Beyond the struggles of the Atrides, clearly contemporary overtones of the growing conflict between France and Germany pervade Giraudoux's play. Between the lines, the author anticipated the spirit of revenge which was soon to bring on the war.

Another important theatrical event in 1937 was the revival of *Right You Are If You Think You Are* at the Comédie-Française, directed by Dullin, which brought Pirandello's consecration in France to its peak. At the beginning of the 1920s, Luigi Pirandello had revolutionized French theater. Over the span of a few years, Dullin and Pitoëff staged *Six Characters in Search of an Author, Henri IV, Right You Are If You Think You Are,* and *The Pleasure of Honesty*; these were windows suddenly opened to a new theatricality—the theater within theater—and new themes—the relativity of truth, the multiplicity of personality, the opposition between life and art. Nearly all important French playwrights from 1937 to 1957 were influenced by Pirandello: Anouilh, Salacrou, Sartre, Camus, Cocteau, Giraudoux, Achard,

Genet, Beckett, Ionesco, and Adamov. For some of them, this influence proved decisive.

Between 1937 and the defeat of 1940, Cocteau stood out by turning his back on experimentation with two neorealistic plays, *Intimate Relations* and *Sacred Monsters*. He claimed that in a period when everyone produced nonrealistic theater, the true avant-garde attitude was to return to realism! Other plays of note include two strong works by Salacrou which received great attention, *The World Is Round* and *When the Music Stops*; Anouilh's rose and dark farces, *Restless Heart* created by Pitoëff and the delightful *Thieves' Carnival* staged by André Barsacq; the very Pirandellian *Le Corsaire* ("The Pirate") by Marcel Achard directed by Jouvet; and of course Giraudoux: *Song of Songs*, and, inspired by a German legend, the charming fairytale *Ondine*, a radiant play, far from the fatalistic pessimism of *Electra* and *Tiger at the Gates*. Not to be forgotten, Antonin Artaud's remarkable manifesto, *The Theater and Its Double*, practically unnoticed on publication in 1938, has exerted a powerful influence on dramatists and directors during the second half of the twentieth century.

1940–1944

It is difficult to imagine now that there actually was any theater at all in Paris under the Occupation. Yet, not only did the theater continue, but in fact those dark years witnessed considerable theatrical activity and even several major works. It seems somewhat embarrassing to realize that everything continued as if there were nothing wrong. "It should have been night but it seemed like broad daylight," wrote drama critic Guy Dumur. "I am afraid that political events do not coincide at all with artistic ones.... It is astonishing to view this autonomous life in the midst of the worst catastrophe that had ever befallen the world.... the theater in Paris carried on as if nothing had happened."[1]

Nevertheless, one should not conclude that the theater that flourished under the Occupation was a collaborationist theater. The Germans had decided not to repress the distractions of the capital, undoubtedly on the theory that this course would be better in order to retain a more efficient control. To be sure, plays had to be submitted

TWO DECADES OF THEATER IN PARIS: 1937–1957

to German censorship, but it did not turn out to be fearsome—the case of *The Flies* in 1943 was exemplary in this respect. Nor were the Germans very present; they were rarely seen in the theaters except for certain German-language performances at the Comédie Française of Schiller and Goethe. (On the other hand, the Opera was always filled with German officers.)

As in other circumstances, the French state was another matter. The Commission for the Organization of Performances (COES) was in charge of everything: the authorization to use a theater, subsidies, travel permits, and professional identity cards for all those working in theaters, including actors, administrators, and technicians. It proved to be a fairly efficient mechanism to keep undesirable people out, notably Jews. But the theaters were not deprived of means even during the most difficult years. They were jammed and seats were inexpensive.

Named to head the Comédie Française in 1940, Jacques Copeau gave back a certain brilliance to the House of Molière; he brought in Jean-Louis Barrault who earned a string of successes both as actor and director, with *The Cid* and *Hamlet,* and especially with *The Satin Slipper* (the start of his great collaboration with Paul Claudel as his leading interpreter). The domination of the Cartel of four directors who had reigned over the interwar years was coming to an end: Pitoëff died at the beginning of the war; Baty left the theater to work exclusively with puppets; Jouvet took his company to South America where he remained until the Liberation—on his return after the war, in the last years of his life, he created very few plays; and Dullin, nearing the end of his career, left his Théâtre de l'Atelier in order to take over the cavernous former Théâtre Sarah Bernhardt, rebaptized (the expression is appropriate!) Théâtre de la Cité.

That is where, in June 1943, Dullin staged Sartre's first play, *The Flies,* yet another variation on Greek myths. Undoubtedly, it was the mythological frame of reference that enabled this subversive play to obtain the green light from the German authorities. But for the public, there was nothing equivocal about the play: by affirming his responsibility for his actions, the Sartrian Orestes incarnated perfectly the theses of existentialism as well as a clear and powerful symbol of resistance, while the tyrant Aegisthus did not fail to recall Marshall Pétain. Moreover, Sartre did not hesitate to spell out his intentions in the theater magazine of the Occupation, *Comœdia:* "Free in con-

TWO DECADES OF THEATER IN PARIS: 1937–1957

science, the individual who has managed to rise so far above himself will only become free in situation if he reestablishes liberty for others, if the consequences of his act bring about the disappearance of the present state of things and the reestablishment of what they ought to be." [2]

However, younger directors were ready to take over. Following his triumph at the Comédie-Française, Jean-Louis Barrault continued for more than half a century to be a notable man of theater whose extraordinary career left its mark on the postwar era. More than anyone else, he was the worthy successor and heir to the great tradition of the "Cartel." André Barsacq replaced Dullin at l'Atelier where he remained faithful to Anouilh—with *Dinner with the Family* as well as two other plays based (yet again!) on Greek myths, *Legend of Lovers (Eurydice)* in 1942 and especially *Antigone* early in 1944. Antigone was one of the greatest moments of the Occupation theater. Less lyrical but more intense than Sophocles' tragedy, Anouilh's play is thoroughly modern in spirit and resonates (in a manner more complex and ambiguous than was thought at the time) with the feelings of France toward Germany. People again thought that, as with *The Flies,* the Germans had let a subversive play slip past, but it seems far from clear that the censor made a mistake. In contrast to Antigone's rather arbitrary "No" to tyranny, the defense by a kindly, disillusioned Creon, of the need to govern, seems convincing.

Other authors whose works continued to be performed include Cocteau *(The Typewriter, Renaud and Armide),* Giraudoux (the very somber *Sodom et Gomorrhe,* featuring Gérard Philippe's first appearance), Marcel Achard, and Stève Passeur. There was also J. M. Synge, Georges Neveux (the mysterious *Voyage de Thésée,* "The Voyage of Theseus"), and a man called Jean Vilar who played Strindberg. *Queen after Death,* Montherlant's first play, went counter to the dominant trend of contemporary French theater: in its thoroughly classical perfection, its sources lie with Racine rather than in the reaction to Antoine's Théâtre Libre.

The most astonishing play during the Occupation years was created a mere ten days before the Normandy landing and three months before the liberation of Paris. In the venerable Théâtre du Vieux-Colombier, where thirty years earlier Copeau had attempted to renew French theater, the first performance of Sartre's *No Exit* took place at the end of May 1944. *No Exit* gains its full impact through the subtle and dramatically powerful mix of two main themes: the theme of *the other* and that of *freedom/bad faith*. By situating his three characters in the hell of a Second Empire drawing room with no exit, Sartre attained an extraordinary concision and economy of means: a minimum of characters, a single, simple plot line presented with an increasing intensity during some seventy-five minutes of performance time, without intermission, without anything superfluous. The now-world-famous phrase "hell is other people" sums up the dilemma of these three "bastards"; the *other* is infernal not only by his very presence, by his glance which reduces everything to the level of object, but also because the *other* destroys the facade shown to the world, the lie behind which one seeks to conceal one's truth to others and to oneself. Orestes had been the quintessential existentialist hero; in their bad faith, the characters in *No Exit* represent the other side of the coin. Inès exclaims: "It's what one does, and nothing else, that shows the stuff one's made of. . . . You are—your life, and nothing else." Applied to Garcin-the-coward, these words crucify him, condemn him to his cowardice, to inauthenticity. The Sartrian hell of *No Exit* has become proverbial, a powerful and universal metaphor.

1944–1949

If Paris had managed to carry on a theatrical activity of honorable dimensions under the Occupation, the departure of the German troops led to a veritable blossoming. The six years following the Liberation were particularly fruitful for the theater. Most of the already established playwrights continued writing; others (especially Camus) joined them to resume the preoccupations of the preceding era and the problem of the human condition. Meanwhile appear the first signs of the tendencies which, since 1950, increasingly dominate French theater: Jean Genet's first plays and a poetic theater—a new phenomenon—with such poet-dramatists as Henri Pichette, Georges Schehadé, and Jacques Audiberti. It is a period of continuity as well as of transition.

Most notable was the theater of commitment, even though it was comprised of only a few authors—mainly Sartre and Camus, as well as Simone de Beauvoir with *Les Bouches inutiles* (Brecht mania had not yet reached France). But given Sartre and Camus's notoriety, it was sufficient for the theater of commitment to dominate.

TWO DECADES OF THEATER IN PARIS: 1937-1957

Camus's first theatrical works were eagerly awaited. The publication of *The Stranger* and *The Myth of Sisyphus* in 1942, when Camus was not yet thirty years old, had made him famous; in love with theater since childhood, Camus quickly felt tempted by dramatic writing. He wrote only four plays (not including his adaptations, particularly Dostoyevski's *The Devils*), and all were important events. *The Misunderstanding,* directed by Marcel Herrand in 1944 at the Mathurins, offers a tangible image of the absurd: the play ends on a plea from the young woman (played by Maria Casarès) to the old servant: "help me, for I need help. Be kind and say that you will help me," followed by a simple and sharp "No!," the response of a universe which is indifferent to the fate of men. But *The Misunderstanding* had a lukewarm reception; Camus's real triumph on stage had to wait for 1945 with *Caligula,* which revealed an original imagination and theatrical technique. In the role of the Roman emperor who discovered that "things as they are . . . are far from satisfactory" because "Men die; and they are not happy," Gérard Philippe became a star overnight. Its theatricality, its play-within-a-play as staged by Caligula, inscribe the play within the great antinaturalist lineage of French theater, whereas Sartre leans to a more realistic form of theater.

Even though it featured the collaboration of a number of well-known artists, *The State of Siege,* in 1948, turned out to be a failure. Staged at the Marigny by Barrault with his new Renaud-Barrault company, its cast included—aside from Madeleine Renaud and Jean-Louis Barrault—Pierre Bertin, Pierre Brasseur, Maria Casarès, Marie-Hélène Dasté, and Marcel Marceau. Arthur Honegger wrote the music and Balthus created the setting and the costumes. By situating his play halfway between Artaud's universe and his own novel *The Plague,* Camus failed to find the right tone; the aridity of *The State of Siege* left the critics unconvinced. With *The Just Assassins* in 1949 Camus made a comeback: this solid play, which investigates possible justifications for political terrorism, was well received and continues to be revived regularly.

During these same years—the golden age of Saint-Germain des Prés and of existentialism—Sartre, by now an international celebrity, had three plays produced at the Théâtre Antoine: *The Victors* as well as *The Respectful Prostitute* in 1946, and *Red Gloves* in 1948. Like Camus's flawed but provocative *The Just Assassins,* Sartre's very successful *Red Gloves* deals with the conflict between political realism and idealism and also touches on the problem of terrorism. It leads straight to the political preoccupations of the start of the Cold War. Several years later, in an increasingly venomous political climate, Sartre was to feel very uncomfortable with his critical portrait of Communist parties in *Red Gloves* and he tried, unsuccessfully, to have a production of his own play forbidden at a Soviet-inspired peace congress in Vienna.

The theater of commitment—which he prefers to call theater of situations—was admirably defined by Sartre during a lecture in New York in 1946. In it, he speaks especially of *Caligula,* of *Antigone,* of *Les Bouches inutiles,* and of his own plays:

> Our plays are violent and brief, centered around one single event; there are few players and the story is compressed within a short space of time, sometimes only a few hours. As a result they obey a kind of "rule of the three unities," which has been only a little rejuvenated and modified. A single set, a few entrances, a few exits, intense arguments among the characters who defend their individual rights with passion—this is what sets our plays at a great distance from the brilliant fantasies of Broadway. Yet some of them find that their austerity and intensity have not lacked appreciation in Paris. . . . Since it is their aim to forge myths, to project for the audience an enlarged and an enhanced image of its own sufferings, our playwrights turn their back on the constant preoccupation of the realists, which is to reduce as far as possible the distance which separates the spectator from the spectacle.[3]

But if the theater of commitment was the leading tendency of the immediate postwar period, it was not everyone's cup of tea; there was also a real thirst for distraction, not necessarily light distraction but at least a breath of fresh air, of fantasy. One of the most popular plays of the postwar years was Giraudoux's *The Madwoman of Chaillot.* The play, staged by Jouvet (back from his long South American exile) in 1945, one year after the playwright's death, belongs in spirit to the prewar era. It was an unforgettable production, starring Marguerite Moreno in the role of the dazzling madwoman who purifies the world by eliminating all the shady characters who seek to exploit it. One and a half years later, Jouvet also staged *The Apollo of Bellac*; it was the last time that the names of Jouvet and Giraudoux shared a billing (Giraudoux's posthumous work *Duel of Angels* was produced by Barrault in 1953).

TWO DECADES OF THEATER IN PARIS: 1937–1957

The presence of Paul Claudel became more and more dominant as the 1940s were ending. *The Tidings Brought to Mary,* created by Lugné-Poë in 1912, was redone in a second version in 1949 by Jouvet at the Athénée, and in a third—and definitive—version by Jean Vernier at the Hébertot in 1948. Most notable was the splendid new version of *Break at Noon*—a landmark event, directed and performed by Barrault in 1948, with Edwige Feuillère and Pierre Brasseur. Although Claudel was then eighty years old, his writing had the overwhelming power of a great dramatist at the peak of his career.

Salacrou, Anouilh, and Montherlant continued to be successful. *The Master of Santiago* lived up to the promise of *Queen after Death* and confirmed Montherlant as an important author. With *Ring around the Moon* (1947) and *The Cry of the Peacock* (1948), Anouilh took a decisive turn towards antirealism. Salacrou's *Les Nuits de la colère* ("The Nights of Wrath") in 1946 turned out to be the best play about the Occupation; in *L'Archipel Lenoir* ("The Lenoir Archipelago"), presented by Dullin the following year, he gave further proof of his penchant for comedy and irony. As for the Renaud-Barrault Company in its new home at the Théâtre Marigny, the eclectic repertory included, beyond the works already mentioned: *Hamlet,* Marivaux's *False Admissions, The Trial,* in Gide's adaptation of Kafka, and Feydeau's *That's My Girl.*

But during these same years just preceding 1950, a new esthetic of theater was born. Following his great success with T. S. Eliot's *Murder in the Cathedral* at the Vieux-Colombier in 1945, Jean Vilar founded the Avignon Festival which was to become the most prestigious theater festival in the world. In his initial seasons he staged Shakespeare, Corneille, Büchner, Montherlant's *Pasiphae,* and Gide's *Oedipus*; the great post-1950 years were to follow.

A striking phenomenon of the period was the appearance of a poetic theater with its burgeoning of poetic imagination on stage. It was the time of Jacques Audiberti's first plays, *Quoat-Quoat* directed by André Reybaz in 1946, and especially *Le Mal court* ("Evil Rampant") (1947) and *La Fête noire* ("The Black Feast") (1948), directed by Georges Vitaly, which reveal a new universe whose density was quite different from that of the established playwrights. The great revelation of the poetic theater was Henri Pichette's *Les Épiphanies* ("Epiphanies") created by Vitaly in 1947 at the tiny Théâtre des Noctambules in a set by Matta. *Les Épiphanies* translate onto the stage an essentially verbal text, but this was no mere dramatic reading of poetry. Rather, it was a complex, formal visualization of a poetic frenzy of rare strength and great beauty.

Paradoxically, the play which best anticipates the 1950s and which serves best as transition between the theater of the Occupation and the postwar period on the one hand and on the other what was to be known as the "new theater" was staged not by a young, innovative director but by the veteran Jouvet. A priori, one can hardly imagine a work farther removed from Jouvet's esthetics than Jean Genet's *The Maids,* yet it was Jouvet who, in 1947, created this play which, with its vigorous and original theatrical idiom, has become one of the masterpieces of French theater. Accustomed to more traditional themes and techniques, the Athénée's audience was unenthusiastic but Jouvet succeeded in introducing to the stage this already scandalous writer. *The Maids* revealed to the public an extraordinarily talented dramatist: the maids' sterile revolt against their employer unfolds in a strange world of incantation and ritual, of exaltation and wild apotheosis within the subtle game of mirrors of a Pirandellian play-within-a-play.

1950–1957

If *The Maids,* *Les Épiphanies,* and *Le Mal court* had been the precursors of a new theater, the real explosion occurred in 1950 with a new manner of using the stage, a new esthetic based on more radical, antirealistic, and metaphoric techniques. In small Parisian theaters, from 1950 to 1953, was born the theater which not only would be dominant in France until 1957 but would extend far beyond: it became the dominant mode of theater in the Western world for decades to come. Commenting on the 1950 season in Paris, theater critic Guy Dumur wrote: "Nothing was coming to an end; everything appeared to be beginning."[4]

1950: *The Bald Soprano* by Ionesco; *The Invasion* and *The Great and the Small Maneuver* by Adamov; *The Knacker's ABC* by Boris Vian; *La Pucelle* ("The Virgin") by Audiberti. 1951: *The Lesson* by Ionesco; *Monsieur Bob'le* by Georges Schehadé. 1952: *The Chairs* by Ionesco; *Capitaine Bada* ("Captain Bada") and *La Nouvelle Mandragore* ("The New Mandrake") by Jean Vauthier; *The Parody* by Ada-

TWO DECADES OF THEATER IN PARIS: 1937–1957

mov; *Nucléa* by Pichette. 1953: *Victims of Duty* and *Maid to Marry* by Ionesco; *Professor Taranne, The Direction of the March,* and *One against the Other* by Adamov; and especially Beckett's *Waiting for Godot.*

In the space of just over three years took place a veritable revolution of an avant-garde labeled as "absurd" or "antitheater." For once this avant-garde did not trail behind other art forms but rather preceded them. Its directors were relatively young: Nicolas Bataille, Jacques Mauclair, Sylvain Dhomme, Roger Blin, Jean Vilar, Roger Planchon, Jean-Marie Serreau, Gérard Philippe. And that was only the beginning! Among the most important productions between 1954 and 1957, one can mention Ionesco's *Amédée, Jack,* and *The New Tenant*; Beckett's *Endgame*; Adamov's *Ping-Pong* and *Paolo Paoli: The Years of the Butterfly*; Marguerite Duras's *The Square*; Schehadé's *La Soirée des proverbes* ("The Evening of Proverbs") and *Histoire de Vasco* ("The Story of Vasco"); Vauthier's *The Character against Himself* (the last three staged by Barrault) and many short plays by Jean Tardieu. It was an unprecedented profusion of theatrical experimentation. This avant-garde quickly reached a sizable public and was soon performed in larger theaters as well as the national theaters. In the best tradition of Paris, this "School of Paris" was international: it included dramatists from many countries who all wrote in French and most of whom lived in Paris—the Irishman Beckett, the Rumanian Ionesco, the Russian Adamov, and the Lebanese Schehadé. It was equally international in its extension: its heirs include Harold Pinter, Edward Albee, Tom Stoppard, Friedrich Dürenmatt, Max Frisch, Slawomir Mrozek, Fernando Arrabal, and Peter Handke.

Two plays stand out from this striking theatrical production, *Waiting for Godot* and *The Bald Soprano.* Each invented a new language of theater, tangible and comprehensible images of the absurd, unforgettable metaphors of the human condition; both have become part of our vocabulary and of our system of reference. Beckett's play brought us memorable images: the two tramps, Vladimir and Estragon, waiting for a Godot/savior who defines himself by the fact that he does not come; their pitiful but marvelous way of "returning the ball" to each other, of filling the void of their abandonment; the tyrant, Pozzo, who is the torturer but also the victim of his servant Lucky. These images of the absurdity of existence do not reach us through rational analysis (as had been the true for Camus and for Sartre) but rather they take a

TWO DECADES OF THEATER IN PARIS: 1937–1957

hold of us directly, viscerally, not intellectually. "one day we were born, one day we shall die," shouts Pozzo, "the same day, the same second. . . . They give birth astride of a grave, the light gleams an instant, then it's night once more." As pure and as hard as a diamond, this metaphor sums up the distress of the characters in the play as well as our own distress.

The dislocated, delirious language of *The Bald Soprano* made available to the spectator a certain grotesque and dehumanized modern world of interchangeable characters with no depth, no reality. The Smiths speak only nonsensical banalities; Mr. and Mrs. Martin do not even recognize each other; the countless people called Bobby Watson are all indistinguishable from one another; the apparently serious "reasonings" yield such "truths" as "Experience teaches us that when one hears the doorbell ring, it is because there is never anyone there": these create the paradoxical double impression of nightmare and farce of Ionesco's world, the radical new element which constitutes his contribution to the theater and, beyond it, to our perception of reality.

The theater of Beckett and Ionesco and of the other avant-garde playwrights of the 1950s takes position against the more realistic theater that preceded it, which usually presented a problem and proceeded to its solution by moving from A to B to C, that is, logically, sequentially. In this form of theater, the spectator tries to find out what will happen. In the new theater, what matters is not what is going to happen (although often very unexpected things happen) but rather the meaning of what is happening. The progression is not A to B to C but X to Y to Z, that is, an illogical, arbitrary progression removed from any system of causality. Disoriented, the spectator remains outside; he is incapable of identifying with the characters. He fails to find a "situation" in the Sartrian sense of the word; he is finally confronted with the irrationality of his own existence, of existence in general. Just as in the "New Novel" which was to triumph several years later, reason, plot, and psychology are downgraded and the only realism for a spectator to latch on to is an interior, metaphoric "new realism."

Yet, as the new theater was gaining momentum, the dramatists of the 1940s persisted in defending a more traditional idea of theater. Sartre presented *The Devil and the Good Lord* (created by Jouvet in 1951, shortly before his death), *Kean* (adapted from Alexandre Dumas père) and *Nekrassov*; with *Malatesta* and *Port Royal*, Montherlant

TWO DECADES OF THEATER IN PARIS: 1937–1957

carried on with his own brand of classicism; Anouilh began the most fruitful period of his career with ever more grating, profoundly antirealistic plays filled with cynical humor, especially *The Rehearsal* (1950), *The Waltz of the Toreadors* (1952), *The Lark* (1953), and *Poor Bitos* (1956).

As for the directors, Barrault, now at the Marigny, continued to stage Claudel *(The Exchange* and *Christopher Columbus)*, Giraudoux, Molière, Racine, and Jean Vilar, appointed to run the Théâtre National Populaire in 1950, gave Parisians the heroic days of the TNP at the Théâtre de Chaillot. He helped them rediscover the classics (Shakespeare, Molière, Corneille, Musset, and Hugo) by stressing simplicity and restraint, by respecting both the text and the actor. With Gérard Philippe, he rejuvenated *The Cid* and *Lorenzaccio* and introduced Kleist's *The Prince of Hamburg*. His production of Pirandello's *Henry IV* in 1957 was an exceptional theatrical event that demonstrated not only Vilar's absolute mastery but also the ever renewed modernity and topicality of the Italian playwright. Vilar's TNP attracted a vast public to the cavernous subterranean playing space of the Chaillot Palace, and managed, as much as it was possible, to create a popular theater within a national theater. His enterprise had a definitive influence on the French theater of the twentieth Century.

Vilar was also instrumental in introducing Brecht to France, but the most powerful revelation of the German dramatist proved to be the performance of *Mother Courage* by Brecht's company, the Berliner Ensemble, at Barrault's Théâtre des Nations festival in 1953. By opposing a political and critical theater to the metaphoric and metaphysical theater of Beckett, Ionesco, and others, and by using the novel techniques of distanciation which, though also antirealistic, differed greatly from those of the theater of the absurd, Brecht opened up one of the major paths of the theater of the 1960s, alongside the one inaugurated by the School of Paris of the 1950s.

1937–1957

During these two decades in Paris, the art of theater thrived alongside the plastic arts, with dramatists as brilliant as the painters. From Giraudoux and Cocteau to Anouilh, Montherlant, Sartre, and Camus, to Beckett, Genet, and Ionesco; from Jouvet, Dullin, and Pitoëff to

TWO DECADES OF THEATER IN PARIS: 1937–1957

Barrault, Vilar, and Planchon; from the Giralducian refinement of the prewar years to the theater of situations of the 1940s, to the theater of the absurd of the 1950s: twenty dazzling years with *Electra, No Exit, Antigone, Queen after Death, Caligula, The Maids, The Bald Soprano, Waiting for Godot,* and *Endgame.* In this diversified production, several common features stand out: an antirealistic theatricality which, rejecting the fourth-wall convention, accepts the theater not as a space for the reproduction of reality but as the privileged place for a poetic vision, an interior, subjective world, a metaphoric representation of life, a critical distance. Moreover, one finds throughout a constant thematic concern with the human condition, even if it is viewed differently by the various dramatists.

These twenty years of theater at the mid-century encapsulate the entire century. They are the continuation of what preceded them since *King Ubu*; they presage what is to follow, after 1957. From the Comédie Française to the tiniest Left Bank stage, Paris was an exceptional home for theatrical creation where all tendencies mingled, from classicism to the most experimental avant-garde. The theatergoing public was in luck. It had a vast choice of modes and esthetics of theater; it could take delight in great spectacles, theater of action and of words, "poor theater" (to use Grotowski's phrase), or costly stagings. All of that and more was offered to the public during these extraordinary twenty years during which Paris was truly the capital of the world of theater.

Translated and adapted from "Vingt ans de théâtre à Paris" in *Paris-Paris 1937–1957* (Centre Pompidou, 1981), 324–32.

CHAPTER THREE

Pirandello and French Theater

Since the first French production of Pirandello by Charles Dullin in 1922 *(The Pleasure of Honesty),* the great Italian dramatist has become probably the most performed author, French or foreign, in Paris. The great revelation of Pirandello occurred the following year with Georges Pitoëff's staging of *Six Characters in Search of an Author.* The date was April 10, 1923. It was a memorable evening that had the effect of an earthquake; French theater would never be the same again. Pierre Brisson, one of the leading Parisian drama critics of the period, wrote: "Overnight, Pirandello conquered his reputation as a sorcerer of dramatic art. It was a window suddenly opened, a flood of dreams freshly clothed on the stage."[1] "It . . . marked a new achievement in the contemporary history of the theater."[2] Pirandello had gone to the very heart of drama, displaying a technique at once boldly modern and immediately comprehensible. French productions of his plays followed at a dizzying pace. "Pirandello 'forever'!" wrote another critic. "Do you like Pirandello? He is being put on everywhere, at the Atelier, at the Renaissance, at the Théâtre des Arts; he is being played in three theaters at the same time—a fact without precedent for a foreign author; it's a rage, an infatuation, a fancy, a craze."[3]

But the critics were not the only ones impressed. Young contemporary French playwrights admired the Italian's treatment of illusion and personality and they saw the medium of theater itself in a new light. They adapted what suited their own needs to produce a new theater, whose antecedents rested at least partially in Pirandello's. Here was the spark that was needed. In Pirandello these young dramatists found themes that reflected the anxieties of the times; they found an exciting technique that brought to the theater the modern forms already adapted by painting, poetry, music, and the novel.

With Pirandello among those standing at the threshold, the French theater entered the modern age. Cerebral content became an ingredient of the theater, just as suspense and psychological analysis had been previously. Pirandello and his successors gave a voice to the uncertainties and the absurdities of twentieth century life. Throughout the 1920s and 1930s, French theater became Pirandellian. Jean Cocteau and Jean Giraudoux were but the most important authors influenced by the Italian. By the time a new generation of dramatists became known during the war and the immediate postwar years, Pirandello was thoroughly domesticized in France.

It is perhaps no coincidence that the man who was one France's leading playwrights in those years is also the playwright who reflects most clearly the influence of Pirandello. In its themes, its treatment, and its general atmosphere, the theater of Jean Anouilh is the most Pirandellian in France.

Anouilh's characters, like Pirandello's, are engaged in the search for escape from life's sordidness, and they too usually choose irreality as the solution to their problems. Whereas Pirandello's plays resemble one another to the extent that they are sometimes thought of as variations on a theme, Anouilh's do not follow a master pattern. We therefore find Pirandello's influence on the French writer diffused and uneven, more pronounced in some plays and less in others. The division into *pièces noires, roses, brillantes,* and *grinçantes* (dark, rose, sparkling, and grating plays) underlines the varying moods in which they are written. Actually, the categories themselves are rather loose, and each includes plays that differ radically from one another. Pirandello's influence transcends the four groups.

One of the Sicilian's themes recurring most markedly in the Frenchman's theater is multiplicity of personality. In the pattern of Pirandello's *Henry IV,* Anouilh's *Traveler without Luggage* (1937) is the

PIRANDELLO AND FRENCH THEATER

story of a man without a present who reaches a point of no return between his past and his future. Amnesia is the convenient vehicle for creating this unusual situation wherein the multiplicity of a man's personality can be ideally studied, for, in his recovery, the protagonist, Gaston, reaches precisely that moment in his life when his past unfolds in direct opposition to his self, revealing the painful dichotomy between the two aspects of his mind. Gaston is as different from the young Jacques who disappeared in the war as it is possible for two people to be; yet they are the same person. By admitting that he is Jacques, Gaston would have to accept the horrid past that his former self had left behind—a past that is unbelievable in view of his gentle nature as a grown man. Therefore he reaches the difficult decision of renouncing his family and a part of himself in order to be true to himself as he now is.

Like Henry IV, Gaston-Jacques has two totally distinct personalities, and in both cases the split occurred as a result of amnesia. Anouilh's basic conception of his hero is wholly Pirandellian. Yet Henry becomes a defeated, tragic figure, whereas Gaston sheds his past in a fairly satisfactory resolution of his conflict by accepting his new role as the little English boy's nephew. The character of Henry brings up the question of insanity, and his difficulty lies in accepting the outside world. For Gaston, neither madness nor the outside world are problems. It is himself he cannot escape. "I'd grown used to myself," says Gaston, "I knew that self well, and now I have to leave it and find another me, and to put that one on like an old coat."[4] He is, to use the Pirandellian frame of reference, a character in search of himself, a man longing for a past, yet having the most unusual liberty of being able to choose it. Anouilh's Gaston expresses it with his characteristic irony: "it frightened people to think of a man living without a past. Foundlings aren't too well thought of, as it is. . . . But a man, a grown man, who scarcely had a country, no place of birth, no background, no name. . . . Good God, the fellow's a bleeding outcast."[5] This liberty is precious to Gaston, and he is not willing to surrender it for the past of a man who had cheated, stolen, lied, crippled his best friend, and stolen his brother's wife. Valentine, like an existentialist, tells him: "It's too easy to live without a memory. You'll have to accept yourself, Jacques. Our whole life, with our fine moral code and our precious freedom, consists ultimately in accepting ourselves as we are."[6]

Valentine does not understand that liberty does not mean accepting what one was but what one is. For Gaston to accept what he is, he must, perforce, deny Jacques. He goes into the future without the burdensome baggage of his past in a supreme affirmation of his freedom, whereas Henry's act of violence—it too a free act—shackles him forever in his world of fiction.

In *Signora Morli, una e due* ("The First and Second Signora Morli"), Pirandello confused a double personality with multiple facets of a single personality. *Mademoiselle Colombe* (1951) is the treatment of a basically similar situation. Anouilh does not, however, commit the Italian's error; instead, he leaves it to his hero, Julien, to think that there are two separate people called Colombe—the innocent, childlike girl he had married, and the worldly wise actress she becomes. "I won't let you throw mud at that girl,"[7] he tells Colombe, referring to the wife he knew before his army service. He can explain the drastic change only by imagining a dual Colombe, when in fact, her life in Paris was merely the catalyst that enabled the carefree facet of her personality to emerge dominant.

Another phase of the personality puzzle is given in *Restless Heart* (1934) and *Antigone* (1942). Here reappears the mask motif: people (women, as is usual in Pirandello also) who appear to the world in two contradictory manners. For Thérèse, a mediocre violinist with a shady past and a sordid background, marriage to the kind and wealthy Florent offers the unique opportunity of escape from the baseness of life. Yet, despite her longing for respectability, she deliberately plunges back into the mire of her former existence. The mask will not adhere to the face that hides behind it, and when it is torn away, Thérèse's personality conflict is resolved through the victory of her baser self.

Antigone is similarly torn in two opposing directions—her instinctive love of life is contrasted with her unrelenting drive for justice, even though the latter necessarily involves her death and the destruction of her city. Like Ersilia Drei and Thérèse, Antigone is bent on self-destruction, and in her case also, the mask of participation in life is not solid enough to ward off her basic nihilism. She epitomizes what Anouilh has succeeded in capturing so well in the heroines of his dark plays—the tragic flaw. But the flaw is not a personality trait exploited by an impassive fatality; it is inherent in the personality structure itself.

Poor Bitos (1956) presents an interesting variant of the multiplicity-

PIRANDELLO AND FRENCH THEATER

of-personality theme. In it, a man is forced to assume a personality not his own, but one which is similar enough so that he glides easily from one to the other. The young public prosecutor, André Bitos, has many enemies. His former schoolmates dislike him for his excellent grades—Bitos, the poor scholarship student, who had spent all his time studying. Others hate him for his methodical, ruthless prosecution of collaborators after the liberation. To get revenge, Maxime arranges a *dîner de têtes,* a gathering at which the participants disguise their heads as those of historical characters.

Bitos is asked to portray Robespierre; others come as Danton, Mirabeau, and sundry figures of the Reign of Terror. The accusations leveled at Robespierre are all too obviously double-edged, and Bitos is forced to defend both himself and his historic counterpart. The climax of the evening turns out to be the reliving of the shooting of Robespierre by the policeman Merda. The gun is not loaded, but Bitos faints and then dreams of himself as Robespierre. The remainder of the play is taken up with the efforts of the guests to placate Bitos, and with the latter's inability to differentiate between those hostile to him and those who have genuine sympathy for him.

Poor Bitos is perhaps Anouilh's most bitter play. Its cynicism is unrelenting and unrelieved. As a result, the spectator is overwhelmed by vitriol and cannot help but breathe more easily when the final curtain rings down. The multiple personality theme is very cleverly exploited by Anouilh. Bitos's personality blends with Robespierre's until the two become one. Robespierre's faults and qualities are Bitos's, their backgrounds the same, their careers similar; and Bitos's fantasy in which he is Robespierre seems perfectly natural. The whole conception of Bitos is well within the Pirandellian concept of personality.

A considerable number of Anouilh's plays involve the exploration of the relativity of truth. Most often, this relativity involves a situation concerning the preservation of peoples' private worlds—a notion which preoccupied Pirandello like Ibsen before him. But while the Norwegian's attitude centered around social protest and the Italian's somber pessimism provoked outrage at man's stupidity, the French playwright's work is permeated by sadness and by an irony, sometimes savage, that accompanies the conviction that happiness is, at best, very difficult to attain and that most human beings move in mutually exclusive spheres.

Both *Ardèle* (1949) and *The Waltz of the Toreadors* (1952) deal with generals' households living in sham, and in both cases a private fiction is allowed to dominate outsiders, with damaging effects. Pirandello maintained in *Il Giuoco delle parti* ("The Game of Roles"), in *Liolà,* and in other plays that each person is entitled to his private idea of himself so long as it does not hurt someone else. Anouilh provides two cases in point.

The marriages in Ardèle's family are pretenses. Lacking the courage to admit that they no longer love each other and are concerned only with their mistresses and lovers, husbands and wives pretend to the outside world that they are happily married couples. This, by itself, would not bring harm to anyone, but they try to impose these artifices on Ardèle, the hunchbacked sister, who falls in love with the equally hunchbacked tutor. Confused and morally twisted, the family members do not even recognize the importance of a true love, and, aware only that the tutor's social position makes a liaison with Ardèle unacceptable, they proceed to break up the romance and drive the deformed couple to suicide.

The children in this play also suffer because of the examples of conjugal relationships set for them. When they play at being adults, they only fight and scream and beat each other. "You know perfectly well," the countess tells her husband, "it is simply a question of avoiding a scandal." [8] But she does not realize that in building a fence of fiction around the family group unwilling members are included who, unable to escape, perish.

General Leon Saint-Pé of *The Waltz of the Toreadors* is guilty of the same crime. The fiction of his marriage, enduring through his wife's illness and his seduction of countless girls, is preserved not so much for appearances as out of cowardice. Without realizing that he is destroying himself and those around him, Leon refuses to end his marriage because he wants to spare his wife. As a result, the patient Ghislaine, his true love, wastes seventeen years of her life, and the General's wife must endure his constant infidelities. Clearly, the proper solution would have been to cut cleanly and swiftly, to avoid ensnaring innocent people in the general's fiction.

The Rehearsal (1950) is one further variation of the sham marriage motif. Into the heart of an aristocratic *ménage à quatre* comes Tigre's love for Lucile, the teacher he has hired for his orphanage. This is an intolerable situation for both his wife and his mistress, not because it involves their love but because it involves their dignity. Lucile is from a much lower station in life. Their solution, to destroy the couple, succeeds with the help of the villain, paradoxically named Héro—a villain of very unlikely motivation.

All these people attempt to protect the world they have created at the expense of other people. Their moral position is untenable, and they either fail completely or destroy themselves along with the outsiders who become entangled in their web. *L'Amour puni* (Love punished) is the subtitle of the last play, and it might well serve for all three, for it emphasizes the defeat of love.

Structurally, *The Rehearsal* differs from the other two plays in a way that is strongly reminiscent of Pirandello. The Count and his friends are rehearsing Marivaux's *The Double Inconstancy,* and the dialogue of the play-in-rehearsal blends with and becomes a part of the words spoken by the characters themselves, just as the situation in the eighteenth-century play is an echo of what is transpiring at the chateau. (The interplay is heightened by the *marivaudage* with which Anouilh endows his dialogue). This intimate relation between a play being enacted and another, included in it, being rehearsed, makes one think inevitably of *Six Characters:* Hortensia says to the Count, as the actors might tell the Father, "You just said we weren't playing ourselves." [9]

The characters are aware that their lives as people and as actors overlap. "I need to spread disgust a bit," Héro explains. "It's part of my role. Not the one in our little play, the other—the one I really play in." [10] And later, Hortensia tells Villebosse, who is anxious for rehearsal to start: "The play is in full swing! Do you mean to say you hadn't noticed?" [11] Life, these characters feel, as does Pirandello, is composed of roles that its participants play.

A little Pirandellian touch, too, is the dropping of the curtain at the conclusion of Act II, as the group rehearses its curtain calls; it brings to mind the accidental curtain in *Six Characters.* Of further interest are the Count's ideas as director for the presentation of the Marivaux comedy. He conceives the play as a direct outgrowth of life, which becomes animated in front of spectators—an approach reminiscent of *Tonight We Improvise:* "Character number stands up and addresses number two. The others listen, intrigued." [12] To prepare for this, an eighteenth-century turn is given to the conversation and the transition is complete. *The Double Inconstancy* emerges slowly, as a perfect illusion, out of a twentieth-century dinner party.

Ring Round the Moon (1947) highlights the contrast between the profound reality of Isabelle, who is actually a sham, and the falsity of the very real characters of the play; truth, as it concerns the validity of their existences, is proven to be relative.

Lastly, two rose plays, *Dinner with the Family* (1937) and *Time Remembered* (1939), clearly illustrate Anouilh's Pirandellian antithesis. Georges, the hero of the first play, belongs to the line of characters who create intricate fictions to compensate for unpleasant facts. To make up for the baseness of his parents and of his best friend Robert, he creates new parents and a new Robert. Beginning in his imagination, this process is then extended to Isabelle, the girl with whom he has arranged a rendezvous in Senlis. Finally, it assumes reality through the physical presence of the "parents" enacted by hired actors. This use of actors is the last stage of the creative process, as evidenced by Georges's advice to the actors: "You must understand however that I did not send for you to have you imagine theatrical fathers or mothers at will. These characters exist. These characters are already half alive. Someone believes in them." [13] These parents came into existence when Georges conjured them up in his imagination, and they became alive when they were impersonated in Senlis. Even Robert recognizes this in saying "appearances are more than enough to create a world." [14]

In *Dinner with the Family,* Anouilh also touches on another Pirandello theme—the art-life opposition. As the hired father and mother rehearse their roles with Georges, they are all so carried away by their inventions that they believe they are participating in reality. They are acting, but the play they are performing is more convincing than the life that gave rise to it. Unwittingly, Georges addresses the actors as if they were truly his parents and they in turn regard him as their son. In a small way, art has imposed itself upon life.

Time Remembered is not one of Anouilh's most effective plays, but it is worthy of attention because of its affinity to *Henry IV.* As in the Italian drama, a man's mind becomes unbalanced by unhappiness in love—in this case, the death of his beloved—and a wealthy relative attempts to create for him the surroundings in which he can maintain the illusion of the past. To foster the Prince's illusion that Léocadia is still alive, the Duchess recreates the places to which the young man had been with his love in the three days they knew each other before her death. But the Duchess then contrives a scheme to bring her nephew back to reality. She hires Amanda, a seamstress who bears a remarkable resemblance to Léocadia, to impersonate the dead beauty, hoping to shock him into the realization that Léocadia is no longer alive. The method used is exactly the same as in *Henry IV;* the result, is different, however, for the Prince is not defeated. He falls in love with Amanda and thereby succeeds in transcending the impasse of his passion for the dead Léocadia.

If Anouilh's theater is thus found to be thoroughly imbued with Pirandello, it must not be assumed that his plays are imitations. Henri Clouard says that Anouilh "frenchifies Pirandello,"[15] but he adds, as many other critics have, the names of Gérard de Nerval, Giraudoux, and especially Musset as influences on Anouilh. Anouilh is no imitator; his theater is highly original. But of course no playwright writes in a vacuum. If, first, Pirandello and, second, Musset are the strongest influences on him, it is proof of Anouilh's originality that he was able to blend different antecedents into a new entity bearing his own individual stamp. Anouilh's great debt to Pirandello resides in the themes that he has adapted an in the Pirandellian flavor of much of his dialogue and atmosphere. His is "a sort of Pirandellian drama of a single character in search of himself and it reiterates the familiar theme of escape from the ugliness of life."[16]

The distinctive contribution of Anouilh is the light touch of the rose and sparkling plays, woven with strands of his peculiar irony, and the more mordant humor of the grating plays with characters so unreal yet alive because of their passions and their foibles. These qualities form the complex of the theater of Jean Anouilh, whose eminence among French dramatists was achieved by a long series of thought-provoking, technically brilliant, and very actable plays.

As acknowledged leader of the existentialist school, as editor of the influential *Les Temps modernes,* as a dramatist whose plays stirred widespread discussion, Jean-Paul Sartre is the foremost theatrical figure of the postwar era. His skill in creating theater out of philosophical attitudes was largely responsible for the vogue of existentialism—a remarkable achievement, for it is rare for a philosophic movement to enjoy real popularity. Moreover, it is the first time that the theater was the instrument of this popularity. Sartre's merit lies in his ability to adapt his complex ideas to the requirements of the stage thanks to simplification and a choice of theatrical illustrations. His plays can be enjoyed by the uninitiated and even by those hostile to his ideas. A pioneer in a virgin field, Sartre set high standards for those who would propagandize a philosophy in the theater.

Sartre left no doubt about what he considers to be Pirandello's influence in France. Asked who was the most timely modern dramatist, he answered: "It is most certainly Pirandello."[17] That Pirandello is very much up-to-date is borne out in Sartre's own theater.

Underlying Sartre's plays is an attack on all pretense in human behavior that tends to turn men away from full acceptance of their responsibilities. This may be equated to Pirandello's concern with pretense as a danger when it harms others. The climaxes in Sartre's dramas occur as the main characters, breaking through their fictitious armor, face themselves and their acts in the stark glare of their liberty. In similar situations, the Sicilian's characters suffer the human anguish of self-confrontation; the Frenchman's feel the existentialist anguish of full responsibility. In the mirror in which the former see their souls, the latter see the absurdity of life.

In *The Flies* (1943), the illusion of guilt is fostered on Argos by Aegisthus and Clytemnestra, with Jupiter the instrument of their deception. The god explains that he enslaves through make-believe, through a form of hypnotism: "For a hundred thousand years I have been dancing a slow, dark ritual dance before men's eyes. Their eyes are so intent on me that they forget to look into themselves. If I forgot myself for a single moment, if I let their eyes turn away."[18] It is Orestes' role to stop the dance and thereby shatter the illusion of culpability that has enthralled the citizens. By killing the royal couple, the hero takes upon his shoulders all the guilt and all the responsibility for past events. He lifts the collective mask of the populace and forces existence on them.

Inès performs the same function in *No Exit* (1944). The only member of the play's unholy trio to see clearly her own reality, she taunts the other two until all their illusions are unmasked. "Well, Mr. Garcin, now you have us in the nude all right,"[19] she says, referring to that same nakedness that is Ersilia Drei's in *Naked* and that of other Pirandellian characters agonizing in self-revelation. Inès possesses the keen insight and the sharp tongue required to make Garcin and Estelle see precisely what they are, what they have done, and how they have concealed their truths behind the pretense of respectability. "Hell is—

other people!"[20] only because they are each other's conscience, the constant reminder of their sordid reality.

Inès also tears down the illusion that life is still possible in the infernal Second Empire drawing room. She makes clear that their visions of the earth are fading, that they have to stay together forever, and that the absurdity of their coexistence is complete because, being dead, they cannot even kill one another. The three have no choice but to accept the consequences of their lives, as Henry IV had no choice but to accept his.

The illusions must be replaced by reality because they have hurt other people. This is the same criterion for behavior that Pirandello expressed. "Certainly the characters in *No Exit* 'half lucid and half overcast' strip themselves naked and wallow in their anguish much as Pirandello's six characters."[21] Garcin and the Father of *Six Characters* express the same objection to being judged on the basis of one isolated act. The Father feels that the Step-daughter had caught him in a brief, unrepresentative moment of his existence and was trying to attach his entire reality to that moment. Garcin, for his part, asks "can one judge a life by a single action?" and Inès replies tersely "Why not?"[22] Likewise, in *The Victors* (1946), Canoris states: "It is on our whole life that each one of your acts will be judged."[23] In Garcin's case, however, that one act is not truly isolated; Inès proves it to be part of his general pattern. Cowardice is his reality and heroism merely the illusion he had created for himself. Because his wife had been made to suffer, Garcin is guilty and is relegated to the hell of Inès's probings.

"The anguished situation, the climate of torment in *Six Characters* is common to all of Sartre's plays and within it Sartre's heroes attempt to realize themselves like Pirandello's partially constructed characters."[24] *The Victors* points this out also. The Resistance fighters of the play are placed in a situation of extreme stress and torture, wherein they see clearly into their own selves. It is a terrible moment of truth. Some come face to face with the image of their cowardice for the first time; others discover that their heroism is tainted by dubious motives. Even those whose valor remains unchallenged find themselves drained of true human emotions, their bond to mankind severed by their singular bravery which sets them above all others. They represent the epitome of suffering as conceived by Pirandello.

The mirror and the face behind the mask shift to the domain of politics in the masterful denunciation of the sophistry of Communist Party practice, *Red Gloves* (1948). The reality that is revealed to Hugo does not concern his self; it concerns the truth about the Party. Hoederer's death is the catalyst. Upon his release from prison, Hugo learns that the man he had killed at the Party's orders has been "rehabilitated" posthumously. His act of murdering a man he respected emerges futile and absurd and the Party a ruthless tyrant with no use for idealism. Nurtured on the illusions of Party justice, Hugo suffers as much in his disenchantment as Pirandello's most moving characters. His raison d'être has been destroyed and he goes willingly to his death.

The Devil and the Good Lord (1951) exemplifies the shattering of metaphysical illusion. What Goetz attempts to do in this epic of atheism is to rid the world of its illusion of God and to force men to behold themselves in all their liberty. It is still basically the same theme of existentialist man emerging from behind pretense to assume his responsibility and freedom.

By 1955, *Nekrassov* proved that Sartre had lived to regret *Red Gloves*. His change of allegiance to the ideology he had condemned would indicate that the author frequently shares his characters' inability to differentiate between fact and fiction. Perhaps his frequent reversals would not prove so embarrassing if he had not marked each stage of his vacillation with a play that lasts longer than his latest attitude.

While *Red Gloves* was a serious, dramatically effective demonstration of the bankruptcy of Communist methods, *Nekrassov* is a farcical attack on anti-Communism, naive in its conception and puerile in its argument. Again the device of illusion is used—a newspaperman's scheme to boost circulation by "creating" a Soviet minister who has escaped and is selling his memoirs. He tries to impose a gigantic hoax on his readers for the sake of his job, notwithstanding the international discord that can arise out of the deception.

Sartre shares two elements with Pirandello: the absurdity both men discern in life and the frequent repetition of the illusion-reality theme. Sartre, however, penetrated to attitudes underlying the dichotomy and charged it with the implications of existentialist thought. His high opinion of Pirandello at the forefront of modern authors is explained by the similarities in their works, similarities which are actually far greater than a superficial glance would suggest.

PIRANDELLO AND FRENCH THEATER

If Albert Camus's theater remains too abstract and lacks Sartre's dramatic flair, his novels, or his *récits* as he prefers to call them, and his long essay *The Rebel* demonstrated his remarkable gifts. After a period of adhering to existentialist thought of a more or less orthodox nature, Camus veered away toward a broader humanism. Always aware of the utter absurdity of man's existence in this world, he is not content to accept this absurdity—his answer is revolt. This revolt is the solidifying bond of mankind, the simple "no" that expresses the refusal to accept the unreasoning tyranny of fate. The positive values that emerge out of unblinking recognition of man's situation are Camus's specific contribution to contemporary literature.

The absurd is the bond between Pirandello and Camus. Like Sartre, Camus understands the absurd in clearer and more conceptual terms than does Pirandello. Human values are implicit in Camus's theater, and perhaps because these values are never explicit, it remains too impersonal, too systematic, and too abstract. These factors have helped deny his theater the unqualified success of his other works.

Caligula (1945) is probably Camus's best endeavor in the dramatic medium. The Roman Emperor, who concludes that only arbitrary action can overcome the absurdity of existence, is a pathetic figure of defeat as he realizes finally that his liberty of peremptory terror was delusion because it was gained at other people's expense. Francis Jeanson compared this play to *Henry IV* because both heroes are alike in their isolation despite their omnipotence in their own realms:

> One will agree that from *Henry IV* (1922) to *Caligula* (1945), the essential preoccupations and themes did not become basically different. It is very much the same denunciation of this world which is not what it ought to be; the same disdain for those who get along with it; the same feeling of solidity; the same pessimism; the same recourse to the choice of the absurd against the very absurdity of existence; the same frenzy of denying and destroying, of pulling the world out from under the feet of those who have them firmly planted on it.[25]

Jeanson points to the similarities between these plays, but one must add that the problem of responsibility, basic to *Caligula,* does not figure in *Henry IV.*

One conversation between Caligula and his friend Cherea is notable for its Pirandellian character:

CALIGULA: Do you think, Cherea, that it's possible for two men of much the same temperament and equal pride to talk to each other with complete frankness—if only once in their lives? Can they strip themselves naked, so to speak, and shed their prejudices, their private interests, the lies by which they live?

CHEREA: Yes, Caius, I think it possible. But I don't think you'd be capable of it.

CALIGULA: You're right. I only wished to know if you agreed with me. So let's wear our masks, and muster up our lies. And we'll talk as fencers fight, padded up on all the vital parts. Tell me, Cherea, why don't you like me?

CHEREA: Because there's nothing likable about you, Caius.... And because I understand you far too well. One cannot like an aspect of oneself which one always tries to keep concealed.[26]

The references to masks concealing the reality of a person, to Cherea's several faces, to the pretense in the relations between people, are very reminiscent of the Italian dramatist. Whether they stem from Camus's knowledge of Pirandello cannot be determined, but they are certainly attributable to him indirectly, for these ideas had, by 1945, become thoroughly naturalized in the French theater.

If a bond seems to exist between the absurdity that Pirandello portrays in personal terms and the one that the existentialists visualize as an impersonal metaphysical reality, there is definitely a bond between Pirandello and Samuel Beckett's *Weltanschauung.* The depiction of absurdity as the dominant aspect of life in *Waiting for Godot* (1953) is so devastating because it is seen, as Pirandello saw it, in a profoundly human light, tempered with compassion for the victims caught in its web.

Vladimir and Estragon encapsulate mankind. Their pathetic efforts to distract each other in their never-ending wait for salvation are an attempt to create the illusion that they really exist, while actually they are merely dangling helplessly at the end of the perfidious rope of life. The great merits of the play are the ultimate *reductio ad absurdum* of the human condition and, despite the prevalent nonsensical atmosphere, its deeply moving quality on the individual level. In this respect, Beckett has contributed something new to the stage. *Endgame* (1957) continues in a similar vein, but it is even darker in mood, less humorous, less humanistic in conception.

PIRANDELLO AND FRENCH THEATER

Pirandello had elicited compassion in his plays, but he did not aim at a generalized philosophy of absurdity; the existentialists dramatized the absurdity of man's existence in this world without ever feeling pity for that trapped humanity; Beckett achieves the synthesis of both. His universal truth prevents him neither from sympathizing with mankind nor from participating in its fate. This reverting to the humanistic tradition is of primary importance in this postwar French theater which tends too much to the abstract. It may explain Jean Anouilh's great enthusiasm at the opening of *Godot:* "I think that the evening at the Babylone [Theater] is as important as the first Pirandello play produced by Pitoëff in Paris in 1923." [27]

Arthur Adamov, whose reputation was made in experimental theaters in the 1950s, reduces absurdity to the everyday life of ordinary people. His universe is often akin to the world of George Orwell's *1984*—a world in which the citizen is helpless against forces which victimize him for no purpose and in an arbitrary way. Adamov depicts the anguish and the senseless terror of the police-state age. His pessimism is so overwhelming that he envisages life for the individual as only an illusion of reason until total absurdity annihilates it.

This horror of the modern totalitarian state is dramatized in *One against the Other* (1953) and *The Great and the Small Maneuver* (1950). The Disabled Man, the principal character—for one cannot speak of "heroes" in Adamov's works—of the latter play, is deprived of all his limbs, one by one, in a senseless persecution by the authorities. Still he maintains the illusion that life holds happiness for him because a woman, Erna, loves him. The reality of the chaos of existence becomes clear for him only at the end as Erna, in an act fully as gratuitous as the quadruple amputation, vilifies him and pushes him out onto the street on his caster—a pathetic stump of flesh facing certain death. He brings to mind Kafka's Joseph K., also destroyed by an impassive fate without ever understanding why.

Although he does not use devices that tend to bring the audience "into" the play, Adamov attempts to make the play transcend the limitations of the stage in order to confront the spectators directly. He achieves this effect by means of what one might call an ultrarealistic technique, that is, not the faithful reproduction of realism, nor the emphasis on sordidness of modern neorealism, nor again the suggestion of a superior reality of surrealism, but a fusion of all three, in which the complete naturalness of the dialogue (to the exclusion of all

PIRANDELLO AND FRENCH THEATER

theatricality), together with the sharp, brutal outline of authority, infers the ultimate absurdity.

Because the language seems spontaneous and because both the situations and the terror are products of a society that is no longer fictitious but is already developing, the audience can identify with the action. As a result, the stage itself becomes more than the traditional boards, curtain, scenery, and so on; it becomes the willing accomplice of the dramatist, inasmuch as the play is projected by means of the stage rather than *on* the stage and is thus given life. Insofar as this is possible in a medium which, despite all efforts, is still artificial, Adamov succeeds in obtaining an additional, convincing dimension out of his stage: "The precursors whom Adamov admits besides [Antonin] Artaud . . . are all playwrights who grasped and gave material expression to the idea of the theater as an autonomous art inseparable from the physical space of the stage: Kleist, Büchner, Strindberg, and Pirandello." [28]

In the two plays mentioned above, Pirandello's influence is restricted to the concept that the life we live is mere illusion and to the heritage of the absurd. It is more widespread in other works. *The Invasion* (1950) stresses the relative nature of truth in a world wherein absolute truth is impossible to attain. The title refers to an unfinished manuscript which intrudes into the life of the family and friends of its deceased author. The laborious struggle of these people to decipher the handwriting and clarify the work ends in a dismal stalemate for, in addition to disagreeing among themselves, they individually find different interpretations for each word until no one is certain of the real meaning. The chief would-be editor finally tears up the manuscript and dies, an apparent suicide. The symbol of the enigmatic opus, whose meaning is impervious to comprehension thus emphasizing the impossibility of determining the truth, is akin to Signora Frola's veil in *Right You Are If You Think You Are.*

The Parody (1952) suggests again that life is lived in an illusion, with reality hidden and far removed. The motions of the characters in the play are, like our own motions, only a parody of existence itself. Lastly, *Professor Taranne* (1953), concerns a Pirandellian type of self-confrontation. The university scholar of the title is incapable of living up to his reputation; as he grows aware of the gap between his true self and the person he is thought to be, he resorts to plagiarizing the ideas of his colleague Ménard. But Taranne cannot endure his own

PIRANDELLO AND FRENCH THEATER

deception any more than he could endure mediocrity. Subconsciously craving to be exposed, he carries to an extreme the act of stripping himself of all deceit: he is caught walking the streets stark naked. He thus shows his true self without the illusions imposed by the plagiarism. Ironically, people mistake Taranne for Ménard when he tries to identify himself. The illusion has even conquered others.

It is evident that Pirandello's ideas infiltrate these five plays in varying degrees. Adamov's theater is compelling and almost frighteningly modern in its emphasis on the suppression of the individual and on the impossibility of communication between people. The absurdity of contemporary life, seen in abstract terms in Beckett's plays, is very concretely pictured in the theater of Arthur Adamov.

Eugène Ionesco represents, together with Adamov and Beckett, the successful new voice in the French theater of the 1950s. His plays place him with the writers of the absurd, but the world of Ionesco lacks the brutality of Adamov or the total despair of Beckett. He does share with the latter one quality, rare indeed among innovators today—humor. Much of his work is filled with jokes, puns, hilarious nonsense, and apparently meaningless sentences that are often uproarious.

His first play, *The Bald Soprano* (1950), seems to have the same basic goal as Adamov's *The Parody*. Like his elder colleague, Ionesco calls attention to the mechanical ritual of living, which creates the illusion of life but which, in fact, is only a parody of it. His subject is that oft-satirized English society of proverbial reserve, lack of humor, vapid social banter, and sentimentality.

In *The Chairs* (1952) and *Amedée* (1954), Ionesco deals with the married couple. The latter play moves on a real and on an illusory level. Amédée and his wife Madeleine find a dead man in their apartment. While this corpse, symbolic of the love that they have killed in each other, grows constantly, taking up more and more room in their apartment until it becomes gigantic, the couple continues to behave in an entirely normal way as if the situation were completely natural. The illusion of the enlarging body becomes a part of their everyday reality.

The Chairs projects the interior existence of a very old couple onto a semicircular stage, which soon fills with chairs. These chairs are occupied by imaginary guests, including the Emperor, entertained by the Old Man and Old Woman. Whereas the illusion in *Amédée* is materialized as a corpse, in *The Chairs* it is left an illusion: the increasing number of imaginary people are reflected only by the ever-larger number of chairs that clutter the stage. Besides this Pirandellian illusion theme, Ionesco suggests also the multiplicity of the Old Woman's personality. Suddenly, she becomes grotesque and vulgar, and the stage direction demands a style of acting "entirely different from her manner heretofore as well as from that she will have subsequently, and which must reveal the hidden personality of the Old Woman."[29] It is her erotic self coming to the fore.

Like Beckett and Adamov, Ionesco attempts to use the theater for new, essentially dramatic expression. These three authors and other avant-garde playwrights such as Neveux, Genet, and Vauthier approach the play primarily as a function of the theater. Therefore, they investigate every avenue of theatricality and invention that might extend the limits of the stage. In Pirandello they found a logical precursor who had tried the same thing. Ionesco explains that "Luigi Pirandello's theater does, in fact, meet the ideal exigencies of the structure, of the dynamic architecture of the drama. He is the manifestation of the inalterable archetype of the idea of the theater which we have in us."[30]

The theater of Georges Neveux is best classified as avant-garde. *Juliette ou la Clé des songes* ("Juliette or the Key to Dreams"), written in 1927, earned him considerable renown at its 1930 production. Since 1940 he has written regularly for the stage. The experimental element of Neveux's works is his technique: the dramatization of a heavily symbolic dream; the encounter with the dead, the living, and the unborn; the face-to-face meeting of a man and his self; the experiencing of an action before it takes place. The content of his theater is, however, surprisingly traditional. His subjects are fate and the human experiences of life and death. Neveux is not a philosophical playwright, and one need not seek a system of thought or a portrayal of the absurd in his dramas. Germaine Brée points out that the "bitter existential revolt against man's 'absurd' condition is completely alien to him. In *Plainte contre l'inconnu* ("Action against Persons Unknown") (1946), he reverses the basic existentialist theme, pointing to the absurd human refusal to accept life, all of life, as it is given."[31] This emphasis on life's positive values is in welcome opposition to the gloom of many of Neveux's fellow experimentalists.

Neveux assigned to *Six Characters* an enormous influence in the history of the modern French theater. On the occasion of the twentieth anniversary of Pirandello's death, a French periodical asked several French playwrights if they had been influenced by Pirandello. Georges Neveux's answer explains what he himself and an entire generation of French dramatists found in Pirandello:

> Pirandello is, first of all, the greatest prestidigitator of the Twentieth Century, the Houdini of interior life. In his most important play, *Six Characters*, he took the very center of the real world and turned it inside out right in front of us, as the fisherman turns inside out the skin of an octopus to lay bare its viscera. But what Pirandello laid bare before us is not only the work of the actors, nor that of the author, not only the other side of the scenery, but something much more universal: the other side of ourselves. It is our inner life which is suddenly found projected on the stage and decomposed there as if by a prism. What are these fantoms, condemned to relive endlessly the same scene (all of a sudden one thinks of *No Exit*) if not the most obscure part of ourselves. These six characters are not only the unfinished creatures of an author at a creative impasse, but also, and more important still, those impulses which each of us keeps within him and does not manage to live out.[32]

This sudden confrontation with one's inner self and these hidden desires are the Pirandellian elements in Neveux's theater. His Pirandellism is always on the human level; he is not concerned with the artist's dilemma.

In *Le Voyage de Thésée* ("The Voyage of Theseus" 1943), the Minotaur that Theseus finds in the labyrinth of Cnossus looks like Theseus himself; it is, in fact, an aspect—the happy side—of the young Athenian's personality that suddenly confronts him. The secret of the Minotaur's deadly power over the many youths sent yearly to slay it was its ability to appear as the hidden self of each of its victims, which paralyzed them in the agony of encounter. Theseus alone has the strength to look at himself honestly, to reject by tearing the thread linking him to his bride, the part of himself that longs for happiness, and to accept his fate by recognizing it in the labyrinth of existence. The Pirandellian mirror in *Le Voyage de Thésée* is the Minotaur.

Self-confrontation is achieved in a more conventional manner in *Plainte contre inconnu* (1946). The six plaintiffs against God or the Unknown—who appear in the prosecutor's office as gratuitously as do

PIRANDELLO AND FRENCH THEATER

Pirandello's six characters on the stage, and who, like them, demand to register their protest against the injustices done to them—are dissuaded from their planned suicide by being afforded a long look at themselves. This is made possible indirectly by the prosecutor. Having attempted and failed to change the determination of the sextet bent on self-destruction with the customary reasons in favor of life, the public servant unwittingly offers them hope. He points out what a perfectly happy man he is, shielded from any conceivable annoyance or misfortune. In so doing, he lays bare the empty existence of a man whose impervious armor shelters nothing within him. Upon seeing what a "happy" man looks like, the six reconsider their decision. Each of them searches deeply within himself and realizes that life is worth being lived; they all choose to resume their lives. The image of his own hollowness is not lost on the poor prosecutor either, and it is he who finally shoots himself.

Additional Pirandellian elements can be observed in Neveux's other plays. Although the employee of the dream bureau in *Juliette ou la Clé des songes* makes it clear that dreams and reality must remain in mutually exclusive worlds for a sane man, Neveux nevertheless punctuates the attraction existing between them. For Michel, the illusory realm of Juliette has far greater appeal than his real life. He is reluctant to abandon his travels through the symbolist maze for the less enchanting, if truer, light of the everyday world.

In *Ma Chance et ma chanson* ("My Chance and My Song") (1940), the dead materialize on the scene when they are needed with the same sort of improvised magic that brings forth Madama Pace in *Six Characters*. Lastly, one element of *Zamore* (1953) also evokes the Italian play. With the help of *la fièvre de tout à l'heure* ("the in-a-little-while-fever"), a condition that enables one to see the near future, the Police Commissioner tells Zamore that he will be killed by Charles Auguste, his wife's lover. From that point on, try as they will to escape their fate, the curious *ménage à trois* plunge relentlessly forward in their destined roles with as little real hope of avoiding the culminating shot as there is for the six characters. The three are, in fact, like characters falling in spite of themselves into the trap an author has set for them.

Neveux's use of Pirandellian techniques and motifs is a good example of how modern playwrights benefit from Pirandello. Neveux is no imitator, and none of his plays is overwhelmingly in the Italian's tradition; but Neveux's theater as a whole incorporates much of what is best in Pirandello.

Jean Genet's *The Maids* (1947) dramatizes a double transfer of personality. The sisters Claire and Solange, Madame's maids, engage in frequent excursions into other personalities, with one "playing" their employer, the other taking her sister's role. On the day of the action, it is Claire who, as Madame, heaps abuse on Solange, whom she calls Claire. What had started as a game for the sisters becomes starkly real. With the "imitation Madame" wearing the clothes and assuming the manner of speaking of the actual Madame, the two lash one another verbally and articulate their resentment against their mistress. Their occasional lapses, when they call each other by their true rather than their assumed names, stress only more strongly how fully immersed they are in their adopted identities. Having prepared a poisoned tea for the real Madame without succeeding in getting her to drink it, Claire, completely consumed by her impersonation, drinks the fatal brew. By accepting Madame's death, Claire fuses into Madame's personality. This alter ego—only an illusion at first—is complete reality at the end. Genet's view of disintegrating personality is directly in the Pirandellian line, with the emphasis on the imagined aspect of multiplicity rather than on the innate one.

Pirandello has been applauded enthusiastically in France since the initial performances of *The Pleasure of Honesty* and *Six Characters in Search of an Author,* and his techniques and propositions have been mirrored with equal enthusiasm by many French playwrights. French plays depicting the relativity of truth, the multiplicity of personality, the art-life opposition, and the overwhelming absurdity of life have become familiar on the Parisian stage during the past three and one-half decades. The striking modernity of his approach appealed to many French dramatists, and the lessons Pirandello taught them were taken seriously. His influence reached a considerable segment of dramatic authors both great and secondary. It was with only slight exaggeration that Georges Neveux wrote: "Without Pirandello and without the Pitoëffs (because one can no longer separate them, the genius of the Pitoëffs having given its form to Pirandello's) we would have had neither Salacrou, nor Anouilh, nor today Ionesco, nor . . . but I shall stop, this enumeration would be endless. The entire theatre of an era came out of the womb of that play, *Six Characters*."[33]

A great part of the French theater of our era was influenced in one way or another by Pirandello, or showed similarities to his work. Some playwrights, like Anouilh, are Pirandellian in a major group of plays; others, like Cocteau, only in one or two plays. While many were directly influenced, others found that their ideas were in accord with his, and others still, especially some of today's younger dramatists, have felt the impact indirectly through their seniors who had already made Pirandellism a part of the French theater. Pirandello is "French" now not only because his plays have been produced regularly in Paris for the past thirty-seven years, but also because his ideas and methods were made essential elements of French dramatic expression during this period. The Sicilian is still a potent force in the contemporary scene.

It is rare for a dramatist to wield a truly extensive international influence. Besides Pirandello, only Shakespeare and Ibsen have left such a legacy, and it is unlikely that either has affected the theater of a single country of any one era more than the author of *Six Characters*. Of all the various forces that combined to mold the theatrical imagination of the French writers of our age, none was more widespread, none more penetrating, and none more productive than his.

The essence of Pirandello's theater is the marrow of contemporary ideas, of modern anxieties and pessimism. This is what the French writers admired in him. Elements of Pirandellism can be detected in the works of other European playwrights: László Krakatos, Kurt Goetz, and Miguel de Unamuno—in whose case similarities rather than influence are seen. In this country, Pirandellian concepts are found in the plays of Thornton Wilder, Elmer Rice, and Arthur Miller. But these are all isolated cases and indicate no concentrated influence by Pirandello on a single country's theater. Even in Italy, where one might expect to find an important school of dramatists influenced by the master, only a relatively few well-known authors reflect Pirandello's contribution. One might mention Gherardo Gherardi, Ugo Betti, Eduardo de Filippo, Diego Fabbri, and Cesare Viola, but they are in no way disciples.

It was France which was most receptive to Pirandello and which adopted him as its own. The Italian, who had been most responsible for liberating his country's drama from simple imitations of French models, turned the tables by giving France bold new ideas and daring techniques. Pirandello's great role in France is an outstanding example of international theater.

From "Pirandello's Influence on French Drama" in *Pirandello: Twentieth Century Views,* ed. Glauco Cambon (Englewood Cliffs, N.J.: Prentice Hall, 1967), 43–65.

CHAPTER FOUR

From Text to Performance: The Dialectics of Contemporary Theater

The theatrical text has always been a pretext for the end product of theater, that is, for performance. The relationship between text and performance, between language and action or movement on stage (or even what we prosaically call "stage business") has varied from generation to generation, as the concept of theater itself has undergone transformation. The dialectic relationship between text and performance is the sign of the dynamics of theater at any given period. Since the 1960s, this dialectic has been particularly active, changing subtly—and at times less subtly—changing generally but not consistently in the direction of primacy of the concept of performance over the centrality of text.

The struggle for performance supremacy is not really new in our time, but the early attempts to downgrade the function of language in theater were relatively few and on the whole ineffectual. The mainstream of Western theater remained faithful to the word in the first half of the twentieth century. The more marked path away from the verbal signifier toward a nonverbal signifier—that is, a path leading away from text and toward the staged performance as the recognizable theatrical entity—corresponds to a gradually shifting emphasis in

64

FROM TEXT TO PERFORMANCE

the signified of theater during the 1950s and early 1960s. The signified
of theater that emerged from these shifts articulated the metaphysical
anguish undermining the apparently safe structures of new societies in
the post-World War II era, past the politicization of the mid- and late
1960s, from Berkeley to the Paris barricades and beyond—when in
the theater, as elsewhere, language was perceived as having a mission,
as having *something to say*—to the generalized disillusionment and
despair of later recent years: a desensitization, a stultification yielding
a theater beyond words, beyond language, a theater which seizes the
world through what is *not* said, what is not sayable, what is unnamable. For the past forty years, the dialectic has alternated from a fairly
balanced position in the early 1950s with the theater of the absurd to
a clear domination by performance subsequently, led by powerful
directors and companies working collectively, leading to a new synthesis characteristic of the new realism of the late 1970s and early 1980s
in which an unarticulated, diminished language maintains a dynamic
tension with noneventful action.

In the theater of the absurd, the dialectic appears quite balanced in
contrast to the mainstream theater of the previous period, totally
dominated by text—for example, Shaw, Giraudoux, Sartre. Genet's
plays are extraordinarily textual and yet fully dramatic or perfor-
mance-oriented, especially *The Blacks* and *The Screens*. For Beckett,
the texture of the dialectic is quite different, but the balance is there
just the same, at least in his early plays. To be sure, Beckett's language
stresses above all the impossibility of communicating and Lucky's
diatribe in *Waiting for Godot* is the perfect sign of the failure of
language. The forlornness of Didi and Gogo, the particular ambiance
of *Dasein,* of being at once in the microcosm and the macrocosm of
the human condition, everywhere and nowhere, is fashioned both by
the text ("Let's go," "We can't," "Why not," "We're waiting for
Godot," "Ah")[1] and by the desolate stage space which frames the
performance while rendering it impossible for the spectator so much
as to imagine anything beyond the stage. The performance blends the
emptiness of language and the nondescriptness of place to produce
that anguish *sui generis* that permeates *Godot* viscerally and finds
verbal expression in the one violent burst of lyricism:

Have you not done tormenting with your accursed time! It's abomina-
ble! When! When! One day, is that not enough for you, one day he went

dumb, one day I went blind, one day we'll go deaf; one day we were born, one day we shall die, the same day, the same second, is that not enough for you? They give birth astride of a grave, the light gleams an instant, then it's night once more.[2]

Similarly, we can speak of a certain balance in Ionesco's theater; *The Bald Soprano* is all text, even if its thrust is to explode language and meaning. The performance aspect requires the actors to play their roles with utter seriousness, unaware that they are describing the emptiness within the void as if their discourse really formed the rational core of a meaningful universe. In *The Chairs,* the balance is maintained: the two key components of this "tragic farce" are the stage chaotically full of empty chairs and the mock triumph of text in the garbled, incomprehensible message delivered by the orator.

The generation that followed Beckett and Ionesco was still fascinated with the problematics of language. Playwrights such as Harold Pinter, Marguerite Duras, and Nathalie Sarraute explored the dramatic potential of silence, but they treated silence as a complement of language, of text, rather than a disappearance of language. It was Peter Handke who, more than any other dramatist of the 1960s, probed the limits of language as theater text. His "Sprechstücke" are events without action that exist solely on the level of text. *Self-Accusation* and *Offending the Audience* are pieces of disembodied text, of pure language, or, as Handke wrote: "spectacles without pictures inasmuch as they give no picture of the world."[3] *Kaspar,* an infinitely more structured work, breaks away from the purely textual nature of Handke's earlier writing to introduce highly complex patterns of performance. Language remains at the core of *Kaspar* (Handke says, "it shows how someone can be made to speak through speaking," and he proposed an alternate title, "speech torture").[4] But *Kaspar* is also remarkably plastic; the main character's struggles against his monitors and alter egos remove this work from the category of pure textuality by frankly acknowledging the performance component.

If Handke represents perhaps the logical inheritance of the theater of the absurd, the counter tendency—away from the text—affirmed itself in the 1960s and became clearly dominant in the 1970s. With Artaud as patron saint, directors in Europe and the United States tipped the dialectic clearly toward performance, away from text, creating idiosyncratic "theater pieces" that are nonreproducible by others, since their theatricality depends entirely on the stage view—or staged view—of a particular type of space: thus Jerzy Grotowski and the Polish Theater Lab, the Living Theater and the Becks, Joseph Chaikin and the Open Theater, Peter Brook, Eugenio Barba, Luca Ronconi, Ariane Mnouchkine and Le Théâtre du Soleil, Richard Schechner and the Performance Group, the Bread and Puppet Theater—to mention only the best known of the first- and second-generation performance directors and collectives.

For his Theater of Cruelty, Artaud had shunned traditional text and postulated that "the director becomes author—that is to say, creator."[5] This corresponds to more than a mere shifting of weight to the director in the perpetual stress and strain among the three main creative forces in the theater: director, actor, playwright. It is nothing less than an esthetic of the performance theater in which the deep effect of the theatrical representation is actually lessened by language (thought of by Artaud as reductive and paralyzing, rationalistic and conventional in nature), and heightened, on the contrary, by (in Artaud's words) "another language . . . to restore its old magical efficacity, its power of enchantment, which is integral to words, whose mysterious potential has been forgotten."[6] For him, language is rigid, limited, incapable of accounting for the reality of phenomena, incapable of describing the smooth surface of things. In Artaudian theory, the text/performance dialectic is one-sided.

Peter Brook, one of the most cerebral and also probably the most eclectic of contemporary directors, addressed the need for a new equation in the text/performance dialectic when he wrote in *The Empty Space:* "Is there another language, just as exacting for the author, as a language of words? Is there a language of actions, a language of sounds?"[7] This search for another theoretical expression Brook has carried on with remarkable lack of dogmatism. He had been drawn to modernist textual theater, with productions of *The Balcony* and *Kaspar* among others; his continuing explorations of Shakespeare (*King Lear*—reread in the light of Beckett's *Endgame*; *A Midsummer Night's Dream* that explored vertical space via a circus setting and metaphor) naturally did not abandon the level of text, even if the emphasis was shared by a highly inventive sense of performance. But in *Orghast,* "written" by the poet Ted Hughes in an imaginary language (invented by him) and performed in Persepolis, Brook detached himself entirely from language to concentrate only on performance elements: movement, sound, and nonarticulated elemental forces. His more recent work with his International Centre for Theater Research at Paris's Bouffes du Nord continues the eclecticism of his stance. *Conference of the Birds, The Iks, The Mahabarata,* and *The Man Who* all downplayed the purely textual element and were essentially performance pieces; on the other hand, Brook's highly acclaimed *Carmen* stripped away layers of operatic tradition to focus on the spare, tragic nature of the text.

The use of artificial language in *Orghast,* which offered no direct meaning, attracted other directors as well. The Living Theater and Grotowski used related techniques at times; Andrei Serban's *Trojan Women, Medea,* and *Electra* (spoken in Ancient Greek, Sanskrit, and Latin) willingly dispensed with verbal communication—but it didn't matter since everyone knew the action anyway—in order to dwell fully on the performance possibilities inherent in the mythic material and in the guttural harshness of language limited to the domain of connotation. This approach is diametrically opposed to the way playwrights such as O'Neill, Eliot, Sartre, and Giraudoux dealt with myth. In a somewhat similar vein was Richard Schechner's *Dionysus in 69* with the Performance Group. It is worthwhile noting that Schechner, also a leading theoretician of performance theater (and what he terms "environmental theater"), approaches staging more from the vantage point of cultural anthropology than from dramatic theory. Performance theory, he states, "is a social science, not a branch of aesthetics." [8]

In the 1970s, the movement away from text encompasses most major experimental theater people: Robert Wilson's startling productions, and especially the indelible *Deafman's Glance* which, as the title emblematically suggests, projected movement and pure visual qualities with no dialogue at all; the Open Theater's extraordinary late works, such as *Nightwalk* and *Terminal,* involving body, movement, and vocal effects but no real text; and Stuart Sherman's strange, short speechless spectacles. For all these and more, the text/performance dialectic was wholly tipped in the direction of performance.

But not all experimentalists are so performance-committed. Le Théâtre du Soleil, for instance, has maintained a careful and even very

FROM TEXT TO PERFORMANCE

special balance between text and performance. Their memorable *1789* used multiple techniques of performance, from marionettes to clown show to gross parody to historic reenactment, but throughout, actual historic debates and speeches blended with ironic reconstitution to provide a very solid textual base. In Richard Foreman's Ontological Hysteric Theater, we see perhaps better than anywhere else the synthesis of the continuing concern with language and a new (or newly rediscovered) concern with the plasticity of stage images and actions. Like Handke, Foreman is a careful reader of Wittgenstein. In the first *Manifesto* (1972) Foreman writes: "Theater in the past has used language to build: what follows what? We use language not to destroy but to undercut pinnings of *there*."[9] Foreman rivets our attention on words and action alike. Repetitions, ultra slow speech, echoing tapes extend the field of audition granted the spoken text; slow motion, stylized and exaggerated movements, concrete sight lines made of drawn strings, all stress the presence of actors and punctuate their movements. These two techniques combine with loud, jarring noises and bright lights flashed at the audience to shake up our perception and oblige us to reconsider our concept of performance.

Like Foreman, the Mabou Mines by and large also choose in their esthetics to deny a dominant role to either text or performance. They are less systematic, however, since the productions of the Mabou Mines involve the work of a number of directors and are therefore less classifiable. Still, whether in the stagings of Lee Breuer, JoAnne Akalaitis, Fred Neumann, or Ruth Malaczech, whether in plays by Beckett or in original works such as *Dressed Like an Egg, Dead End Kids,* the various "Animations," or *Prelude to Death in Venice,* text and action are equally central.

The most recent theater trend is the new realism, which has commanded attention in a number of countries—and may well be seen to link with esthetic imperatives in other forms of artistic expression. The bankruptcy of values, the vacuity of mass-produced, mass-marketed behavior patterns, the lack of dimension, of real meaning in the lives of late twentieth-century men and women fill the strange, new, essentially nonverbal plays of dramatists such as Franz Xaver Krötz, Botho Strauss, Michel Deutsch, Jean-Paul Wenzel, Tilly, the collective of the Théâtre de la Salamandre of Tourcoing, Spalding Grey, Elizabeth LeCompte, and the Wooster Group. If they do not form a school, certain points in common are nevertheless discernible: concentration of surface realities that seem to conceal no greater, hidden meanings (somewhat reminiscent of the early novels of Robbe-Grillet), a *dramatis personae* composed of very ordinary people who speak little or not at all, and who say nothing much even when they are speaking, who do things and at times commit angry or violent acts—ordinary people whose behavior and inarticulateness reveal a profound emptiness and despair. The settings may be naturalistic in their precision, but there is no return here to nineteenth-century modes of realism. These plays are more allusive, full of suggestion, and the formal behavior of the characters is but the tip of a deep, distressing emotional iceberg set in a frame of reference that is, by implication, political. It is a curious use of text that is wholly downgraded to favor performance values, which are, however, equally and deliberately flat and unemotional.

In Krötz's *Request Concert* the single character, deprived of language, suffers a veritable implosion of her existence, culminating in her utter abandonment, a void that can be filled, at best, with an overdose of sleeping pills. Significantly, not a word is spoken in the entire play. Krötz expresses his esthetic in terms of a reaction against the antirealistic conventions that have become the mainstream of theatrical expression. He stated that he "wanted to break through an unrealistic theatrical convention: garrulity," thus making clear his disparagement of text. "The most important 'action' of my characters is their silence," he goes on, "and this because their speech doesn't function properly. They have no good will. Their problems lie so far back and are so advanced that they are no longer able to express them in words." [10] Krötz's performance theater seeks a new truth, one deprived of language—a deprivation more sociopolitical than metaphysical—a truth beyond language and text.

Seen from the vantage of the permanent dialectic between text and performance, the most notable aspect of the forty years of theater has been the giving way of the concern with language to a reaction against language in favor of a purer level of performance (purer in the sense of being less dominated by text). This has been the most experimentally oriented period in the history of the theater, and much of that experimentation has concerned language directly. We have come around 180 degrees—from the theater of the absurd to a period of true performance theater and then a tentative return to forms of realism, and

FROM TEXT TO PERFORMANCE

with it a conscious downgrading of language. But lest things seem too easily schematic, it must be remembered that Beckett, Pinter, Sam Shepard, and others continue to write, continue to keep the text predominant in a still very dramatic theater.

Adapted from "From Text to Performance—The Dialectics of Contemporary Theater," *Proceedings of the 10th Congress of the International Comparative Literature Association* (New York and London: Garland Publishing, 1985), 275–79.

INTRODUCTION TO GIRAUDOUX, COCTEAU, ANOUILH

I have a real weak spot for the French theater between the two world wars. In the 1920s, it generated exciting experimentation in theatrical forms, much of it under the impulsion of Pirandello; by the 1930s, the avant-gardism of the previous decade gave way to a wise, witty, mature period—one of the most satisfying of the entire century. For me, Giraudoux, Cocteau, and Anouilh are, with Sartre, the outstanding, the most enjoyable playwrights before the revolution of the theater of the absurd in 1950.

I was once asked how, as a lover and specialist of Beckett, I could like Giraudoux. To me this sort of question makes no sense. The one in no way cancels out the other and I have no difficulty in responding very positively (though differently) to the plays of two very dissimilar but great dramatists. Each offers me a distinct, rich universe; I don't want to have to reject the one in the name of the other. Jean Vilar, the celebrated director and founder of the Avignon theater festival, once stated that between Claudel and Adamov, he chose Adamov. I find that a reductive attitude. I want both Claudel *and* Adamov, and I certainly want both Giraudoux (and Cocteau and Anouilh) *and* Beckett. I don't want to be forced to choose, even if Beckett for me is in a category by himself, the *ne plus ultra*.

Giraudoux, Cocteau, and Anouilh were, each in his own way, marvelous dramatists, especially in their bringing substance and remarkable theatricality to their reinterpretation of Greek myths. The best the French theater of the interwar years had to offer is precisely their reworking of the stories of Œdipus and Antigone, Electra and Orestes, and other Greek mythic heroes and heroines. Each created his own, idiosyncratic universe based on the Greek one, highlighting a modern approach that illuminates the classic, well-known stories and is illuminated by them. Giraudoux's language introduces us to a very special world, far removed in spirit from ancient Greece even if the stories are those of the Trojan war, of Electra, and of Amphytrion; Cocteau's Orpheus and Œdipus are Greek heroes deflated but also reenergized by modern readings; Anouilh's many Greek plays are profoundly contemporary in spirit, transformed from the Aeschylus, Sophocles, and Euripides models on which they are based, while retaining the universality that is the hallmark of myth. The works of these three playwrights, profoundly French in their writing and their nonrealistic dramaturgy, rank at the very top of dramatic creativity in the first half of the century. I have never tired reading them, seeing them, or teaching them.

CHAPTER FIVE

About Jean Giraudoux

In a time when many French dramatists have become well known to playgoers in the United States, it is paradoxical that Jean Giraudoux, acclaimed by most critics as one of the most illustrious and original French playwrights of the twentieth century, is by comparison little known to the American public. To be sure, his best works have been performed on Broadway, some with considerable success (notably *Tiger at the Gates*); but the enormous impact of Giraudoux's work in his native country has never been felt by audiences this side of the Atlantic.

This fact cannot be dismissed merely by attributing it to a general lack of interest by American audiences for French plays. It is true that Gallic stage successes have sometimes failed dismally in New York, but this is hardly the rule. Anouilh, Ionesco, and Beckett, for instance, have been well treated here, while Genet enjoys an even greater reputation in the United States than in France. Why then are Americans not equally impressed by Jean Giraudoux, a writer who has been called "the most original dramatist of our time"?[1]

The answer, it would seem, lies in his language. The enchantment, the brilliance of Giraudoux's theater stems, above all, from the en-

75

chantment and brilliance of his language. His is a French of subtle phrases, of sparkling, *précieux* images and metaphors, luxuriant without any trace of self-consciousness, remarkably refined in its aristocratic elegance. Giraudoux is the heir of that great tradition of French letters which for centuries has stressed grace in expression. More than any other writer in the era between the two world wars, he kept alive this classic inheritance.

Since his language is of fundamental importance, Giraudoux loses much in translation. This loss, in general, is not the fault of his translators; many of his plays have been rendered into English by such gifted writers as S. N. Behrman, Christopher Fry, and Maurice Valency, all remarkable manipulators of the English language, and the latter equally adept in French. Rather, the difficulty is that English is not properly suited to the verbal pyrotechnics of Giraudoux's French, and that the finely chiseled conceits of his idiom, enhancing as well as expressing his thoughts, leave the English-speaking spectator a trifle disoriented. A Giraudoux is best savored in French!

It is through language that the immensely rich universe of Giraudoux's theater emerges—a literate, loquacious theater whose very cornerstone is sophisticated discussion. Among the finest scenes in his plays are those in which two characters debate, or one character expounds with great poetic imagination the essential point of contention at the heart of the drama: Hector and Ulysses weighing the arguments for and against war in *Tiger at the Gates;* Alkmena sparring with Jupiter about infidelity and friendship in *Amphitryon 38;* the Supervisor likening a Civil Service career to a marvelous voyage of discovery in *The Enchanted;* the Ragpicker's impassioned "defense" of the world's exploiters in *The Madwoman of Chaillot.* In every case, the play is built on a fundamental contrast, intellectually conceived and developed through the dialogue of articulate people.

If contrast underlies his plays, Giraudoux's life, as well, is not without its share of opposites—the renowned writer who is also a successful diplomat, the novelist of repute who abandons his genre for the theater, the cosmopolite who remains at heart linked to the small towns of his native Limousin.

It was in Bellac, a town of some three thousand people, not far from Limoges, that Jean Giraudoux was born in 1882. No great cathedral, no museum, no noteworthy industry sets Bellac apart as a point of interest. In fact, its importance to Giraudoux stems from its very insignificance—it is a provincial town like any other in France, and, as such, it inspired in him a love not only for his birthplace but for all similar places where simple, good people, average Frenchmen, dwell. When his father, a tax collector, was transferred to nearby communities, Jean felt in no way *dépaysé*. Many years later, after having seen much of our world and having come to know many of its great figures, Giraudoux still remained essentially a Limousin, firmly rooted *en province,* treasuring humble virtues above all others.

His earliest successes in life were of an academic nature. He was a brilliant student at the Lycée of Châteauroux and, in his early twenties, at the famous Ecole Normale Supérieure in Paris, where he graduated first in his class. To have been a *normalien* is perhaps the best recommendation a young Frenchman can have as he seeks a career; to have graduated at the head of the class is more than a recommendation, it is an attestation of the highest possible intellectual capacity, which automatically opens numerous doors. After a scholarship in Munich, Giraudoux went to Harvard in 1906 for a year as a lecturer in French. He was to return there a decade later during World War I, when, having been wounded at the front and decorated, he was sent by his government as a military instructor, first to Portugal and then to the American university. His impressions of the United States were set down in a book entitled *Amica America*.

After passing brilliantly the required examinations, he entered diplomacy in 1910 and moved through a wide variety of posts on his way up the ladder of the Ministry of Foreign Affairs. At one point, he was Chief of Press and Information Services; other assignments took him to leading cities of the world. Following the outbreak of war in 1939, Giraudoux's final assignment as Minister of Information included the insurmountable task of propagandizing the moribund Third Republic. Soon after the creation of the Vichy regime, he resigned, profoundly discouraged, thus terminating a very distinguished governmental career.

Throughout these years of public service, Giraudoux led a double life; his private commitment was to literature. His debut in literature came with *Provinciales,* a collection of stories published when he was in his mid-twenties. During the following two decades, the young diplomat wrote a series of novels and short stories that earned for him considerable renown and a reputation as a skilled, if overly *précieux,* prose writer. Giraudoux was already forty-six years old when he turned to the theater. At the urging of Louis Jouvet, he dramatized his successful novel *Siegfried et le Limousin* (calling it simply *Siegfried*) and gained immediate acclaim. The year was 1928. During the remaining fifteen years of his life, he wrote fourteen more plays which placed him securely at the very head of his country's dramatists. All but one of these were staged by Louis Jouvet. This brilliant actor-director and the writer formed one of the most fruitful theatrical collaborations of modern times. They complemented each other perfectly. Like his mentor Jacques Copeau, Jouvet's fundamental approach to theater was through the text. This innate respect by a director for the written word proved fortunate in the case of an author whose theatricality, essentially verbal, does not rely on striking stage effects. Jouvet and his superb company played Giraudoux with precisely the proper emphasis, speaking his lines with a clarity of diction that gave them their full value.

Opinions vary as to which is Giraudoux's greatest play, but any listing of the finest French plays of our century would surely have to include all or most of this half dozen: *Amphitryon 38, The Enchanted, Tiger at the Gates, Electra, Ondine,* and *The Madwoman of Chaillot.* Deliberately conceived in a lesser key, two of his one-acters, *Paris Impromptu* and *The Apollo of Bellac,* are small masterpieces as well. In these and in his other plays, there is inherent a universe that is Giraudoux's very own. It is a poetic universe, with all the luster, transparency, and sparkle of a diamond—where the impossible is commonplace and only the prosaic inconceivable. Typical of Giralducian enchantment are Isabelle's pupils in *The Enchanted,* those pert little girls for whom good and evil in the world are caused by The Harmonizer, with Arthur responsible for such minor frolics as caterpillars climbing up school inspectors' trousers. For them, a tree is "a tall person who is rooted to the ground," a zero the best of grades because it most closely resembles infinity, their classroom the great outdoors where they write on "blueboards." If the Inspector is outraged by such education, it is merely because he is too pedestrian to breathe in the purity of their atmosphere. In this rarefied surrounding, Isabelle is not to blame for allowing herself to be attracted towards death by the Ghost; rather, her shortcoming is in not treasuring life. Consequently, the remedy devised by the supervisor is apt: by immersing Isabelle in the noises of everyday existence, he succeeds in leading her back to life.

Giraudoux excels in his female characters of all ages—from the old (Aurélie, The Madwoman of Chaillot) to the mature, married woman (Andromache, Alkmena), to that most ethereal and perfect of all his creations, the young girl, charming, innocent, beguiling (Isabelle, Ondine, Agnès). If, as has been claimed, much of Giraudoux's theater is a battle of the sexes, it is generally one in which feminine delicacy and fragility oppose masculine clumsiness and lack of imagination. These women, "interstellar creatures who have chosen the earth . . . sleep and live with man, a terrestial creature." [2]

This relation is exemplified in the story of Ondine, the ethereal water sprite who renounces her aquatic realm for love of a bold knight, despite the warning that he will die if he deceives her. For the pure Ondine, love is total in what it gives and what it demands. Alas, Hans, unlike his mate, is only human. In reaching for Ondine, he had exceeded himself. He had attained an unaccustomed height at which he could not linger; insensitive to the world of nature, he falls back to earth, stifles in the totality of love that is given to him and finally deceives Ondine, thus sealing his death. This tragic denouement could not be avoided in Giraudoux's scheme of things, for once Hans had perceived perfection, he could neither do without it nor live up to it.

The battle of the sexes, tragic and charged with allegoric significance in *Ondine,* is again tragic and allegorical in the last work to be produced during Giraudoux's lifetime, *Sodom and Gomorrha,* a somber and uncharacteristically pessimistic view based on Genesis. Significantly, in the play it is not righteous men who are needed to ward off destruction, but a couple in love. However, for Jean and Lia, passion has not managed to survive a few years of marriage. They have grown so far apart that only bitterness remains. Clearly they have failed the test, and the world is destroyed. But even in this grim scene, Giraudoux's irony and wit are not absent. Following the total annihilation, the voices of the twosome are again heard, still bickering:

THE ARCHANGEL: Will they finally stop talking! Will they finally die!
THE ANGEL: They have died.
THE ARCHANGEL: Then who is speaking?
THE ANGEL: They are. Death has not been sufficient. The scene continues. [3]

Ironic, these lines, but also infinitely sad! Coming as they do at the end of his life, during a time more depressing than any previous one, they reveal his discouragement. Perhaps it is not entirely coincidental that despite their differences in significance, these final words foreshadow those of Sartre's *Huis Clos,* a year later (1944): "well, let's get on with it."

For Alkmena and Andromache the battle ends in decided triumph, for, unlike Lia's marriage, theirs are founded entirely on virtues. Thus, by counteracting the rapacious Jupiter's various ruses, Amphitryon's wife eventually succeeds in imposing her purity on him. Once victorious, she offers him the noblest gift mankind has to bestow, that quality unknown to the gods—friendship. Giraudoux's humor is at its broadest in this tale, but tempered always by sufficient irony to keep *Amphitryon 38* from becoming farcical.

More elevated in tone and sober in outlook, *Tiger at the Gates* is a well-nigh perfect blend of wit and loftiness. Its theme is that tortuous period of simultaneous preparation for war and desperate attempts to avoid conflict, a theme whose contemporary significance did not escape the audience in 1935, and continues to be uncomfortably meaningful in 1963. Among the numerous brilliantly and originally conceived characters, Hector and Andromache loom large in their blend of public virtue and domestic tenderness. Hector, the victorious general weary of war, who longs to live in peace with his wife and the child she will bear, is Giraudoux's most noble creation. Discounting the prevalent nationalistic sentiment in Troy, he argues, pleads, and reasons in a heroic, albeit futile effort to reverse destiny and human folly, hoping that, by returning Helen to the Greeks, his countrymen might ward off catastrophe. In his majestic oration to the dead, Hector extols the fallen warriors, but in so doing he throws the weight of his words in favor of life. Peace, so costly to win, must henceforth be preserved; Hector closes the gates of war and prepares to send Helen back to Menelaus.

Andromache fully endorses her husband's pacifism. She trembles for him when he is in battle, more worried about his life than about his glory. But if war is folly, war for no reason is utter absurdity. Andromache begs Helen to love Paris. Then, at least, the destruction to follow, no less horrible, would not be totally devoid of sense. It is for sanity's sake and for the sake of the man and the unborn child she loves that she not only endures Ajax's insults, but is proud of Hector for not letting himself be provoked by the Greek's slap. Ironically, when the two giants of the Homeric world, Hector and Ulysses, meet to weigh the arguments for peace and war, it is the noble Trojan princess who tips the balance. Ulysses, with the overwhelming weight of historical destiny on his side, is about to opt for conflict when, in a sudden spurt of generosity, he changes his mind because Andromache's eyelashes remind him of Penelope. Here, for one fleeting moment, woman's innate longing for peace and order triumphs over the inanity of men and all is well with the world. If Lia had been Andromache and Jean Hector, Sodom and Gomorrah would not have been destroyed. But, of course, tragedy will not be denied; the jingoistic poet, Demokos, has his revenge even in death—the Trojan War will take place. "The Trojan poet is dead," says Cassandra "And now the Grecian poet will have his word."[4]

In this imaginative rendition of the prelude to one of ancient history's momentous events, Giraudoux has tempered the seriousness of his theme with some of his most tender scenes as well as with his cunning wit. No pages in his works are more moving than those in which Andromache and Hector, like any ordinary husband and wife, rejoice in the prospect of having a child. They are profoundly human, but not witty, for they who judge the situation ominous can have no taste for humor. In contrast, Helen, who unwittingly precipitates the debacle, is enveloped by Giraudoux's humor. The men of Troy adore her no less than does her abductor, for she is to them the symbol of their collective virility. Of course, their admiration is not entirely symbolic in nature—they are not beneath peering up at Helen's anatomy as she strolls on the ramparts. Giraudoux's mordant irony is evident in his very concept of her. She is, after all, the cause of the tragic happenings; it would be fitting if she had sufficient stature to be worthy of her role in history. Giraudoux, instead, depicts her as a flighty conceited girl whose only quality is her beauty. Events present themselves to her in bright colors or in dull grays; she instinctively associates herself with the former. Thus the author shows momentous decisions hinging on the vivid imagination of an egotistical mental lightweight. As if to punctuate the absurdity of it all, Giraudoux ends his play with the gates of war opening and revealing Helen kissing young Troilus.

Even though *The Madwoman of Chaillot* boasts all the characteristics of Giraudoux's other plays—sharp irony, subtle wit, sparkling language, highly individualized characters, and remarkable theatricality—it is yet quite different from all of them. The irony is sharper, the wit more concrete, the dialogues just as sparkling, but with a new whimsical quality. The characters are individualized to the point of being outlandish and often grotesque caricatures; the theatricality is more apparent and more essentially linked to the very concept of the play.

The circumstances surrounding the production of *The Madwoman of Chaillot* in December 1945, were unusual. For the first time Jouvet was on his own; Giraudoux had died the year before. From *Siegfried* in 1928 to *Ondine* in 1939, Louis Jouvet had introduced each of the Limousin's plays. The two men had depended on each other. They would consult on such matters as interpretation and corrections in the text; whenever the producer was beset by doubts, the author would gently reassure him. But now, Giraudoux was gone. Not only could Jouvet no longer ask his advice, but he even had to choose from among the variant texts extant. Moreover, several unknown factors came into play. Would the writer who had captivated audiences in the thirties appeal to those of the postwar era? The prevailing mood had, after all, changed perceptibly; it was more serious, even grim, and a fantasy might be out of place, especially when viewed against the rising current of existentialist literature, full of philosophic import and not given to comedy.

Jouvet himself was marking his return to Parisian footlights after four years of performing in South and Central America with his company. He could not help but wonder whether he would still be able to assess the theatrical pulse of the French capital. More than ever, Jouvet was prey to the anxieties attendant upon a new production. Nor were his worries lessened by the fact that *The Madwoman of Chaillot* required a large cast at a time when it was extremely difficult to obtain funds even for a two-character drama. But help was forthcoming. A public appeal by Jouvet for props and costumes for the fanciful work brought forth a flood of articles in response; more important, a government subsidy was granted which made the production possible.

The play was an immediate triumph. Giraudoux and Jouvet had come back to Paris to reclaim their ever-faithful audiences. The one, posthumously, proved that he was not out of tune with the times—the times were out of tune and urgently needed good, highly sophisticated comedy; the other reaffirmed his artistic eminence and, until his death six years later, remained clearly a leading director of the French stage. *The Madwoman of Chaillot* ran for 297 performances at the Théâtre de l'Athénée—the longest run of any play by Giraudoux. In the title role, the veteran actress Marguerite Moreno capped a lifetime's career with her remarkable portrayal. Jouvet played the Ragpicker, whose second-act trial defense is the climax of the play. Two much-praised sets by the renowned designer Christian Bérard, depicted the bustling terrace of the Café Chez Francis on Place de l'Alma and the mysterious cellar in Chaillot, the gateway to the bowels of the earth.

The appeal of *The Madwoman of Chaillot* is not surprising. It is readily comprehensible, perhaps the most easily accessible of Giraudoux's major plays. The multitude of characters who parade on stage fall neatly into two groups: the good people of the world and the bad—or, in the author's terms, the simple folk who enjoy the ordinary pleasures of life, and the power-thirsty, money-minded "dealers" of society who defile everything their hands touch. The delineation is so evident that no one need wonder what the author means, or which side he favors. There are only heroes and villains—nothing in between. Irma epitomizes this conception of life. In her monologue ending the first act, she declares that she hates ugliness, bad people, evening, the Devil, slavery, death; and loves beauty, good people, daytime, God, liberty, and life.

Since life, however, does not reduce itself to clear-cut choices, how can a play with so singularly ingenuous an outlook be so well received? How could the most sophisticated French dramatist of his time write it? In fact, the simplicity is deliberate and, rather than betraying a naïve Weltanschauung, it is symptomatic of a poetic vision. Giraudoux condenses the myriad complexities of the eternal opposition between good and evil into a highly imaginative situation involving stock characters and four delightful madwomen. Only by resorting to such a nonsensical scheme as the oil exploitation of the Paris subsoil and by treating wildly improbable conspirators could Giraudoux treat this timeless subject without becoming involved in an exercise in topical social commentary. For, despite numerous contemporary allusions, *The Madwoman of Chaillot* is not an indictment of an age; it addresses itself to the perennial greed, cunning, and ruthlessness of mankind. When the Ragpicker's mock defense becomes, in effect, an indictment of the moguls of modern commercial-industrial civilization, his vitriol could just as easily have been directed at avaricious Roman patricians or wily feudal barons.

Germaine Brée quite correctly labeled *The Madwoman of Chaillot* a modern masque, pointing out the resemblance to the ancient form: stylized language, disguises and costumes, the transparent confrontation of virtue and vice leading inevitably to victory for the former. The similarity can further be seen in the atmosphere of gay improvisation that marks the play and invests it with a prodigious theatricality. Giraudoux maintains a careful distance between stage and audience, as if to remind the spectators that theater, essentially, is illusion. He makes the illusion real for us while insisting that it is, nevertheless, illusion; he does not pretend to give it the consistency of reality.

In a sense, then, the roles of illusion and reality have been reversed. Supposedly, the various businessmen and the prospector live in the realm of fact, while Aurélie and her zany cronies are relegated to their private pretenses. But for us, these men have no reality; theirs is a world of utter madness where they plot feverishly to turn Paris into a vast oil field. The madwomen on the other hand, despite their carefully elaborated fictions of invisible dogs and imaginary suitors, grow in credibility until their fantastic solution for ridding the world of its parasites strikes us as logical. The evil legions descend to subterranean death; the long-imprisoned good people are released; the birds start singing again. Illusion triumphs over reality.

In a much more obvious way, *The Apollo of Bellac* also deals with an imposition of illusion on reality, of beauty on ugliness. The secret Agnès learns so well from the mysterious gentleman is simply that the male of the human species thrives on flattery. The most repugnant of men will believe that he is handsome if a woman merely tells him so. Such flattery, far from being reprehensible, is highly desirable for it has the power to transform darkness into light, to make life more tolerable by embellishing the mirror in which we see ourslves reflected.

It is quite proper that the incarnation of beauty—the Apollo of Bellac—is imaginary. Beauty, itself, resides only in the imagination of the observer who has the magical power actually to make attractive what he deems attractive. In *The Apollo of Bellac,* this power is granted to Agnès, a lovely young girl possessing all the many charms Giraudoux discerns in her sex and her age.

ABOUT JEAN GIRAUDOUX

The author tells, with the verbal grace so characteristic of him, the brief tale of how Agnès learns to use the key to men's hearts. The playlet is all dialogue, as brittle, sparkling, and pure as fine crystal. Like crystal, it must be enjoyed for its fragile qualities—examine it too closely and it shatters. It is perhaps the ideal vehicle for the presentation of Giraudoux's outlook on life that stresses above all the need to poetize, to give free rein to imagination, and to treasure what little we have in this world. The President is wise to marry Agnès; in the reflection of her eyes, everything is metamorphosed, himself included. Agnès, too, is wise to marry him, his ugliness notwithstanding; beauty is where she wants it to be, nowhere beyond that. The Apollo of Bellac does not exist.

Giraudoux sent the manuscript of this work to Jouvet in Rio de Janeiro, where it had its world première in 1942, with Madeleine Ozeray and the director in the principal roles. The author left to his friend the choice of a place of origin for the imaginary Greek god. Jouvet accordingly selected a different small town in the Limousin and named the play *The Apollo of Marsac*. Later, when it was published following its first French performance in 1947, the location was changed to Bellac because a manuscript prepared by Giraudoux himself, revealed that the author had selected his birthplace.

Louis Jouvet died in 1951. Jean-Louis Barrault staged the last remaining work of Giraudoux, *Duel of Angels,* in 1953, bringing to a close the long literary career of the writer-diplomat. His enchanted universe remains, inviting us to cross its threshold. It is a universe that has not aged. Writing at a time when the French theater was convulsively exorcising its antiquated realistic traditions, Giraudoux was not content with mere innovation. His theater represents a process not of destruction, but of rebuilding through poetry, through brilliant manipulation of the French language, through gentle irony a world complete unto itself, peopled by a rich and representative assembly of men and women engaged in the often discouraging yet exhilarating business of living.

Adapted from Jean Giraudoux, *La Folle de Chaillot* and *L'Apollon de Bellec,* edited by Tom Bishop (New York, Dell, 1963), 9–21.

CHAPTER SIX

Jean Cocteau Revisited

During his lifetime, Jean Cocteau was one of the most widely discussed literary figures, revered by many, reviled by others who considered him a mere clown. In the course of nearly six decades in the limelight, Cocteau tried his hand at most forms of literary expression as well as many outside the realm of literature: poetry, theater, novel, criticism, cinema, ballet, and painting. This very diversity has been a source for attacks on him, for some critics interpreted it as proof of Cocteau's dilettantism. Moreover, the very foundation of his esthetics generates controversy since it relies on a constant change of forms and on a conscious desire to scandalize and shock the public in order to rivet its attention.

Critical reaction to Cocteau followed an uncertain curve during the course of his career. During his most inventive period, in the dozen years following World War I, he was misunderstood by the establishment and hailed as an innovator by a minority concerned with new forms. By the mid-1930s, *The Infernal Machine* won the admiration of many of his former antagonists — "a masterpiece of the modern theater"[1] and "one of the legitimate triumphs of the antinaturalistic theater,"[2] in the words of two eminent critics Francis Fergusson and Eric Bentley, respectively.

86

JEAN COCTEAU REVISITED

Not surprisingly, the last years before his death five years ago were not his proudest, artistically speaking, and they help cloud even more his true merit. Writing in 1961, Jacques Guicharnaud called him "an understudy of genius," with a signature rather than a style. "The general impression is," he adds, "that Cocteau has always something to do if not always something to say."[3] This excessively harsh judgment may be the result of the weaker late works casting a shadow on Cocteau's heroic period; in any case, it proves to what degree he succeeded in doing something he wanted more than anything else: to irritate. He irritated with his works and with his life, with startling techniques and striking images, with his fondness for opium, his conversion to Catholicism, and his election to the Académie Française. Everything he did or wrote was intended to rouse from lethargy—and let the chips fall where they may.

Perhaps no one responded to the bait more feverishly than François Mauriac, himself a perennially controversial figure. In the weeks following Cocteau's death, when he was widely eulogized by many and when most of his enemies were content to remain silent or to print bland praise, Mauriac laced into his late colleague with characteristic nastiness, unable to contain his disapproval of everything for which Cocteau had stood:

> His death yields up to me the secret of the uneasy feeling which he gave me: I am astonished that he was capable of doing something as natural, as simple as dying, something so unstudied. This time he is not trying to pass off for a sleeping poet; he is the sleeping poet. I am sure at last that he really is what he appears to be and what he no longer pretends to be, since he is dead.[4]

It is time to revisit Jean Cocteau and to attempt an assessment of his real worth. It is perfectly clear that some of Cocteau's work is second-rate, contrived, and derivative. But that is not really the question; it is more important to ask what the *positive* elements in his works are. The theater appears to be the most logical place to evaluate Cocteau's best qualities, not only because he probably gave the most of himself to that genre (with, perhaps, the cinema a close second), but also because it is in the theater that he functioned most successfully as an innovator. Neither in the novel nor in poetry, for instance, did Cocteau contribute anything new; in the theater he did, and it is precisely as an innovator that Cocteau has left much of his mark.

It is true, of course, that Cocteau thought of himself primarily as a poet, but for him poetry is an all-embracing term, and he speaks readily of such terms as "graphic poetry," "poetry of the theater," "cinematographic poetry," and so on. Thus, to speak of Cocteau the dramatist is in no way to neglect the poet. They are one and the same.

In the post-World War I period, a generation of playwrights deliberately went about revolutionizing the French theater in order to liberate it from the restricting sterility of the realistic tradition. Cocteau's place in this upheaval is striking. He introduced new themes and techniques to the stage, but most importantly, he contributed his own, very personal esthetics—which one may appreciate or reject today but whose originality at the time is undeniable. The foundation of this esthetics is mystery, magic, illusion,[5] and it is here that we discover his "poetry of the theater." The mirror, an object that crops up frequently in his works, is the symbol of mystery, par excellence, the gateway leading from the world of the real to Cocteau's peculiar realm of magical enchantment.

His approach to the theater as medium was particularly novel and paved the way for other avant-garde thrusts in later years by other playwrights, including many of those now in the limelight. For Cocteau insisted on maintaining a careful distance between the stage and the audience in order to stress the basic unreality of the dramatic phenomenon. This, possibly Cocteau's major contribution to the theater, is not to be confused with Brecht's famous *Verfremdungseffekt,* whose purpose is didactic. The French writer's main concern was to make a definitive break from the naturalistic molds left over from the nineteenth century. His preface to *The Eiffel Tower Wedding Party* serves as a veritable manifesto. He begins in a typically tongue-in-cheek manner, by referring to a line from the play itself: "A remark of the Photographer's might do well for my epigraph: 'Since these mysteries are beyond me, let's pretend that I arranged them all the time.' This is our motto par excellence" But after brushing the esthetics of surrealism—(from which he never remained far removed even though he never embraced it entirely)—"I try to paint more truly than the truth"—Cocteau develops his basic notion of theater: "The fact is that I am trying to substitute a 'theater poetry' for the usual 'poetry in the theater.' 'Poetry in the theater' is a delicate lace, invisible at any considerable distance. 'Theater poetry' should be a coarse lace, a lace of rigging, a ship upon the sea."[6] Cocteau will not attempt to make his public believe in the reality of what is transpiring on the stage; he *wants* his public to be aware that it is watching a play, an illusion which is not reality, but which, thanks to poetic truth, may be "more real than reality."

In the preface, Cocteau stresses another important aspect: "Every living work of art has its own ballyhoo ("parade"), and only this is seen by those who stay outside. Now in the case of new work, this first impression so shocks, irritates, angers the spectator that he will not enter."[7] This notion of the relationship of new forms vis-à-vis the public is basic not only for Cocteau but for many avant-garde movements.

In his early plays, Cocteau emphasized the visual aspect of the dramatic representation, and in so doing, he anticipated such contemporary playwrights as Ionesco and Adamov. Objects, particularly, played a major role—objects which are often displaced in unexpected settings and which at other times appear to have some sort of independent life (e.g., the broche in *The Infernal Machine*). In his dramaturgy, he relied heavily (too heavily, undoubtedly) on theatrical tricks such as his famous mirrors through which characters step into other worlds. These tricks endow his plays with their air of mystery, but there are times when Cocteau abused them with the facility of a prestidigitator.

If the techniques are at times excessive, Cocteau tends to play down the magical aspects of his theater thanks to his clear prose style, this *style blanc,* lucid and devoid of grandiloquence, which gives a classic aspect to his avant-garde plays. Moreover, if the spectator is suspended in a realm removed from his own, he eventually manages to find himself, since the themes of even the most puzzling Cocteau plays are familiar: man, his fate, the drama of the self, and the role of the poet in the world.

Viewed from the perspective of the post-World War I era, Cocteau's modernity is remarkable. For Robert Kanters, he is modern right down to his fingertips.[8] Cocteau's initial foray into avant-garde writing was precipitated by Serge Diaghilev in a by-now legendary conversation on the Place de la Concorde, a half-century ago. The renowned director of the Ballets Russes, walking with Nijinsky and Cocteau, then twenty-eight years old, turned to the young poet and said: "Astonish me!" The immediate result of this exhortation turned out to be the ballet *Parade* which created a veritable sensation in 1917. But at a time when all forms of artistic expression were being completely revolutionized by such men as Diaghilev, himself, Picasso, Apollinaire, Stravinsky, the poets of "Dada," and so many others, to "astonish" became for Cocteau an esthetic formulation basic to the new spirit that was in the process of being shaped.

The very essence of his avant-garde outlook is his insistence on saying "no" to established forms at the very moment that they have become established. The experimental writer always seeks newness and considers constituted structures tyrannical. Cocteau was forever prepared to change the rules of the game. But this readiness also led him at times to return to outdated techniques in a strange reversal. Thus he explains in the preface to the naturalistic play *Intimate Relations* that he will no longer write experimental theater because experimentation had become hackneyed. The true avant-garde attitude of the late 1930s, he claimed, consisted in no longer writing avant-garde plays! It is obviously not difficult to point out the absurdity of such a statement; Cocteau, himself, knew his position to be illogical, but he maintained it out of a continuing fondness for paradox and scandal.

Yet for Cocteau scandal was not a matter of personal publicity—it was his way of upsetting and shocking his spectators so that they would pay attention and approach works with more or less open minds. Neal Oxenhandler entitled his study of Jean Cocteau *Scandal and Parade*, thus punctuating the two vital elements that comprise his theater. Cocteau himself said with his great flair for paradox and epigrams that "one must know how far one can go too far ('Il faut savoir jusqu'où on peut aller trop loin')."

Three of Cocteau's early works for the stage are particularly significant. *Parade*, in 1917, attempted a synthesis of various forms of art. Cocteau wrote the scenario for the ballet, Erik Satie composed the music, Picasso painted the sets, and Diaghilev's Ballets Russes, with Léonide Massine, performed the choreography. This search for pure theater—a combination of pantomime, ballet, music-hall variety show, and play—proved to be a brilliant marriage of the arts, the first avant-garde theater in France since *King Ubu* two decades earlier and a powerful impetus to theatrical iconoclasm.

The Eiffel Tower Wedding Party four years later, also "mixed media," as one might put it today, is much more recognizable as a play. It is permeated by a carnival atmosphere of gay improvisation and humorous inventiveness, as Cocteau for once dispenses with mystery and esoteric symbolism. The plot, if one may use that term, involves a wedding dinner at the first-floor restaurant of the Eiffel Tower during which odd things happen. The expressionistic technique is new and strange: two loud speakers, placed at either end of the stage, not only comment on the action like some impersonal, electronic chorus, but even speak the lines of all the characters in the play; a large old-fashioned camera enables people to appear and disappear unexpect-edly. Through this use of stage devices, Cocteau succeeds in poetizing such banalities as a wedding dinner and tourists on the Eiffel Tower. Perhaps most significantly, the preface served Cocteau as a manifesto for antirealistic theater.

These early plays, by their very breaking of precedent, were in-tended for a limited audience. They caused a great furor in a rather small circle. *Orpheus,* directed and played by Georges Pitoëff in 1926, earned Cocteau his first real success. *Orpheus* marks a significant moment in the development of the modern French theater, since Coc-teau was the first of the modern playwrights to refashion and modern-ize Greek myths—before Giraudoux, Gide, Anouilh, and Sartre. In going back to Greek mythology, Cocteau tapped an immensely rich vein, which later yielded some of the finest French plays of the 1930s and 1940s, including his own *Infernal Machine.* Greek gods and he-roes were to become familiar figures on the Paris stage; but in 1926 they served the shock value that Cocteau sought as he forced his audience to break its normal habits in order to discover a new mean-ing in the ancient archetypal situations. Cocteau's most striking weapon against his audience was the liberal use of anachronisms. Orpheus, dressed in a sweater, uses a typewriter, receives telegrams, and possesses a birth certificate, while rubber gloves and electric ma-chines are the instruments of Death and her Biblical helpers, Azrael and Raphael. Heurtebise, a character invented by Cocteau is a guard-ian angel and a glazier—two anachronisms rolled up into one—and there is much stage business concerning a magic horse tapping out messages in Morse code. Clearly, the spectator, not used to such techniques (it was not until years later that one would become accus-tomed to it), was obliged to reconsider the entire tale and to seek new implications.

For behind this external dazzle, Cocteau was dealing with a serious theme: the unlimited power of poetry for transforming life and the painful but necessary discovery of self by the individual. Through the use of analogies and verbal sparkle, the play escapes from the domain of reality as Cocteau ushers us into a poetic universe of mystery and magic. As he had announced in his manifesto, the author attempts to have his illusion accepted—and accepted *as* illusion and not as reality. Thus, the prologue announces at the outset that art involves a difficult equilibrium and asks for the public's rapt attention for the play about to be performed. Moreover, during the course of the spectacle, one of Death's assistants, in need of a watch, turns to the audience to borrow one. This deliberate interruption of the action is Cocteau's way of reminding the public that what it is witnessing is not life but an imitation of life wherein the reality of metaphoric truth compensates for verisimilitude. This is what Cocteau meant by "poetry of the theater"; it is a far cry from the fourth-wall convention of the realistic stage which would have people believe that they are the privileged spectators of the private lives of the characters, with one wall removed so that they can peek in, undetected.

These various innovations made of *Orpheus* an outstanding date in the development of French avant-garde theater. Without it, Giraudoux could not have written *Tiger at the Gates* nor Anouilh, *Antigone,* to name only two works. And if *Orpheus* has aged by now, it is still eminently playable today. Most important in Cocteau's own evolution, it paves the way for his greatest work, *The Infernal Machine.*

Cocteau's original treatment of the Oedipus legend must be considered on the borderline of the avant-garde and accepted, "classical" theater. Not that *The Infernal Machine* reverts to some older form of dramaturgy; rather, it is the entire French theater which progressed from 1926 to 1934, and what shocked earlier only surprised eight years later. The avant-garde movements of the 1920s were beginning to stabilize and to become widely accepted. The experimental success of *Orpheus* helped to make possible the much broader success of *The Infernal Machine.*

Cocteau reinterpreted the myth to render it more accessible to the modern spirit. He does not attempt to improve on Sophocles; his aim is to restate a familiar situation for contemporary man, in his own terms. To this end, the structure employed by Cocteau is a direct help: the first three acts are modern in tone, heavily Freudian, with ironic overtones of Hamlet and contemporary allusions, part farce, part parody, full of double meanings and devoid of heroic spirit. But the fourth and final act, entitled "Oedipus the King" brings us directly into the tragic and mythic world of Sophocles, with the myth now

JEAN COCTEAU REVISITED

perfectly accepted by the spectator and charged with a new significance. The first three acts display a certain fairy-tale character—the
knight who kills the dragon, marries the princess, and lives happily
thereafter. But at this point the tragic machinery of the fourth act
makes itself felt and leads inexorably to the fated conclusion. Cocteau
protests against the essential nature of the human condition, against
the pain and misery of life, against destiny; however, it is the protest
not of a philosopher or a social thinker, like Sartre, but rather that of
a poet and a humanist.

Cocteau's concept of the well-known characters is highly inventive.
Oedipus, until his elevation to tragic stature at the end, is a fatuous,
ambitious, not very sympathetic young man; Jocasta is a foreign-
accented, aging nymphomaniac; and the Sphinx is a beautiful young
girl who, tired of killing, gives Oedipus the answer to her riddle. Only
Tiresias is a tragic character throughout, and this despite the fact that
Jocasta calls him "Zizi."

As in his other plays, Cocteau goes to great lengths to underline the
unreality of *The Infernal Machine.* He removes all elements of suspense by having first a Voice and then Anubis relate the events twice
before they occur. Thus the spectator is free to concern himself mainly
with understanding Cocteau's particular intentions and points of emphasis. As before, there is a wealth of brilliant paradox and witty
epigrams ("The gods exist, that's the devil of it") but on the whole
these entertaining devices, by their profusion, do the author more
harm than good. They tend to give an impression of superficiality
when in fact they are meant to reaffirm the life of the myth.

Following *The Infernal Machine,* Cocteau wrote a fantasy, *The
Knights of the Round Table,* then naturalistic plays such as *Intimate
Relations, Les Monstres sacrés,* and *The Typewriter,* next romantic
plays such as *Renaud et Armide* and *The Eagle Has Two Heads,* and
finally *Bacchus,* an unsuccessful play with philosophic pretensions.
These plays add nothing new to the contemporary French theater,
unless it be the delicate and psychologically profound treatment Cocteau gives in *Intimate Relations* to the theme of incest which was at
that time still taboo in literature except for the Oedipus myth. It
would be expecting too much of Cocteau to have remained in the
vanguard all of his life; no one has managed that for the entire span of
a long lifetime, not even Picasso. How would it have been possible for
him, near the end of his days in the 1950s and early 1960s, to write in

the manner of Ionesco, when he was two or three generations removed from the dramatists of the absurd? And if he had done so, would he not have been attacked for being imitative?

Every writer must be put in his proper perspective. Cocteau's avant-garde contribution was immensely valuable. His avant-garde theater is not like today's which attacks language and bases itself on a vision of life as absurdity; but in order for playwrights such as Ionesco, Beckett, and Genet to write as they do, the theater needed first to experience the avant-garde thrust of the 1920s in which Cocteau played such an important role. It was then that the French theater was firmly placed under the sign of antirealism, and that valuable new theatrical forms and techniques were explored. Most French experimental dramatists of the post-World War I era have been relegated to total oblivion (e.g. Jean-Victor Pellerin, Simon Gantillon, Bernard Zimmer); Cocteau remains very much alive. And if the accusation that he followed trends rather than set them is justified in some cases, it certainly is not true for *Parade, The Eiffel Tower Wedding Party, Orpheus,* or *The Infernal Machine.*

Cocteau was not the most profound of thinkers and he was not the greatest French playwright of the century. But he was a serious artist who played a nonnegligible role in the development of the French theater and who created a few works of first quality. Nor are his masterpieces limited to the theater; with *The Infernal Machine* mention must be made also of at least one novel, *The Holy Terrors,* the poems of *Plein chant,* some of his drawings, and certain films, *The Blood of the Poet, Orphée, Beauty and the Beast,* and *The Eternal Return.* Of the unity of Cocteau's diversity, Robert Kanters wrote: "The great theme (of Cocteau's work) for forty years is not a minor theme; it is the theme of Orpheus, that is to say, of poetry tearing life away from death."[9]

An important niche among contemporary writers is due him—not among the very greatest, perhaps, but right below them. Now it is up to posterity.

From *The American Society Legion of Honor Magazine,* XLIV, 3 (1968): 139–51.

CHAPTER SEVEN

Anouilh's *Antigone* in 1970

One of the most striking features of the French Theater between the two world wars was undoubtedly its rediscovery of Greek myth. Many of the finest dramatic works of this period retell the ancient legends of Hellenic tradition in contemporary, twentieth-century terms: Jean Cocteau's *Orpheus* and *The Infernal Machine*; André Gide's *Oedipus*; Jean Giraudoux's *Amphytrion 38, Tiger at the Gates,* and *Electra*; Jean Anouilh's *Antigone, Legend of Lovers (Eurydice),* and *Medea*; and Jean-Paul Sartre's *The Flies.* It seems no mere coincidence that almost all the major playwrights for two decades should turn at one time or another to the reinterpretation of Greek myths; similarly, it is probably not by chance that the "new dramatists" since 1950 have completely renounced this return to ancient sources. For the playwrights mentioned as well as for others, the timeless stories of Oedipus, Orestes and Electra, Medea, Orpheus, and the heroes of the Trojan War lent themselves admirably to an analysis of the human condition. After all, what great myth has to offer to posterity is a restatement structured along poetically pregnant lines of the essence of man's experience. The greatest insights concerning man's relationship to his universe, to his fellow men, and to his own truth are

95

equally valid in every era and in all societies. At the same time, by resorting to very well known characters and events, the playwrights in question were able to make more palatable to the wide theatergoing public various, fairly new dramatic techniques. That Giraudoux, Cocteau, Gide, Anouilh, and Sartre were so successful in adapting Greek myths is probably the principal reason why later writers such as Beckett, Ionesco, and Genet shunned these very techniques and themes, since they consciously wanted to react against the sort of theater written by their predecessors.

Francis Fergusson has pointed out in his brilliant study, *The Idea of a Theater,* that for the classical Greek dramatist and for his public for whom theater played a necessary, integrated, and ritualistic role in cultural life, the myths had a comprehensive meaning and were understandable on a variety of levels, whereas modern playwrights, creating a theater which does not fulfill the same social function, can only explore partial facets of these same myths. Thus, for instance, Cocteau's *The Infernal Machine* cannot hope to express the same unity of human experience that Sophocles succeeded in capturing in *Oedipus Rex*; instead, he concentrates imaginatively on a psychoanalytic approach to the hero's quest for truth and his destruction by a malign destiny. The portrayal of countries wavering between war and peace in Giraudoux's *Tiger at the Gates* is particularly pertinent to the political realities of Europe in the mid 1930s. And Sartre's Orestes in *The Flies* is the apt spokesman of the existentialist ethic, proclaiming the freedom of man, his unlimited potential, and his awesome responsibility.

In basing himself on Sophocles' *Antigone,* Jean Anouilh also decided to stress only some parts of the thematic content of the ancient play. In so doing, he created a brilliant, taut tragedy which, with the passage of time, seems not only the most remarkable of all the French reinterpretations of Greek myths but also the most relevant to the 1970s. By discarding everything in Sophocles' play which does not focus on the opposition between Creon and Antigone and by sharpening the validity of the positions of the antagonists, Anouilh dwelled on aspects of the Antigone myth that were only latent but not developed in Sophocles. Similarly, a close reading of the play today brings out values of particular significance that were not clearly noticeable at first. Since it was first performed in Paris under the occupation, in 1944 (it was written in 1942), critical attention was focused initially on the political context. To some, Antigone appeared the incarnation of the spirit of resistance in France; her uncompromising "no" to the tyrannical king Creon represented France's refusal to yield to the Nazi occupier. Others accused Anouilh of writing an apology for collaboration—Creon's case is well founded and his acceptance of necessary compromise appears in line with a realistic approach to life in general and to government in particular.

A quarter of a century after the end of World War II, Anouilh's *Antigone* has lost none of its power even if we no longer look at it from the perspective of occupation-resistance. In fact, the latter approach strikes one as being excessively limiting and tends to obscure more permanent values in the play which take on ever increasing significance for us.

It is perfectly justified for a modern author to select carefully from the mythic material at his disposal and to make certain alterations in order to suit his needs. In fact, the Greek playwrights did no less. One need only compare the contrasting interpretations given the Orestes-Electra legend by Aeschylus, Sophocles, and Euripides respectively. Using the same basic structure, each of the three was able to order events and character analysis to suit his own needs. In contemporary times, Giraudoux's handling the same Orestes-Electra myth is as different from Sartre's as both of theirs are from the ancients' and from, say Eugene O'Neill or T. S. Eliot. Sophocles' *Antigone* pits the individual (Antigone) against the state (Creon), and of course Anouilh retains this basic conflict. But in the ancient play, we are presented also with a clash between the laws of religion and the laws of state— a clash that becomes meaningless in contemporary terms and which Anouilh appropriately dismisses. The French author significantly excludes the character of Tiresias whom Sophocles had used to uphold the cause of religious tradition. While remaining very close to events in the Greek work, Anouilh's tragedy does away with everything superfluous to the central Creon-Antigone opposition, which casts the individual against the state, purity against compromise, the idealistic against the realistic. In return, Anouilh is able to probe depths of Antigone's character which are only latent in Sophocles. His Antigone is more human, stronger by contrast, and heightened in dramatic effect by being confronted with a more worthy opponent. Anouilh's Creon is no simple tyrant and accordingly, when catastrophe engulfs him at the end, he does not rush to recant his moves but merely suffers his fate stoically and with a wise understanding of the tragic irony of life. The simplicity of Anouilh's storyline is more classically austere than Sophocles' and the tension is even more acute. Moreover, the modern spectator is more intimately involved than he might be in viewing the Greek prototype, since Anouilh carefully draws him into the play thanks to the use of modern, Pirandellian dramatic techniques, a neutral setting, and an astute use of anachronisms which demystify the myth and bring it within everyone's reach. Anouilh's Antigone becomes very much like the existentialist heroine: she is not the product of a curse but chooses freely in a given situation and defines herself through her acts.

The essential lines of Anouilh's plot follow Sophocles'. After the fall of Oedipus, his two sons Eteocles and Polynices quarreled over who should succeed their father as King of Thebes. It was decided that they would reign in alternating years, but after having been in power for the first twelve months, Eteocles declined to yield his reign. Polynices there upon organized an alliance with neighboring kings and attacked his native city. In the ensuing battle, the two opposing brothers killed each other in single combat. Following the Theban victory Creon, brother-in-law of Oedipus and next in line of succession, became king and struggled to restore order to the country. He decreed that Eteocles be given a hero's burial but that no one be allowed to render the usual honors to Polynices's body since he was a traitor to Thebes. It is at this point that the action of the play begins. Oedipus's daughter, Antigone, decides to oppose Creon's edict and throws dirt on her brother's body as a symbolic gesture of burial. She stands alone in her opposition to her uncle, the King, and even her sister, Ismene, thinks she ought to yield to Creon's authority. Antigone is arrested by the guards assigned to watching the body. She is brought before Creon who sentences her to be entombed alive. When the sentence is carried out, Haemon, Creon's son and Antigone's fiancé, commits suicide over her body. On hearing the news, Creon's wife, Eurydice, kills herself and the circle of tragedy is complete.

Within this general framework, Anouilh shifts all dramatic emphasis on the meeting between Antigone and Creon during which her fate is sealed and the dramatic tension reaches its highest peak. Anouilh heightens the effect of the scene by giving us a glance at the antagonists beforehand and by enabling us thus to realize that they are set on a collision course. At the very outset of the play, the Chorus (played by a single character in this modern version) describes Creon in a sympathetic light. We find out that the King is interested in music and "rare manuscripts" and that he would prefer to spend his time in the "antique shops of Thebes" (a delightfully anachronistic notion) but, like a conscientious workman he has accepted to do a job because someone must lead the state. At the same time, Antigone is presented as unalterably opposed to all compromise, realizing full well that her opposition will entail her death. In a tender scene with her fiancé, she bids him farewell without offering any explanation and in effect draws a line on her life before confronting Creon. The Chorus can now exclaim that the tragedy will now unfold by itself: "In a tragedy, nothing is in doubt and everyone's destiny is known . . . tragedy is restful; and the reason is that hope, that foul deceitful thing, has no part in it" (24).[1] We modern spectators can approach the tragedy in precisely this way, since we know Antigone's fate and therefore cannot react with any suspense as to the possibility of a favorable outcome. The tension which grips us is based on conflict not on hope.

In their scene together, Creon and Antigone are not unlike two boxers, parrying, sparring, looking for an opening and then landing a telling blow, hurting the opponent and being hurt in turn. They are worthy antagonists because Anouilh has made his Creon into a more human and more credible figure than Sophocles' King. The latter wasted no time on subtlety; for him, Antigone's opposition was an intolerable challenge and he quickly orders her to be executed. The most notable aspect of Anouilh's Creon is that he does not want to execute Antigone. He seeks to avoid this calamity not only for political reasons but, perhaps even more convincingly, because he is fond of his little niece, no matter how difficult a girl she may be. He tries a variety of approaches to dissuade her from her resolve, but in the face of her obstinacy he eventually yields to what he obviously considers the even more compelling reasons of state which demand that his edict be observed.

At first he is confident that everything can be worked out. He will get Antigone to renounce her folly and he will easily do away with the only witnesses to what she has done, three guards. And he thinks that Antigone acted so brazenly because she counted on the immunity of her family relationship. When Antigone quietly assures him that such was not the case and that she was sure in fact that he would have to have her put to death, he scornfully accuses her of sharing in the pride of Oedipus. "You come of people for whom the human vestment is a kind of strait jacket, it cracks at the seams. You spend your lives wriggling to get out of it. Nothing less than a cozy tea party with death and destiny will quench your thirst." (30). But, he announces, a new hour has come to Thebes, the country needs peace and order and not another tête-à-tête with destiny. Creon now speaks with some feeling of her intended marriage to Haemon in paternal and somewhat paternalistic tones. He even reminds his niece that the first doll she ever had came from him.

But he does not score in this first round, for Antigone remains determined as ever to cover her brother's body a second time. He reminds her that even if she were to do so, he would have the earth removed again but Antigone is satisfied to reply that "what a person can do a person ought to do" (32). He next tries to dispel the religious reasons which might compel Antigone to bury her brother—which are all important in the Sophocles play—and he succeeds in drawing from her an admission that she does not believe in the religious practice itself. It becomes clear that Antigone is acting only for herself. It is important for Anouilh to dismiss thereby the Greek religious values since for a contemporary audience they can have no valid meaning, neither in ancient terms nor even transmitted into a modern Christian framework. We enter the very crux of the opposition as Creon explains in some detail the political necessity for his decision. It may not make too much sense he admits, but following a revolution and in order to impose the authority of the state on the mob, he must insist on being obeyed. Antigone contemptuously retorts that he has committed himself on the road to expediency, that he has said "yes" to compromise and that her role is to say "no" and to die. Creon's defense takes the form of a brilliant, extended metaphor. He compares himself to a man who, on a ship floundering in a storm, agrees to take the helm and to lead it to safety. In order to rally the mutineering crew, in order to save the vessel, the new captain may have to be brutal, but his job was to say yes and to save the ship. "It is easy to say no. To say yes, you have to sweat and roll up your sleeves and plunge both hands into life up to the elbows." (37). But Antigone remains adamant.

At this point, the lines are already drawn in the fatal opposition which can readily take on a new significance in the light of the conflict between the young and their elders—a conflict which has always existed, but which has become particularly exacerbated in recent times in all western societies, on both sides of the Iron Curtain. What separates Antigone from Creon is the proverbial "generation gap." Antigone is the purist whose ideals are unsullied and who is willing to die for them. Creon is the practical, older man who knows that life is not what it should be and who tries to make the best of what it is. They are of course both right, each in his own way and this is what makes Anouilh's tragedy so compelling. Virtue opposed to vice does not make for a very good theater. Anouilh opposes Antigone's virtue with another kind of virtue less noble but more possible and if Creon's pragmatism appears obscene to Antigone, her inability to see life as it is makes her incomprehensible to him. Such is, after all, the wall of misunderstanding which separates the generations today. The young reject the hypocrisy and the mistakes of their predecessors without pretending to know how to find all the answers themselves while their parents condemn the younger people for nihilism even though they acknowledge the generosity of their impulse.

Now, Creon plays his trump card. It is to his credit that he plays it only after having tried every other means of convincing Antigone since he knows that what he is about to tell her will wound her. That he should have waited before destroying her illusions until he has exhausted every avenue of further proof of Creon's good will and of the fact that he is a very human, and in many ways a likeable character. What he reveals to Antigone is that both of her brothers were worthless creatures—spoiled, perfidious, power-hungry, and disdainful of their father. He demonstrates irrefutably the absurdity of a cause fought in the name of either of the two brothers and he stresses his point by revealing that the bodies of the fallen Polynices and Eteocles were so mangled that they were unrecognizable and that he selected at random one for the pomp of burial and the other as a symbol for scorn.

The immediate effect is overwhelming. Antigone is crushed and all the fight has gone out of her. She is left a pitiful, weak young girl who suddenly finds out that life is not what it should be. Creon, it would seem, has won, but at this moment he commits a fatal tactical error. Because he feels sorry for his now helpless niece, Creon attempts to spark in her some enthusiasm for life. "Go and find Haemon. And get married quickly, Antigone. Be happy . . . Life is nothing more than the happiness that you get out of it" (41). The King should have left well enough alone and should, perhaps, have given Antigone a chance to meditate on her grief in solitude. Instead, he allows Antigone to dwell on the notion of happiness and to discover how little it relates to her notion of herself. She feels that the sort of happiness Creon is talking about is tantamount to compromise, that it means sacrificing one's ideals, and in Creon's case, accepting a lie as the basis of the political foundation. When she rejects finally the kind of happiness Creon offers her, she does so in terms which clearly oppose her as a representative of the virtue of the young to Creon as a symbol of the tired world of adult appeasement. "I want everything of life, I do; and I want it now! I want it total, complete; otherwise I reject it! I will *not* be moderate. I will *not* be satisfied with a bit of cake you offer me if I promise to be a good little girl. I want to be sure of everything this very day, sure that everything will be as beautiful as when I was a little girl. If not, I want to die!" (42–43). Creon clearly has lost. He now knows that he cannot find any way to patch things up, to keep things going, and when Ismene enters and announces that she will pick up where Antigone left off, the King realizes that faced with the contagion of rebellion, he has no recourse but to condemn his niece to death.

There is a measure of truth to Creon's subsequent reflection that Antigone was bent on self-destruction: "Death was her purpose, whether she knew it or not. Polynices was a mere pretext. When she had to give up that pretext, she found another one—that life and happiness were tawdry things and not worth possessing. She was bent upon only one thing: to reject life and to die" (45). There is a fanaticism to Antigone's behavior, but it is the fanaticism of the young who desperately need life to be something more than a series of adjustments. The tragedy of this play is the same as that confronting us in our current lives—that maturity means, among other things, the realization of the limitations of reality while the generosity and immaturity of youth will have no part of anything less than absolutes.

After Antigone is led away, Anouilh offers us one last, brief, and splendid scene to give final relief to the tragic confrontation between generations. Haemon goes to see his father to plead for Antigone's life. Whereas Sophocles' Haemon had spoken as a dutiful son and had urged that the girl be spared for the sake of his father's political advantage, his modern counterpart speaks only in the name of love. The answer he receives is, of course, unsatisfactory. Creon will not change his mind and calls on Haemon to accept the burdens of manhood. Whereupon Haemon movingly takes a step back and attempts to assess his father as a man; he no longer recognizes the giant he had admired as a little boy and he is dismayed to find his one time idol reduced to human size. "Was it of you I stood in awe? Was that man you?" (46). Creon is equally moving in his reply which is, once again, a model of realistic, unsentimental evaluation of life: "The world *is* here, Haemon, and you *are* alone. You must cease to think your father all-powerful. Look straight at me. See your father as he is. That is what it means to grow up and be a man" (46). Once again, here on the level of father and son, is the microcosm of the dramatic upheaval of growing up. There is no right and wrong; there are only two inalterably opposed sides.

If Anouilh's portrait of Antigone seemed somewhat harsh up to this point, her last scene presents her in a much softer light. Gone are her iron will and her sarcasm; she is a frail creature facing death and she is afraid. Her vulnerability is contrasted to the crass guard who watches her and whose insensitivity counterpoints the tender farewell letter she writes to Haemon. The determined rebel turns out to be also a very human being. Without this final, revealing glimpse, we might have been tempted to dismiss Antigone as an extremist who scorned the treasure of life. But now we know that she is clearly not that, that she, too, would have preferred to live, and that her rebellion entailed for her the greatest sacrifice. It is only in this light that she finally assumes her true heroic proportion.

Antigone's greatness is not gained at Creon's expense, for his suffering lifts him to heroic proportions also. The cost of maintaining order has been a high one indeed—much higher than he had dared imagine. The death of his niece is only a beginning; the double suicide of his son and of his wife are symbols of the terrible toll that life exacts. And yet, Creon remains conscientious to the end, yielding personal considerations to the necessities of his office. He cannot even afford to dwell on his grief. There is a cabinet meeting that for him takes precedence over everything else. He indulges in no self-pity nor does he bother to curse the fates. His despair is revealed in a single sentence spoken to his page: "Never grow up if you can help it" (52). Life, then, is the culprit and it is futile to try to place the blame anywhere else. What Antigone attempted to do was right: what Creon sought is right too, from another point of view. The struggle is classic and the solution has yet to be found by any man.

Anouilh's play is still valid in 1970—in fact, it seems more valid than ever—because the timeless dilemma of its conflict is especially relevant to an age which has witnessed the formation of a deep, ominous chasm between the generations. Anouilh attempted to treat his theme as objectively as he could and his objectivity serves well the contemporary analogy. Neither the point of view of the young nor that of the adults is entirely justified nor entirely misguided. As the Chorus puts it while speaking of tragedy: "he who kills is as innocent as he who gets killed" (24). This is the tragic nature of the human condition which Anouilh has seized so masterfully in his very up-to-date *Antigone*.

From *American Society Legion of Honor Magazine* (XLIV, 2, 973): 41–53.

INTRODUCTION TO BARRAULT

No one had a greater passion for, a greater dedication to, the theater than Jean-Louis Barrault. He lived and breathed it; the theater was his total commitment. He lived on theater the way others live on love. He gave himself to it with extraordinary energy and generosity; the theater was his family, his country, his religion, his raison d'être.

I met Jean-Louis Barrault and Madeleine Renaud early in the 1960s, when they were in New York with their company. We became friends at once and remained close until they died in 1994. In 1981, my friend, painter Paul Jenkins, and I invited Barrault to do a one-man show in New York. Paul had admired Barrault from afar but had not met him. One day, I brought Barrault to Paul's studio on Broadway; it was mutual love at first sight. To pay tribute to his idol, Jenkins rented the handsome Alice Tully Hall at Lincoln Center and created a splendid lithograph to publicize the performance; together, we organized a memorable evening of *Le Langage du corps* as a benefit for our Maison Française.

Barrault arrived from Paris in the morning on the day of the performance, went straight to Lincoln Center to inspect the stage, had lunch with us, and then rested up for a bit before preparing his performance. Despite the six-hour time difference, and despite his then seventy-one years, he showed no sign of fatigue. He gave himself fully—and with great success—for the hour and a half of his one-man show, took part in a brief ceremony in his honor on stage, and ended the evening at a supper for him, surrounded by New York theater people. It was a routine that would have exhausted anyone else. But Barrault insisted on performing also for students at New York University. Thus, the next morning, before taking a plane back to Paris, he showed up at

INTRODUCTION TO BARRAULT

Washington Square and spontaneously redid his entire show to the wild applause of hundreds of students. Barrault could not have been happier than in the midst of these enthusiastic young people. Until the end of his life, he remained young at heart and young in spirit.

CHAPTER EIGHT

Jean-Louis Barrault

The career of Jean-Louis Barrault is the stuff that makes legends. Since World War II, he has dominated the theater in France; as actor, as director, as the head of a great theatrical enterprise, he has put his stamp on the activity of thirty-five years as has no other theater person in his country, and probably in any country. He is the epitome of what the French call an *homme de théâtre*, a creative genius who has invested the theater with his extraordinary energy, vision, and talent. He has carried on a venerable French tradition of these *hommes de théâtre* that goes back to the turn of the century with André Antoine and continues uninterrupted to World War II with figures such as Aurélien Lugné-Poë, Jacques Copeau, Louis Jouvet, Charles Dullin, Gaston Baty, and Georges Pitoëff. If Barrault has been able to carry that torch so brilliantly for a third of a century, it is because his torch burns with the incandescent intensity of a unique passion.

His acting career began exactly fifty years ago when he was taken on by the legendary Dullin as a student and bit player. By 1935, he staged his first work, a dramatization of Faulkner's *As I Lay Dying*, influenced by the great pantomimist Étienne Decroux and the theoretician Antonin Artaud. This first attempt at creating what Barrault

107

termed "total theater"—a blending of text, movement, mime, masks, music—created a sensation and launched the twenty-five-year-old actor/director on his ascent. Artaud himself added a chapter in a second edition of his seminal *The Theater and Its Double* to discuss and praise the Barrault/Faulkner work. In 1940, Jacques Copeau invited Barrault to join the Comédie Française. He played Hamlet, directed Racine and Shakespeare, but, most importantly, created Paul Claudel's monumental *Satin Slipper* and began his long, fruitful association with the great Catholic poet/playwright. Barrault also worked in films, notably in Marcel Carné's masterpiece, *Children of Paradise*. Generations of movie buffs will forever recall Barrault's sensitive portrayal of the mime Baptiste, which earned him a place among the great exponents of pantomime of our century. During these war years, he married Madeleine Renaud, one of the Comédie Française's most famous actresses. The two had met in 1936 and were immediately attracted to each other even though (or because) they came from very different worlds. Renaud was already a celebrity; she hailed from an upper-middle-class family and was the wife of a respectable actor also of the Comédie Française. Barrault was a young firebrand who hung out in Saint-Germain des Prés and espoused radical concepts of theater. In the following decades, they became a legendary couple— legendary in their devotion to each other and in their devotion to the theater.

In 1946, together they left the hallowed Comédie Française to strike out on their own. They formed the Compagnie Renaud-Barrault which, after countless triumphs and obstacles, is still going strong. During that time, Madeleine Renaud established herself firmly as the leading actress of the French stage, the *"grande dame"* who put her stamp on a stunning variety of roles ranging from Molière and Marivaux to Beckett's isolated mouth in *Not I*; meanwhile, Barrault organized, created, directed, acted, and breathed life into a succession of exciting theatrical enterprises which were always eclectically dynamic and avoided doctrinaire positions. He established a very special dialogue with his public.

The first home of the new company was the Théâtre Marigny in the gardens of the Champs-Élysées, an elegant house that lent itself admirably to Molière, Giraudoux, Shakespeare, Anouilh, Racine, and Montherlant. It was here that Barrault staged several Claudel plays, including the universally hailed production of *Partage de Midi (Break at Noon),* starring Edwige Feuillière, Pierre Brasseur, and Barrault. In the latter years of the decade at the Marigny, Barrault created a studio theater in a smaller space in order to present the works of avant-garde authors.

By the end of the 1950s, André Malraux, Minister for Culture under General De Gaulle's Fifth Republic, installed the Renaud-Barrault Company at the nationalized Odéon-Théâtre de France. Barrault made the state-subsidized, venerable Odéon into one of Paris's most creative theater spaces. Besides performing more classics, more Claudel, more recognized modern masters, Barrault took certain risks and opened the doors of his theater to the major new voices that were making themselves heard. He produced Ionesco's *Rhinoceros* and Beckett's *Happy Days* (which provided Madeleine Renaud with one of her greatest triumphs); he was among the first to stage the works of Marguerite Duras and Nathalie Sarraute; he invited Roger Blin to direct Genet's *The Screens,* an event that caused a scandal and near-riots. Ensconced in an establishment position, Barrault managed to produce nonestablishment theater. He was provocative and he continued as always to be inventive, to bring together artists of all sorts to collaborate on theatrical creativity.

What put an end to the glory days of Barrault at the Théâtre de France was the student revolt and barricades in May 1968. Students occupied the Odéon, which they viewed as a symbol of "bourgeois culture." To be sure, it *was* a state-run enterprise, but it remains one of the ironies of that tumultuous month of May that the crowd descended on the Odéon rather than, say, on the Comédie Française. Barrault was surely not the enemy. But the Comédie Française is on the Right Bank, while the Odéon is on the path to the Latin Quarter and the Sorbonne, the prime target of the students' initial dissatisfaction. For days (and nights) on end the theater was occupied and served as a forum for heated discussion and overheated confusion. Barrault expressed his sympathy for the students and tried but failed to control the volatile situation. He refused to carry out the Ministry's order to cut the electricity for the several thousand young people camping in the hall. For this insubordination, he was dismissed when order was restored.

Ever the optimist, unshakable in his faith in the art of the theater,

Barrault regrouped his company, hired a wrestling arena, and within six months produced one of his most original and inventive productions, *Rabelais,* a multimedia spectacle based on the life and work of the great Renaissance author of *Gargantua* and *Pantagruel.* The Renaud-Barrault Company toured many countries with *Rabelais.* They had traveled extensively in their earlier incarnations (including two visits to New York); the rollicking *Rabelais* rejuvenated them and brought them new, young spectators. In New York City, they performed at the City Center. But their greatest triumph undoubtedly was in the mammoth Zellerbach Theater at the University of California in Berkeley. On this campus, whose student riots had predated May 1968 in Paris, Barrault, Renaud, and *Rabelais* conquered thousands of students with a profound message of liberty at the very moment that the Kent State killings set off new and bloody rioting all around them.

By 1974, a new, even bolder challenge presented itself to the veteran couple. Against great obstacles and at the cost of incurring great personal debts, they succeeded in creating a new theater—an abandoned railway station across the Seine from the Louvre, on the Left Bank. With the courage, energy, and tenacity that had always characterized this extraordinary pair and that would have been the envy of people half their age, Renaud and Barrault set about building. The seven years at the Théâtre d'Orsay must rank as one of the most glorious periods in any theater's history. Going to the Théâtre d'Orsay proved to be the sort of complete theater experience for which spectators longed; everything in it was conducive to the appreciation of the theatrical event. The main auditorium, functional, attractive, and comfortable without trying to be elegant, had excellent sight lines and a spacious, adaptable thrust stage; a fine small theater (a Renaud-Barrault tradition) was particularly suited for experimental works. The foyers were covered with exhibits, displays, and backdrops of numerous past productions, often executed by the greatest modern painters. With its modestly priced meals and drinks, the restaurant enabled spectators to come early and stay late, to talk theater, to mingle with members of the company, and usually with Madeleine Renaud and Jean-Louis Barrault themselves. There was nothing like it in Paris. The public flocked to Orsay; the theater was almost always full—and it was filled with a very young public. With no sizeable subvention and with a typically ambitious and demanding schedule, the Compagnie Renaud-Barrault managed to keep its head above water—no mean feat for any theater. Barrault created spectacles based on a number of major writers including La Fontaine, Voltaire, Diderot, and Nietzsche. He produced, again, Claudel, Ionesco, Beckett, and Duras. Madeleine Renaud scored one of her major triumphs in *Harold and Maude*. Both worked very hard, and both enjoyed it immensely. Their love of theater and their total devotion to it made the Théâtre d'Orsay a very privileged place, a temple of theater arts.

And then last year, the Barraults were once again forced to move. The government needed the old terminal to create a museum and the theater had to be dismantled. With a Sisyphus-like refusal to submit and with Herculean energy, Barrault (now seventy years old) and Renaud (past her eightieth birthday) refused to stop doing the one thing they know and love. They picked up the wood, the steel, the lights and all the rest, negotiated with the State for a new space, and got ready to move their company into yet one more home in what seems like an endless diaspora. Less than three months ago, the latest in the Barrault-Renaud miracles took place: the opening of the splendid new Théâtre du Rond Point, at the Rond Point des Champs-Élysées (in a former ice skating rink known as the Palais de Glace). Once again, Barrault's energy and imagination made the impossible possible, and once again, with youthful vigor, this extraordinary theatrical couple set out to work. They reproduced the large and small auditoriums from Orsay, created new foyers and a space for the restaurant. In addition, always eager to try new things, they are preparing to launch an international theater club with the ambition to make it a home-away-from-home for theater people the world over. "Theater people," Barrault has been known to say, "have only one nationality: the theater itself."

Years ago, Barrault had breathed life into an international theater festival called "The Theater of Nations." Now, in his stunning new theater, barely across the street from the Marigny where his company started thirty-five years earlier, he will be able to receive actors, actresses, directors, playwrights, and critics from the whole world. With Barrault, with Renaud, they will feel at home and be welcomed in a place that breathes the very essence of what theater is and has always been. A new theater, a new start, an old love, a lifelong commitment. A young man of seventy who has created an extraordinary living monument that promises to remain as a legacy to the theater of France and to theater in general.

Program text for the June 1981 presentation of Jean-Louis Barrault in *Le Langage du Corps* at Alice Tully Hall.

INTRODUCTION TO IONESCO

Ionesco was one of the first great figures of French literature I met. The year was 1960. I was already enthusiastic about his work, which I knew well. I was particularly attracted to his radical theater esthetics and to his manner of questioning the very notion of realistic theater. We met at the Paris apartment of our mutual friend, the poet Alain Bosquet. I recall my surprise in finding myself in the presence of this short, mischievous-looking man bubbling over with humor: the Ionesco I found was much more *sympathique* than I had imagined. I had not pictured him so relaxed, so easy of access; after one or two whiskies, we were off on a long discussion of *The Chairs*, antirealism in the theater, and the influence of Pirandello. It was the start of a long friendship which remained intact until his death in 1994. For thirty-five years, in Paris or in New York, we saw each other regularly, always with great joy.

At NYU, we awarded him an honorary doctorate in 1971. His acceptance talk at Washington Square was marvelously funny. I can see him now, resplendent in a purple academic gown, relating (in French, of course) the history of his difficult relationship with the English language. In the 1950s, he told us, he had tried in vain to learn English. This failure gave him the idea in part for *The Bald Soprano* (which reflects the absurdity of old-time language textbooks replete with pointless and even absurd sentences). Later on, he claimed, he gave it another try but had no greater success. "And now," he went on, "that an American university is willing to grant me a doctorate without my speaking a word of English, there is no further point in learning it."

Once, when I drove Ionesco home after a dinner in Paris, he got out of the car and then thrust an arm through the window to say good

INTRODUCTION TO IONESCO

night. My dog "Beckett," fearing some intruder undoubtedly, grabbed his hand and grazed the skin. Ionesco had a little scratch. "Call up *France-Soir,*" he said in a burst of laughter, "tomorrow they can put a headline on page one, 'BECKETT BITES IONESCO.' "

CHAPTER NINE

Ionesco on Olympus

"Were you surprised to be selected to the Académie Française?" was the question asked of Eugène Ionesco, the granddaddy
of modern avant-garde playwrights, following his recent, unexpected
election to that most conservative of establishments. Ionesco replied
quickly and with obvious sincerity: "Yes, I was surprised. But, you
know," he added after a second's reflection and with a trace of puckish
humor barely visible on his otherwise deadpan face, "I am always
surprised. I go through life perpetually astonished at everything that
happens around me." Looked at objectively, Ionesco's entry into the
French Academy represents a milestone of sorts—and a very curious
one. The "forty immortals," as they are known, embody the peak of
intellectual respectability. It is rather amazing to imagine the author of
The Bald Soprano, The Chairs, and other plays that irritated many
and baffled most Parisians in the early 1950s resplendent in a new
academician's green uniform fitted to his roundish, unimposing frame,
taking his prized seat next to such traditional writers as Jules Romains,
Marcel Achard, François Mauriac, and Marcel Pagnol.

To be elected, a writer, a philosopher, a statesman, or a historian
must wait for a seat to become vacant (when one of the forty dies),

115

must declare his candidacy, pay courtesy visits to as many of the thirty-nine survivors as he can in the hope of winning their votes, and then await the results. The procedure is only slightly less formidable than a papal election, and in the more than three centuries since Cardinal Richelieu founded the Académie Française, only the distinguished playwright Henry de Montherlant, ten years ago, was elected even though he refused to present his candidacy. Many illustrious authors through the ages have not sought membership and would probably have been refused if they had. The list of nonmembers includes Molière, Pascal, Rousseau, Balzac, Gide, Camus, and Sartre.

Ionesco felt that his candidacy was a good joke to play on the establishment. He had an impressive precedent: near the end of his life, in 1955, the onetime *enfant terrible* of French letters, Jean Cocteau solicited and gained admission to the august body. Asked how a man so imbued with the spirit of avant-garde could seek to join the seat of traditionalism, Cocteau quipped that, since so many important writers refused to have anything to do with it, the true spirit of avant-garde was to belong.

Ionesco's penchant for paradox is not limited to his plays; his wry irony is turned on himself as readily as on others. Upon greeting his visitor following the Academy election, the dramatist declared with mock seriousness: "I am a very academic person. After all, I have been a member of the College of 'Pataphysics for years and hold the exalted title of Satrap. And the uniform of the Académie Française will be nothing new to me. 'Pataphysicians also wear uniforms—invisible ones." The College, a tongue-in-cheek association of particularly literate wits in France and abroad, was founded to propagate the ideals of the iconoclastic turn-of-the-century playwright Alfred Jarry, the author of *King Ubu* and the founder of 'Pataphysics, "the science of imaginary solutions." "The College is really much more formal than the Academy," Ionesco went on. "If you were visiting Ionesco the 'Pataphysician, protocol would require you to bow down to me and to withdraw when you leave without turning your back to me. But since it is Ionesco the Academician you are coming to see, a simple handshake will be perfectly adequate." With that, he thrust his hand out amiably.

It is not really so incongruous for this formal honor to befall the man who just twenty years ago launched the theater of the absurd. The avant-garde of 1950 is no longer shocking today. Ionesco has been played the world over and even at that other citadel of conservatism, the Comédie Française; his plays are taught in universities, and he is the subject of countless Ph.D. dissertations; his own theater has evolved along less radical, though still unconventional, lines; and his influence in France and elsewhere has been considerable.

When *The Bald Soprano* opened in Paris on May 11, 1950, it was greeted mainly by anger or indifference. There were few instant supporters for this puzzling work, labeled an "anti-play" by its unknown, Rumanian-born author with an obvious flair for ambiguity. But with the passage of time, a sizable public responded to this metaphor of the emptiness of our prosaic lives and of the difficulty in communicating, to this dislocated language full of nonsense and non sequiturs. *The Bald Soprano* marked the opening of the massive assault on traditional theater in the 1950s, soon joined by Beckett, Adamov, and others in France, and eventually by playwrights in other countries.

The theater of the absurd had an English phrase book at its origins. Trying to learn English, Ionesco used a text whose sentences—like those in many foreign language manuals—were platitudinous and nonsensical. He suddenly found himself thinking about language itself and about communication or the lack of it based on language. Ionesco never did learn English (although he later wrote a playlet called *French Lesson for Americans,* which became the basis of a first-year French book used in American colleges), but he produced the hilariously funny yet anguishing *The Bald Soprano,* whose tragicomic image of life underlines the clichés of conformity, the dehumanizing stresses of modern society, and the breakdown of language as a means of communication. Like Beckett's *Waiting for Godot,* it has become a contemporary classic, no longer enigmatic to a vast public. For the past twelve years, it has run continuously for more than four thousand performances at the tiny Left-Bank Théâtre de la Huchette.

The first, most inventive period of Ionesco's production—the 1950s—consists exclusively of short, radically anti-realistic plays marked by a proliferation of objects, by language gone insane, and by a surrealistic brand of humor that coated a tragic conception of the absurd. However grotesque the old man and woman in *The Chairs* (1952) may be, their frantic efforts to pass on an incomprehensible message to posterity, as the stage fills ever more with invisible people and perfectly visible chairs, echo the nightmarish quality of our existence. Ionesco called it a "tragic farce"; his particular blend of these two contradictory elements is highly original. *Jack or the Submission* (1955) is the taming of an individualist by a coercive society—young Jack is made to admit that he adores hashed potatoes—while the value of words is again under fire. "All we need to designate things," says a character, "is one single word: cat. Cats are called cat, food: cat, insects: cat, chairs: cat, you: cat, me: cat, all the adverbs: cat, all the prepositions: cat. It's easier to talk that way."

In the 1960s, Ionesco turned to writing full-length plays whose central figure is an Everyman named Jean or Bérenger. The transition came with *The Killer* (1959), one of his strongest works, which deserves to be better known in the United States. The real turning point was *Rhinoceros* in 1960. Catapulted to fame far beyond the previous avant-garde in-circles, thanks to major productions in many countries (Jean-Louis Barrault at the Théâtre de France, Laurence Olivier at the Old Vic, Zero Mostel and Eli Wallach in Leo Kerz's New York staging), Ionesco seemed to some of his early admirers to have turned conservative in dramaturgy as well as in politics. Bérenger's struggle to remain a man even though everyone else had become a rhinoceros can be viewed as antifascism, anticommunism, or a glorification of individualism. Ionesco came under heavy ideological attack from the Left, during which many a scathing subjunctive was exchanged, notably with Kenneth Tynan. In reality, the metaphor of *Rhinoceros* relates more to man's solitude in an increasingly mechanistic society than to politics. As to the play's dramatic technique, there is no doubt that it signals a departure from the zany innovations of his early plays; but if his recent plays, beginning with *Rhinoceros,* appear less "avant-gardish," the answer is not only that Ionesco tempered his experimentation but more importantly that the techniques of the theater of the absurd, a true avant-garde in the 1950s, had become accepted forms in the 1960s.

Exit the King (1962) is perhaps Ionesco's finest play. It is certainly his most moving, most human work, and it comes as close to being classic in its lines as is conceivable in contemporary terms. *Exit the King* is a profound meditation on the meaning of life and the need to die. Although poignant and tragic, it is also full of Ionesco's finest humor, which heightens rather than mitigates the tragedy. It is his most intensely personal work, one that translates into universal terms his deepest anxieties and his obsession with death.

IONESCO ON OLYMPUS

Written for a Comédie Française production in 1966 and performed at Stockbridge, Massachusetts, last summer, *Hunger and Thirst* is a rambling, pessimistic, uneven play. Its last act, one of the most dramatic moments in all Ionesco, again enraged the Left since it satirized Marxist and Brechtian viewpoints via two clowns called Tripp and Brechtoll. Long opposed to the notion of commitment, Ionesco has repeatedly attacked engaged theater in general and Brecht in particular. And if the German dramatist is no longer here to defend himself, there is no shortage of his disciples and admirers who have taken up the challenge and regularly roast Ionesco over critical, Brechtian coals.

After a silence of four years, Ionesco premiered his most recent play, *The Killing Game,* at the splendid new Düsseldorf Theater earlier this year. As in *Exit the King,* the theme is mortality, but this time on a grand scale and in allegro tempo; all the characters, all the people in a city die in a proliferation of death, like so many pins knocked down by a bowling ball. "I wanted to go beyond the absurd," Ionesco confided, "to underline the scandalous aspect of death—an elementary truth that people know but dismiss too readily." Acknowledging that this theme is treated by many if not most authors, Ionesco has come to consider man's mortality as the basic theme of his works and the primary concern of humanity. Like Camus's *The Plague, The Killing Game* is inspired from Defoe's *The Journal of the Plague Year.* This modern dance of death carefully avoids the tragic, thanks to a constant dose of derision. It is a very funny play, although somewhat reminiscent of Ionesco's earlier writings.

The Killing Game is not the first work Ionesco has premiered in Germany. Since heavily subsidized German theaters are relatively free of the financial difficulties that often confront serious theater in France, he finds conditions there more promising for a satisfactory production. The new play will finally be created in Paris next fall, under Jorge Lavelli's direction.

Now fifty-seven years old, as much frightened as flattered by fame, Eugène Ionesco lives quietly in Montparnasse with his wife Rodika and their twenty-four-year-old daughter Marie-France, a few doors from La Coupole where he frequently dines with friends. He is an anguished man, haunted by thoughts of death (as nearly every page of *Fragments of a Journal* testifies), harassed by occasional bouts with illness, despondent over what he deems the chaotic state of the world, terrorized by opening nights, perennially dissatisfied with his own

IONESCO ON OLYMPUS

work, and constantly at odds with critics whom he considers to be interested only in negating, in destroying. These attacks of insecurity often make it difficult for him to work, for when he manages to flee from outside fears, he becomes an even easier prey to the personal hell of his solitude.

Ionesco often—too often—writes articles or gives interviews to explain what he meant in his works as if he were afraid the plays could not speak for themselves. Frequently solicited by newspapers and magazines to write on issues of the day, he pronounces himself readily on such topics as the Near East conflict and Biafra. These articles sometimes get him into trouble. Recently, a German court ordered rectified several pages of a collection of Ionesco's pieces in which he had accused playwrights Peter Weiss and Rolf Hochhuth of pro-Nasser, anti-Israel sentiments and of being conspicuously silent on some issues while speaking out loudly on others. Hochhuth was even singled out as having been pro-Nazi. This sort of amateur politicizing has earned Ionesco a rightist reputation.

While Ionesco would agree to be identified with a center or slightly right-of-center rather than a leftist position in the French political spectrum (although the traditional Right-Left dichotomy has been badly blurred in recent years and no longer means much of anything), his plays are not really political in any sense unless one chooses to dub them rightist only because he refuses to make them leftist. For Ionesco, theater transcends political and social problems to deal exclusively with a metaphor of the human condition in general, far from the doctrinaire arena. In contrast to the Brechtian or Sartrian "theater of education, of answers," as Ionesco has termed it, he opts for a "theater of questions. The poet is neither prophetic nor omniscient. He sees problems where others don't, but he offers no keys for possible solutions. Besides," he added dejectedly, "there are no solutions right now for the human condition. Socialism as well as liberalism has failed. Life is unlivable." [1]

Ionesco is skeptical about the more recent trends in theater. He considers the current "revolt of directors against authors and the revolt of actors against directors" of merely technical interest, and rather elementary at that. "There can be no theater without a text." As for nudity, he considers the "outpouring of erotic neuroses . . . a little more daring than the Folies Bergères" and no more than a passing phase.[2] His own plans for the near future involve writing a modern version of *Macbeth* ("Why not borrow from the classics? Countless other playwrights have") and a new-found interest in directing. He has already directed some of his plays in Germany and Switzerland, and he is increasingly attracted by the challenge and responsibility of staging his own works.

The role of steadying his troubled soul falls mainly to the charming, diminutive Madame Ionesco, his childhood sweetheart, a sharply intelligent ex-philosophy student. She is his staunchest supporter and most severe critic, at once launching pad and life preserver—a vital influence. Despite the frequent controversies in which he finds himself, despite the many anxieties that gnaw at him, Ionesco remains a soft-spoken, gentle, unassuming man whose quizzical, rotund face reveals his humor as much as his obsessions. He is naturally witty in a completely spontaneous manner. When told last fall that Samuel Beckett had been awarded the Nobel Prize, Ionesco, delighted at the news, replied impishly: "We really deserved it." So far, no word from Beckett with *his* reaction to Ionesco's election to the Académie Française. But Ionesco, the poet haunted by thoughts of death, reacted with a healthy dose of self-mockery to his new status as an "immortal." "I no longer have to fear death now," he smiled. "In fact, I had always thought myself to be only half-mortal, or perhaps three-fourths mortal, but I felt that there was at least a small part of me, maybe only one one-hundredth, that was immortal . . . the best part."

From *Saturday Review* (May 16, 1970): 21–23, 91.

$$\boxed{\text{D}}$$

INTRODUCTION TO JEAN GENET

At a bar in Greenwich Village, at the start of the 1970s, I sit with a rather short man, on the thin side, his face pale, his eyes intense, at times filled with enthusiasm. The man is Jean Genet. He is speaking about the Black Panthers at whose invitation he has just come to the United States. Genet is fascinated by them, by their radicalism, their paramilitary organization, their counter-government replete with a bevy of ministers; he admires their courage and he wants to help them. If I did not share his enthusiasm, I respected it because of my profound admiration for Genet, the writer. I was deeply touched by his kindness, his gentleness, and an unexpected fragility. I had a feeling he did not realize what was in store for him.

I had invited him to give a lecture at NYU; he chose "Poetry and Revolution" as his topic: "Doesn't the subject bother you; it might trouble the university administration?" I smiled and reassured him: no, our administration was not in the least concerned and we were delighted to have him. Our largest auditorium was packed, but unfortunately, the lecture was a complete flop. As Genet mounted the platform, I found him tense, anguished. This was not a man with stage fright; he was a man under surveillance. And in fact, he was. I do not know what agreement he had made with his Black Panther escorts, but clearly, he seemed trapped. After rambling on, unfocused, for about a quarter of an hour, he yielded the floor to the "Minister of Culture" of the Black Panthers who launched into a tough political harangue. The audience became restless, and soon, many left.

Several weeks later, at the end of his stay, Genet came to see me in my office. He was no longer the same man; something had changed since our first meeting: his eyes revealed only disappointment and sadness. Speaking of the Black Panthers again, he felt that he had been exploited and misunderstood. He had really hoped to help them, and in return he had been scorned. Scorned as a white man, scorned especially as a homosexual and as an ex-thief. I would have preferred to talk with him about his plays but the failure of his undertaking was obviously a source of such intense pain for him that he could not talk about anything else.

I never saw Jean Genet again.

CHAPTER TEN

Role Playing in Jean Genet's *The Maids*

The opening of Jean Genet's *The Maids (Les Bonnes)* is one of the most brilliant scenes of the contemporary theater. Dispensing entirely with exposition, it plunges us straight into the heart of what we will only eventually understand to be a ritual enacted regularly by two servant sisters. Initially disconcerted by the bizarre behavior of a "mistress" and her maid, the spectator discovers the stylized game of domination that links them. Not until the alarm clock rings to end the scene can we fully comprehend the significance of what has transpired, yet we are carried along by a crescendo of tension and a tantalizing power play that tears apart yet binds the two women. The scene takes some fifteen minutes—fifteen minutes during which we find ourselves enthralled in a strange, stifling atmosphere where nothing is "normal," where identities seem fluctuating, where the most startling behavior appears carefully rehearsed. This is pure theater—the unfolding of a dangerous, intriguing ceremonial.

As the play begins, we are perplexed by the comportment of "Madame." Although the maid, "Claire," is also strange in her oscillation between craven humility and aggressiveness, "Madame's" tone and gestures, "exaggeratedly tragic," [1] according to Genet, astonish us. She accuses her maid of coveting her clothes, of allowing herself to be

125

seduced by Mario, the milkman, of being hideous. This is hardly the way a mistress would normally talk to her maid! Even more surprising, "Madame" includes herself in her comments about Mario: "A ridiculous young milkman despises us, and if we're going to have a kid by him. . . . " (37). We are equally disoriented when the maid imperiously imposes a dress on her mistress and then humbly tells her, "I'll follow you everywhere. I love you" (39).

Quickly, then the tone mounts. "Madame's" exaltation grows ever more manic ("the devil [is] carrying me away in his fragrant arms. He's lifting me up, I leave the ground, I'm off") as the maid's servility turns to assertiveness ("There's no need to overdo it. Your eyes are ablaze. . . . Limits, boundaries, Madame. Frontiers are not conventions but laws. Here, my lands; there, your shore—" [42]).

This admonishment leads to the most startling moment in the scene. "That'll do!" decides the maid, "Now hurry! Are you ready?"; and "Madame" replies "Are you?" (43–44). With that exchange, their positions are inverted. Now it will be the maid's turn to hurl invectives at her mistress and she goes at it with pent up gusto: "I'm ready.—I'm tired of being an object of disgust. I hate you, too. I despise you" (44). By this time, the spectator may have suspected that the two women are involved in a ritual enactment; with the obviously planned reversal of roles, the ritualistic nature of their contest becomes at last clear.

The maid now laces into "Madame" with remarkable violence; she accuses "Madame" of denying her everything beautiful and of lusting for the milkman (an amazing reproach for a maid to make against her mistress!). She is so consumed by her anger that she makes a potentially fatal mistake: in her rage she spews forth "For Solange says: to hell with you." "Madame," panic-stricken, tries to rectify: "Claire, Solange, Claire" (44). We are led to understand that "Madame" is not the only one playing a role; the maid herself has transferred her identity from Solange to her sister Claire. As we eventually realize, the daily ritual consists of a double displacement: one of the maids enacts "Madame" while the second one takes on the role of the first. Solange, who is playing Claire, finally catches on to her mistake, just in time to save the game-playing: "Ah! Yes, Claire, Claire says: to hell with you!" (44).

Without this recovery, the ritual would have collapsed; real hatred would have supplanted the more exalted venting of ceremonial hatred, and the stylized liberation of attacking "Madame" would have been lost in favor of the more pedestrian attacks of one sister against the other. Solange almost let the game get away. Had she maintained her own name, Claire would have become Claire and "Madame" would have evaporated. Fortunately, Solange gets back on track; the ceremony continues and accelerates menacingly as Claire-"Madame" slaps Solange-"Claire" and threatens to kill her just before the alarm clock puts an end to the ceremony. Quickly, the disguise is removed, props replaced, the room spruced up. All becomes normal again—although in the twisted world of *The Maids*, normal is a relative term.

The sisters' daily excursion into structured fantasy is their way of surviving their stifling reality. Their staged revolt against "Madame" relieves them of the necessity of revolting against the real Madame. It is their carefully devised yet poorly executed safety valve which enables them to put up with what they deem their wretched lot. The fact that the real Madame, when we see her midway in the play, is clearly not the tyrant the ritual makes her out to be changes nothing in the maids' perception. Their need to revolt is real, but their desire to revolt is undermined by their fascination for Madame. Thus, they content themselves with a mock revolt, aimed as much at one another as at Madame—a stylized enactment of revolt deliberately circumscribed to end just short of murder. When Claire takes on the role of "Madame" and reprimands Solange who has taken on "Claire," it is an opportunity for the sisters to play out intricate master-slave relationships, to be at once sadistic and masochistic, and especially to act out a virulent yet virtual revolt against their mistress, safe in the knowledge that the revolt remains just between them. Only at the end of *The Maids* will the revolt, for the first and only time, go to its logical, tragic conclusion. With the realization that they will be discovered as the authors of anonymous denunciations of Madame's lover, having failed to kill the real Madame with the poisoned tea just as they have always recoiled from killing the fake "Madame" in the ritual, Claire and Solange give at last stunning reality to their ceremony and an apotheosis of meaning to their lives by playing out the murder on themselves.

Since the sisters view themselves as subjugated servants, only a crime could confer on them the authenticity they seek, but their revolt remains on the level of imagination. Their condition of slavery really suits them; they are satisfied to transcend it only on the level of myth. Thus they *play* at revolt, participating in the fiction now as rebel now

ROLE PLAYING IN JEAN GENET'S THE MAIDS

as object of the revolt. The value of the exercise for them is ritualistic; it enables the sisters to give vent to the loathing which consumes them while continuing to be the subjugated slaves they aspire to remain. Their ritual becomes a play-within-a-play: the maids *play* a drama and their enactment, which has the consistency of *a* truth eventually becomes their *only* truth. By play's end, the transfer of personality is total as illusion triumphs over reality. The role of "Madame" has so completely taken hold of Claire that she dies for it in a perfect fusion with the mythical character she at once admires and detests. This complex interplay between reality and illusion, both being elements of theater and representation, constitutes what Martin Esslin has called "a hall of mirrors" in which truth becomes indistinguishable from fiction. Here, as in his other plays, Genet forces to their ultimate limit the paradoxes of the "theater-within-the-theater" strategy made famous by Luigi Pirandello.

The Maids is a fine example of a theater of cruelty as theorized by Antonin Artaud in his *The Theater and Its Double*. For Artaud, fascinated by oriental theater with its use of ceremonial and magic, theater should serve as a catalyst for crisis, like the plague to which he compares it, in order to force the spectator into a confrontation with his or her metaphysical reality. For Genet, the agony of the maids' painful suffering in a climate of latent violence and eroticism is intended to elicit a similar confrontation from the spectator. In his introduction to the play in French (not translated in the American edition), he wrote:

> These ladies—the Maids and Madame—go off the deep end. Like me, every morning in front of my mirror when I shave, or at night when I'm bored stiff, or in a forest when I think I am alone: it is a tale, that is to say, a form of allegorical narrative whose primary aim may have been, when I wrote it, to disgust me with myself by showing and refusing to show who I am; the second goal being to create a sort of discomfort in the audience.[2]

The audience's discomfort is heightened by the erotic nature of the sisters' dialogue within their ritual. Beyond the maid's adulation of "Madame's" beauty and declarations such as "I love you" and "You want to see me naked every day," the very structure of the ritual mimics the sexual act. The first part of their ceremonial interplay might be viewed as arousal, leading to the "Are you ready?" "I'm ready" that separates foreplay and the sexual act. Already before "Are you ready?," "Madame" was getting exalted, leading the maid to cry, "[in ecstasy] Madame is being carried away!" and to admonish "Madame" to slow down: "There's no need to overdo it. Your eyes are ablaze" (42). With her "I'm ready," the maid becomes the dominant partner; when "Madame" is slapped, she is visibly excited while Solange resorts to equivocal language: "I'll finish it up" and "I'm going to finish the job" (46). But the scene—or the symbolic sexual act—remain unfinished; the alarm clock sounds, the two maids are spent, and, for a brief moment, tender with each other. Their language continues the double-entendre: "you didn't get to the end," "you're never ready. I can't finish you off." "We waste too much time with the preliminaries" (46–47).

When, near the end of *The Maids,* the ritual is resumed, this time to a tragic conclusion—or climax—the sexual nature of the interaction is even sharper. It is Solange, at first, who forces the resumption on a recalcitrant Claire; intuiting their danger, Claire is reluctant to become "Madame" again and to enter a new phase of the ceremony whose outcome she cannot anticipate. But Solange forges ahead: "Let's drop the preliminaries and get on with it. . . . Let's get right into the transformation. . . . I'm quivering, I'm shuddering with pleasure. Claire I'm going to whinny with joy!" And when Claire reappears, transfigured in her white dress into "Madame," Solange forgets her own orders and ecstatically exclaims, "You're beautiful!" But by now, Claire has fully assumed her role and commands, "Skip that. You said we're skipping the prelude. Start the insults." Since Solange is incapable of doing so, Claire prods her with her own, feverish insults: "Servants ooze. They're a foul effluvium drifting through our rooms and hallways, seeping into us, entering our mouths, corrupting us. I vomit you!" The technique is effective. "Go on," Solange pants, "Go on! I'm getting there, I'm getting there." But she is slow in "getting there," and after several more "Go on, go on!"s, Claire, like an exhausted lover, calls out "Please hurry. Please! I can't go on. You're . . . you're . . . My God, I can't think of anything. My mind's a blank. I've run out of insults. Claire, you exhaust me." Just in time, Solange succeeds: "Stop. I've got there" (85–87). And with that, the final process of transcendence is under way. This time, they do surpass themselves in a rapturous climax of death and sublimation.

ROLE PLAYING IN JEAN GENET'S THE MAIDS

If I wrote that the initial ritual is poorly executed by the maids, it is because Claire and Solange are maids and not actresses and their impersonation of "Madame" and "Claire," respectively, is necessarily flawed. An actress playing only "Madame" and "Claire" could do so perfectly, but the actresses who perform *The Maids* must play Claire and Solange perfectly but must impersonate "Madame" and "Claire" with enough artifice to make it clear to the audience—and this right from the opening scene—that they are not really actresses but maids performing the roles. Hence the posturing, the exaggeratedly tragic tone and gestures, the occasional confusion between their roles and their real selves. The actress playing Claire playing "Madame" needs to let Claire's personality appear behind the stylized, figurative mask she assumes as "Madame." It is a particularly demanding role of major proportions. Thanks to the complexity of the three characters (for Madame is herself a fascinating character, though less textured than the maids), Jean Genet's *The Maids* (1947) stands out as one of the first great works of the "new theater." Almost six years before Beckett's *Waiting for Godot* in 1953, with a dramatic technique whose innovation is interior rather than formal, *The Maids* not only presages Genet's own plays to come but also announces a major shift in theatrical expression at the mid-century.

$\boxed{\mathsf{E}}$

INTRODUCTION TO TILLY

Among the most brilliant younger playwrights in France today is Tilly. Though not a prolific author, his five plays in fifteen years have made a powerful impact. His is a strikingly original voice. With irony and minute observation, with a keen sense of theatricality, he dissects French society and, by extension, Western society in general. *Delicatessen* in 1980 revealed a brilliant, new talent. The play introduces us to an inarticulate lower-middle-class family—a butcher, his wife, and their ne'er-do-well son—three very simple characters, at first glance ill-equipped to hold center stage. Yet, their modest existences become fully viable, even tragic, in this short play whose drama and eventual violence builds coherently thanks to Tilly's keen understanding of the human psyche and thanks to his unerring sense of theater devoid of flashy stage effects.

Tilly followed *Charcuterie fine* with *Spaghetti bolognese* in 1982 and then *Trumpets of Death* in 1985 and *A Modest Proposal* in 1987. In this most recent play, as in the earlier ones, the milieu is the lower middle class, its mediocrity, its hypocrisy, its latent violence, and its bigotry. *A Modest Proposal* deals with a dangerous subject: the racism that permeates a segment of contemporary French society.

Tilly turns his back on a century-long tendency towards nonrealistic theater in France by embracing fully the fourth-wall convention familiar to realistic theater of bygone days. We are meant to believe fully in what happens on stage, in the room we see, with the fourth wall mysteriously become transparent so that we can watch as privileged voyeurs what "real" people are "really" doing and saying. But this is no mere reversal to outmoded forms of nineteenth-century realism. The precise observation, the accent on the quotidian, the humble, and the painful yields a wider perspective, a tragic view of daily humilia-

INTRODUCTION TO TILLY

tion compounded by humor which makes us wince with the pain of recognition. Tilly does not explain, he demonstrates, and he does so without stylization, with no theatrical tricks, with a purity of dramaturgy that makes us forget we are in the theater. Without didacticism, he challenges us to think, to judge, to react to a world without pity.

CHAPTER ELEVEN

Interview with Tilly

TOM BISHOP: Many labels have been suggested to describe your work, such as theater of the everyday and hyperrealism. How do you react to such points of view?

TILLY: I pay no attention to that. I am satisfied to write and direct plays, and that's all. And when people talk to me about naturalism, hyperrealism, and the like, it's not my problem. I never think in these terms; I've never thought in these terms.

TB: Nevertheless, when you write a play and you direct it, it involves the fourth-wall convention and the stage/audience relationship. Looking at your plays, one feels that you do in fact use the fourth-wall convention—in a different way, to be sure, without reverting to naturalism. Are you aware of this use of convention and do you reflect on the stage/audience relationship?

TILLY: Not when I write, but I do when I direct. When I direct my plays, these matters become very important. What I do is to ask my actors not to "perform." It's as if there were only one person looking at them. During rehearsals, I am alone with them, perhaps with an assistant, we are two at most. I ask them to work as if someone were

133

INTERVIEW WITH TILLY

looking at them through a half-opened door or through a window or through a keyhole. It is voyeurism.

TB: The spectator becomes a privileged voyeur, then?

TILLY: Yes, that's how I approach it.

TB: And you ask your actors not to concern themselves with this voyeur, don't you?

TILLY: Yes, not to concern themselves with anything, as if they were alone, as if the public did not exist.

TB: Yet at the same time, it's the public that carries them in what they do.

TILLY: Of course. I have just directed *Charcuterie fine (Delicatessen)* in Lausanne and will do it again in Paris this Fall at the Théâtre de la Colline. It is the first play I wrote and this was the first time I staged it. There have been several projects to revive it, but I wanted to keep the rights for myself because I really felt like directing it. It is as timely now as it was fifteen years ago.

TB: When you wrote *Charcuterie fine,* for instance, did you have in mind some form of realism or naturalism in the lineage of Antoine,[1] some notion of fourth-wall convention? I would imagine not, but I wonder just the same.

TILLY: No. When I was writing, not at all. I really didn't have these references because I don't have a great theater culture. Often I am asked about people I haven't even heard of.

TB: So you weren't encumbered by all that?

TILLY: No, I was not, except perhaps unconsciously, because I had after all worked a good deal in the theater as an actor and I was never really satisfied with what I did. But I was never satisfied either by the work of others, by their way of speaking; somehow, I found all that really bizarre.

TB: But now that you are also a director, surely you are familiar with Antoine's work, even if you didn't know him at the outset?

TILLY: Yes, I am, because when I studied theater, I learned a lot about Antoine.

INTERVIEW WITH TILLY

TB: Neither you nor I ever saw Antoine's work, yet we both know enough about what he did to realize that what you try to do is not unrelated to his attempts to renew the theater, even if the two are very different. But it seems to me that no one can see *Charcuterie fine* and think of Antoine with respect to the *subject* of the play. For me the difference is that you deal with less obviously "dramatic" situations, less spectacular ones. When you work with your actors, it's as if you were working under a microscope. And your work with them is a cooperative effort.

TILLY: At least I try. There are actors who find things and to whom I therefore give a lot of leeway; but there are others who don't work that way. I don't really give them instructions in this area. I am very insistent when it comes to moving on stage, to gestures, the economy of gestures, of glances, of movements. Everything has to be very, very precise. I ask precision of them. From that point on, they are closely locked into their work, so to speak; it's as if we were working more and more on a tightrope. At the start, I lead them across a river on a wide bridge; by the end, we finish the crossing on a tightrope. That's where we need to get to: from that point on, they keep their balance in order not to fall into an excess, even two excesses. They could fall into a "boulevard" or commercial excess or into another one that is not really more intellectual, but, let's say, more theatrical.

TB: I assume that when you say "theatrical," you mean the word in quotation marks; it is almost pejorative, isn't it? If it is "theatrical," it is already removed from what you are aiming at.

TILLY: Yes, that's exactly it.

TB: Still, it is theater.

TILLY: Yes, of course, but not "theatrical."

TB: You have been described as having a passion for being exhaustive.

TILLY: I don't know what that means.

TB: You are supposed to have a passion for being exhaustive, obsessive with respect to the use of sets, stage accessories.

TILLY: Yes, that's true. If plays are not staged as written, it can be a catastrophe. When it comes to the banality of the dialogue, everything beyond the dialogue must be kept closely in check.

TB: It is difficult to speak of banality.

TILLY: Last year, I saw *Charcuterie fine* performed in a provincial theater where the play lasted 20 or 25 minutes longer than what I just did. Silences are extremely important.

TB: Twenty to 25 minutes longer! You must have suffered.

TILLY: Yes, I did.

TB: Let's talk about *A Modest Proposal.* You may remember that we talked about it several years ago, and that I suggested then that your play should work well in the United States because the problems and the mentality involved are analogous, even if they are not quite the same, even if the frame of reference is not the same. You don't favor "Americanizing" it, do you, of making it more recognizable for Americans?

TILLY: No, I don't think so. France was a colonial power in Africa. One could transpose the play to Vietnam for a production in the United States, but it's not the same form of racism and I don't see the advantage of doing it. In the play, only the protagonists know why the black man winds up going back to Africa. They treated him very badly, but no one else really knows. That is certainly a danger.

TB: Do you consider it to be a political play?

TILLY: Political or social, I don't know.

TB: But not political in that it involves some precise French political scene? Like the people around Le Pen?[2]

TILLY: Somewhat. It's closer to somewhere between Chirac and de Villiers.[3] But the young woman could be a follower of Le Pen.

TB: When you wrote the play, all that did not yet exist, I believe. Was Le Pen already a political force?

TILLY: Yes, I think so. I recall a roundtable discussion in Avignon.[4] Someone spoke of Le Pen, he was being talked about. I remember that I didn't want to speak his name because I thought that he was already being paid too much attention.

TB: That's right. That was the time when people thought it best not to talk about him because it helped him too much. Since then, he has helped himself. . . . Can you tell me what playwrights interest you? Influenced you? Whom do you like to read? Whose plays do you like to see?

TILLY: I never go to the theater. Or very, very rarely. I haven't lived in Paris for the past year and a half, and don't intend to live there again.

TB: But even when you started, was there no one . . . ?

TILLY: Yes, I did go to the theater a great deal then, but for a good number of years now, I haven't been going any more.

TB: I might imagine that you were not indifferent to Chekhov, for instance.

TILLY: You're right. In fact, he was the first dramatist I appreciated. When I was in school, I liked neither Molière nor Corneille. But I liked Racine and I liked Chekhov—I like him still, in fact. I find his language superb, extraordinary. And later on, when my studies were over, I really discovered Chekhov; it was fantastic. And then Ibsen. Those were the two, Chekhov and Ibsen.

TB: Do you know the theater of Franz-Xaver Krötz and Botho Strauss?[5]

TILLY: No. I saw one play by Krötz—I don't remember which one—but I only found out later that it was by Krötz. It was very good.

TB: I ask you that because Krötz especially is close to your universe, to your concerns, to your esthetics.

TILLY: I have been asked about him before. That was the only play of his I saw.

TB: That must have been *Through the Leaves*, a play with some similarities to *Charcuterie fine*. There is also a woman who owns a butcher shop. In any case, you and Krötz, and to some degree Strauss, are at the center of an important current in contemporary European theater.

TILLY: I saw one play by Strauss. The text seemed interesting but I didn't like the production. I found the staging boring.

TB: Are you writing a play right now?

INTERVIEW WITH TILLY

TILLY: No, I am doing a film, my second film. I haven't written a play for some time. I simply don't write for the theater anymore.

TB: You mean the theater is finished for you?

TILLY: I don't know. I have been on this film for a while; it takes a long time. And then, all I want now is to live in Brittany and write. Last year I began a play, and then I stopped. There are things I want to do, but what bothers me more and more is what comes afterwards, that is, to try to get a production together, to stage the play. I don't really much feel like doing that anymore, in Paris or elsewhere. What I do feel like doing now is to write.

TB: Well, I look forward to seeing you again this Fall, in New York, when you will come for the production of *A Modest Proposal* at UBU.

From Tom Bishop, preface to *A Modest Proposal,* by Tilly (New York: Ubu Repertory Theater Publications, 1994), xiv-xx.

Jean-Louis Barrault and Madeleine Renaud receiving Medal of the Center for French Civilization and Culture. Paris, 1985. *Personal collection.*

Nathalie Sarraute receiving the Medal of the Center for French Civilization and Culture. *Personal collection.*

In Virginia Woolf's *Freshwater* with Florence Delay. New York, 1983. © *Chantal Regnault. By kind permission of Chantal Regnault.*

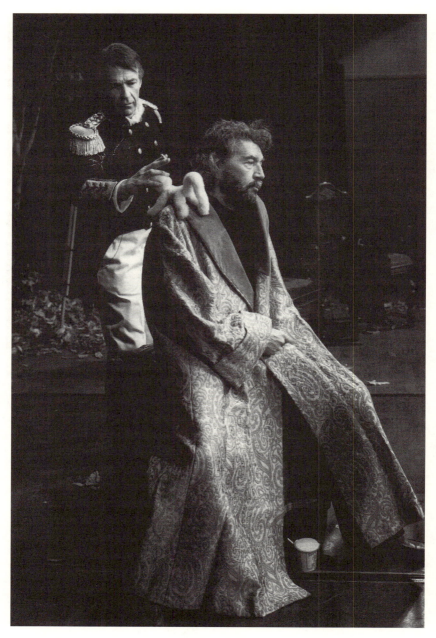

Rehearsing *Freshwater* with Alain Robbe-Grillet. New York, 1983. © *Chantal Regnault. By kind permission of Chantal Regnault.*

Curtain call after *Freshwater*. Nathalie Sarraute, Alain Robbe-Grillet, Eugène Ionesco. New York, 1983. © *Chantal Regnault. By kind permission of Chantal Regnault.*

Eugène Ionesco addressing New York University convocation after receiving honorary doctorate, 1971. *Personal collection.*

The author with Alain Robbe-Grillet at an NYU colloquium. Paris, 1981. *Personal collection.*

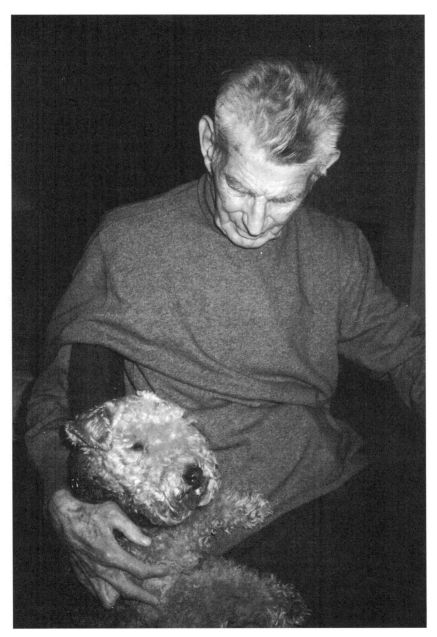

Samuel Beckett with the author's dog Winnie. This photo, taken by the author in late 1989, is probably the last photograph of Beckett. *Personal collection.*

With the leading writers of the "New Novel," (from l. to r.) Robert Pinget, Claude Simon, Alain Robbe-Grillet, and Nathalie Sarraute. New York, 1982. © *Dominique Nabokov. By kind permission of Dominique Nabokov.*

☐F☐

INTRODUCTION TO SARTRE

One of my great regrets is that I never met Sartre. I read him early on, in 1948, I think, thanks to a young undergraduate instructor (Floyd Zulli, who was later my colleague), who was in touch with what was most recent and exciting in France. Zulli's class was a revelation for me—it opened my eyes to modern French literature which I barely knew, to Proust, Malraux, Camus, and Sartre. Sartre had become famous in France in the previous three years, but he was not yet well known in the United States. I read *No Exit* and *Nausea* for Zulli's class in twentieth-century French literature. For my term paper, I wrote on Sartre's theater which, at that time, included only three other plays. I was excited by existentialism and fascinated by Sartre's theater. Three years later—by which time Sartre had written several more plays, including *Red Gloves* and *The Devil and the Good Lord* (which I saw in Paris)—I wrote my master's thesis on his theater. When I began my doctoral dissertation on "Pirandello and the French Theater" in 1954, I wrote to a number of French playwrights whom I considered somehow directly or indirectly influenced by Pirandello, Sartre among them. He replied quickly and kindly in the affirmative and expressed his great admiration for the Italian playwright. If I had been more daring, I would have followed up on that letter and asked to meet him. But I was too timid in those days and did not know how to go about such matters. Besides, Sartre was then the most famous writer in the world and I would have needed not only courage but "chutzpah." Later, I learned; since the early 1960s, I have met any number of writers, intellectuals, and artists, but these meetings happened usually organically rather than at my request. I went on to teach seminars on Sartre, to write on him, and to meet many persons close to him. I wrote to him to invite him to New York University when he was supposed to go to Cornell in 1965 for a series of lectures; but he canceled the trip in protest against American involvement in Vietnam. The opportunity never presented itself after that and I never got to meet Sartre.

CHAPTER TWELVE

Sartre, A Life

Like Voltaire in the eighteenth century and Victor Hugo in the nineteenth, Jean-Paul Sartre dominated the intellectual life of twentieth-century France to an extraordinary degree. His immense production, his diversity and his enthusiasm call to mind the figures of the Renaissance; his fervent wish to be an uncompromising witness to his time links him with the great political and social thinkers of the Enlightenment. When Sartre was to be arrested for civil disobedience, General de Gaulle vetoed the move with the comment that "you don't arrest Voltaire."

Like Voltaire, Sartre also was a conscience for his time, often wrong and subject to massive blind spots but courageous in his commitment and eager to engage in polemics. More than anyone else's, his work resonated with the major problems of literature and esthetics of his era, while his political and social thought reflected the dilemma of modern man in the years centered on World War II.

For a biographer, Sartre's life presents a bonanza of opportunity accompanied by the built-in risk of writing about a man already thoroughly depicted and discussed not only in the remarkable volumes of Simone de Beauvoir's memoirs but in Sartre's numerous autobiographical writings. The first biography appeared in France in 1985, five years after his death. Written by Annie Cohen-Solal, it was highly praised and is scheduled to be published here later this month. Now comes a volume by Ronald Hayman, the British biographer of Kafka, Nietzsche, and Brecht. Mr. Hayman successfully counterpoints the public and the private man and highlights the frequent contradictions that mark Sartre's actions and writings.

Reviled and revered (he was awarded the 1964 Nobel Prize in literature but refused it), Sartre was a controversial intellectual in the limelight. In his private life he was no less intriguing. His fifty-year open relationship with de Beauvoir was as legendary as were his numerous liaisons (always fully reported to her). He pushed himself to work unrelentingly with the help of various drugs, relying on other pills for his short nightly sleep; he often drank excessively, and he chain-smoked all his life. The fact that he was short, unattractive, and startlingly cross-eyed in no way hampered his amorous conquests, but it was a cause of never-ending distress to him. He traveled the world over, met most of the leading political, artistic, and intellectual figures and was consulted, solicited, and quoted; heralded as the "pope" of existentialism, he ranked as an international superstar. His work earned him substantial sums, but he had no use for money and spent it freely to support friends and causes. Nearing the end, he wondered how to provide for the costs of his funeral.

Fame did not come quickly to Sartre—certainly not quickly enough for him. Before he could make his mark, he had to cope with the burden of family. The death of his father when Jean-Paul was only a year old was a loss compensated by his mother's entire attention and affection; but Mme Sartre's remarriage when he was twelve was for him an unmitigated catastrophe. Despite the love and care lavished by his maternal grandparents, Sartre was inconsolable, and remained so. Later, many of his biographical writings concentrated on writers who suffered a similar loss literally (Baudelaire) or metaphysically (Genet, Flaubert).

The man who fought bourgeois values and took an oath of lifelong hatred of the bourgeoisie was born in 1905 into a middle-class family. That accident of birth rendered impossible his ardent desire in later years to communicate one-on-one with the working class. He would bend over backward—to the point of becoming supine at times—to defend the Soviet Union as the sole source of dignity for the proletar-

SARTRE, A LIFE

iat. But he could never feel at ease with the working class other than in theory.

If his family was not able to provide the advantages of a proletarian background, or ease the burden of his ugliness, it did encourage him early on to turn to books—and that proved to be his redemption. In *The Words,* Sartre describes the immense joy of reading, the escape it provided from the world and the promise it held for eventual acclaim.

By the time he entered the prestigious École Normale Supérieure, in 1924, he had already written extensively and published several pieces. As it did for so many other brilliant young Frenchmen, "Normale" proved to be a powerful catalyst. Sartre read extensively in philosophy and literature. Some of his classmates were to be important to him for much of his life: the young writer Paul Nizan, his closest friend until he was killed in action during the war; Raymond Aron, his early mentor in the mysteries and delights of modern philosophy; and, of course, Simone de Beauvoir, whom he met in 1929. Their rare communion of minds began with joint preparation for the redoubtable *agrég-ation* examination. Sartre came out first in this nationwide competition and de Beauvoir was second, a result emblematic of their entire association—at the top always, but with Sartre in the lead. They decided on a relationship of shared experiences, travels, and love with no exclusivity and above all with no lies. They carried off this difficult balance extremely well, although it was far from easy: Sartre's need for amorphous conquests was practically unquenchable, and de Beauvoir did not always remain indifferent to his affairs. But Sartre felt comfortable only in the company of women and, except for Nizan, had no use for the friendship of men.

Following a year's immersion in Berlin in the philosophies of Edmund Husserl and Martin Heidegger, Sartre tasted his first success with the publication of *Nausea* in 1938 and the short stories subsequently collected as *The Wall.* Until the war, as Mr. Hayman shows, he stayed away from political commitments, very much like Mathieu, the protagonist of his novel *The Age of Reason.* But his attitude changed with the war; army service (in the meteorological corps), a German prisoner-of-war camp, the occupation made him realize that Olympian detachment was no longer possible in a world dominated by war, deportation, torture, and genocide. After the liberation, he evolved the notion of literature as commitment, the logical result of a fundamental concept of Sartrean morality—man's realization that he is free and therefore responsible for his actions.

In the wake of World War II, Sartre and his existentialist philosophy were suddenly catapulted to international fame. In his novels and especially in his plays, he managed to provide simple, accessible illustrations of his massive book *Being and Nothingness*. However inadequate the Manichaean concepts and vocabulary of Sartre's ideology may seem today, they were well suited to the immediate postwar period. Good had triumphed over evil, the choices between democracy and fascism, resistance and collaboration, were clear-cut; it seemed reasonable to speak of good and bad faith, of authenticity and inauthentic cowardice, of freedom and determinism.

With the advent of the cold war, the revelation of Soviet concentration camps, and the return to internal politics of peacetime, black-and-white oppositions became more difficult to justify. Having been an outspoken anti-Communist immediately after World War II, Sartre tried during the cold war to find a synthesis of political and moral action aligned somehow with the Soviet Union. His very successful 1948 play, *Dirty Hands* (or *Red Gloves*), critical of the inner workings of the party, proved to be an intense embarrassment to him several years later when it was produced in Vienna at the same time that a peace congress supported by Moscow was held there. Many friends parted company with him: Raymond Aron, Arthur Koestler, Maurice Merleau-Ponty and, especially, Albert Camus. An increasingly marginal figure, Sartre recognized his own failure to translate his political beliefs into meaningful political change: "For a long time, I took my pen for a sword," he wrote in *The Words* in 1963. "I now know we're powerless." Literature as political action is not effective, but "I still write. What else can I do?" During the May 1968 revolt, Sartre joined with the students fighting the status quo and the establishment. This was a new, Maoist ultraleft, hostile to the Soviet Union, disdainful of the French Communist Party. But by then Sartre was no more than a symbol, and his voice no longer carried far.

In Mr. Hayman's biography, the best pages are devoted to Sartre's political activity and to his many travels, especially his two stays in New York soon after the war. But at times Mr. Hayman bewilders the reader with so much detail that even chronology becomes muddled; he traces the labyrinth of Sartre's amorous life with an attention to minutiae, although he remains strangely silent about the nature of the

SARTRE, A LIFE

physical relationship with de Beauvoir. Based on a close reading of all their works as well as on other sources, notably the Cohen-Solal book, Mr. Hayman's *Sartre: A Life* is solid, factual biography but lacking in originality or point of view. The writing is undistinguished and sometimes flawed; but as a full-scale study of this literary giant's life, the book is useful.

Fifty thousand Parisians followed Sartre's coffin in 1980, through Saint-Germain-des-Prés to the Montparnasse cemetery. Only Victor Hugo and Voltaire were paid a similar tribute by their fellow citizens. Jean-Paul Sartre was not the best writer in the world, nor the most profound thinker, but he incarnated the enthusiasm, the anguish and the contradictions of his era with a compelling honesty and an intelligibility that gave him his singular role as an intellectual in the world arena.

From *New York Times Book Review* (June 7, 1981): 11.

CHAPTER THIRTEEN

No Exit

Sartre's first play to be performed, *The Flies* (1943), received a lukewarm critical reception at first and its popular success came later. Soon afterwards, Sartre wanted to try his hand at theater again and began to write a play which was to become *No Exit (Huis clos)*. In *The Prime of Life*, Simone de Beauvoir relates that one of Sartre's friends whose wife was an actress suggested to him that he write a play for her and for another actress. With that in mind, Sartre had to take into account the following imperatives: write a play that would not be expensive to stage and could be performed in Paris as well as in provincial cities. Thus he needed a work not requiring a substantial investment: few characters, a single, simple set, no costumes. Moreover, since it was to be performed by three friends and since Sartre did not want to favor one of them over the others, he aimed for roles of equal length and importance and a situation that would have none of the characters leave the stage: "That meant that I had to have all of them on the stage at the same time and all of them had to remain there. Because, I thought, if one of them goes off, he will be thinking as he exits that the others have better parts than he has."[1]

Thus he settled for a solution that provided *no exit* for any of the

146

three. Sartre had already been struck by the oppressiveness of isolation in the *Stalag*, the German prisoner-of-war camp in which he was held from 1940 to 1941. After investigating several possibilities which might justify the detention he sought for his characters, he struck on the idea of placing them in a form of hell from which they cannot escape. Once these basic problems were resolved, Sartre wrote very quickly (mostly at the Café de Flore); it took him but two weeks.

Sartre had recently met Albert Camus; the two writers liked each other and Sartre asked the author of *The Stranger* to stage the work and to play the role of Garcin. But it was not this project of enthusiastic amateurs which finally saw the light of day. *No Exit* was finally entrusted to the new director of the Théâtre du Vieux Colombier, Annet Badel, who hired professional actors and Raymond Rouleau as director. Thus it was in this venerable Left-Bank house, where thirty years earlier Jacques Copeau had labored to renew French theater, that the first performance of *No Exit* took place on May 27, 1944.

The play is remarkable for its concision and economy of means: a minimum of characters, a single action staged with no intermission for seventy-five or eighty minutes, with nothing superfluous. Sartre himself links the starkness of *No Exit* (and other plays of the period, like Anouilh's *Antigone,* Camus's *Caligula,* and de Beauvoir's *Les Bouches inutiles* ["Useless Mouths"] as well as its moral and metaphysical concerns to the preoccupations of France in the process of redefining itself. If the problems Sartre poses in *No Exit* are individual in nature, they also concern the national conscience at a turning point in the history of the country when the notions of liberty, responsibility, bad faith, and so on, were also interpreted in the light of the experience of the war, the defeat of France, the occupation, and finally of liberation and victory.

Themes and Content

The principal theme of *No Exit* is linked to the third part, "Being for Others," of *Being and Nothingness,* and especially to chapter 3, "Concrete Relations with Others." In his vast theoretical treatise, Sartre analyzes in great detail our relationships with the Other—relationships which are necessary but which distort subjective reality. The individual needs the Other; it is only through the Other that one can know oneself, that one can see oneself. What we know of ourselves directly, what we feel within ourselves is pure subjectivity, the intuition of being without the least confirmation as to its truth. Hence, recourse to the Other who views objectively. That is, the Other sees me from without, without taking my subjectivity into account; if I wish to know how I am *objectively* (and I cannot not want to know), I am obliged to address myself to the Other. But if the Other is objective with respect to me, it means that he has reduced me to the status of object. For me, I am a subject—the only one conceivable—but for the Other I can only be an object. If I am obliged to turn to the Other to know the being that I am, how can I fail to consider myself a prisoner of this outsider's glance which tends to reduce me to a thing. And since the Other cannot take into account what I am for myself above and beyond all else, that is, a subjectivity, I conclude paradoxically that the Other holds the secret of my being and yet at the same time, he projects to me an image of myself which is not the right one. The *real* image is not available to anyone, and certainly not to some Other rather than to another Other.

In *No Exit,* this dilemma leads to the celebrated formula "Hell is— other people!," a phrase that has become world famous but which is more complex than one might think. As he utters these words, Garcin finally grasps the reality of his situation. His intuition comes to him through the massive bronze statuette that has been waiting on the mantelpiece; through it he understands at last that he is in hell. He has become like the statue: a pure object, immutably fixed by the glance of the others, a *thing,* and nothing more. The system of psychological torture at work in *No Exit* is brilliantly adapted to the three characters. Thus, *"Hell is—other people!"* applies not only to the principal philosophic thesis of the play, but also, literally, to the reciprocal relationships among Garcin, Inez, and Estelle. The events of the play demonstrate that each plays—and can never cease to play—the role of torturer for the others.

The link between *No Exit* and *Being and Nothingness* is underlined by the fact that the play, at first, was called *The Others.* "So you see that relations with other people, encrustation and freedom, freedom as the other face of the coin which is barely suggested, are the three themes in the play," wrote Sartre.[2] To the extent that "encrusting" and "freedom" are two faces of the same problem, they could be considered a single theme. For to be encrusted is to be not free; it is to refuse the fluidity of life, change, constant becoming. Sartrean freedom implies first of all that man accepts responsibility for what he is by refusing all bad faith. But the characters in *No Exit* are not free because they lie to themselves as much as they lie to the others, because they conceal their own potential freedom beneath ready-made and false formulas. In *The Flies,* Orestes attains his freedom by finally accepting full responsibility for what he does and what he is. In *No Exit,* Sartre presents the other side of the coin: weak, spineless characters who do everything possible to avoid looking at themselves squarely.

In "What Is Existentialism," Sartre wrote: "Man is nothing else than his plan; he exists only to the extent that he fulfills himself; he is therefore nothing else than the ensemble of his acts, nothing else than his life." [3] In *No Exit,* this discovery is slow, painful, and incomplete: the characters' bad faith is too engrained to yield easily. Sartre succeeds brilliantly in theatricalizing this attachment to lies and to self-deception. The three characters all conceal their freedom, each in a different way and for different reasons. They are not equally oblivious but they are all guilty; they are all encrusted and none is free.

In *No Exit,* Sartre treats the theme of sequestration for the first time on stage. With several characters enclosed in a space, the focus is on the impossibility of solitude given the glance of the Other. The suffocating atmosphere in a drawing room with no exit is not only a brilliant and necessary dramatic convention which forces the three characters to be condemned to each other, it is also the mainspring of the plot since the three only reveal themselves progressively as they realize that they no longer have a future, that all notion of becoming is cancelled out by the limits of their prison. This imprisonment, this promiscuity of the threesome enable Sartre to give the maximum resonance to the last line of the play, "Well, well, let's get on with it." The closed circle will continue endlessly.

If *No Exit* is exemplary for exploiting the parameters of sequestration, Sartre returned to this theme in other plays, notably in *The Victors* and *The Condemned of Altona* but also to a lesser degree in *The Respectful Prostitute* and *Red Gloves* (or *Dirty Hands*). Sartre's profound sense for the theatrical shines in this exploration of human relationships sharpened, accentuated, and exacerbated by forced coexistence within a closed space.

The room with no way out of *No Exit* represents hell—a metaphoric hell of course. It has nothing in common with the popular mythology of hell: no circles of suffering, as in Dante, no instruments of torture, no devil. Against these "traditional" notions, Sartre proposes an apparently normal drawing room, except for the fact that it has no windows and that the door does not open. This enables the dramatist to suggest a hell which does not depend on some infernal place but on those who are placed in it: the others. Thus hell no longer consists of instruments of torture but of voices of another people digging up the past, examining the reasons behind acts—a detested presence which destroys seclusion, which bursts illusions. It is an unusual hell, but also a stunningly efficient one.

Meaning

No Exit takes on its full resonance thanks to the subtle and dramatically powerful blend of the two main themes: the theme of the Other and the theme of freedom. Within the context of the play, the Other is infernal not only by dint of his very presence (which would suffice) but also because the Other tends to oblige the individual to go beyond the facade that we all present to the world to hide the truth from others—and from ourselves. Thus we attain the culminating point of "Hell is—other people!" by means of two different but interlaced paths which come together at the end.

The Other

The notion of the Other enters into play almost from the beginning, when Inez appears. Up to that point, there was no conflict: Garcin was alone to face this unknown universe that the Valet described laconically. Garcin tried to understand, tried to situate himself in relation to this *afterwards* (that is, after death), and he was able to do it calmly, even methodically, for he was alone. With Inez's arrival, the calm disappeared not only because she is the one who asks the tough questions (although Garcin was to realize that only later) but also, simply because she is there, because her very presence is inhibiting. Estelle's arrival will multiply the feeling of inhibition and discomfort. "It bores you having me here" Garcin tells Inez, adding that he, too, would have preferred being alone: "I'd rather be alone. I want to think things out . . . to set my life in order." Their mutual promise to respect each other's needs last merely until Estelle's arrival. That is when the real infernal game begins, cleverly orchestrated by the author through variations which, in turn, oppose each to the two others, collectively and individually.

The contemplation that Garcin longs for is impossible—at all times, the two others interpose themselves by their presence, disturbing the silence and preventing the defense mechanism of self-deception. Estelle can no longer lie to the others nor to herself because Garcin and Inez track her with their questions until her last veil of illusion falls and she stands revealed not only as an egotist and a narcissist (which she had acknowledged in her first "confession") but also as that which she had wanted to hide at all costs, a horrible infanticide. As for Garcin, he is harassed only by Inez. Estelle asks him nothing; for her he is a man capable of satisfying her and that is enough for her. She needs to know no more.

But Inez wants to know everything. She attacks the journalist ferociously and with hatred, to take revenge for his presence and to inflict pain on him. Her relentlessness against Garcin and her victory over him make up the central conflict in *No Exit* around which the play is built. Like his partners, Garcin is finally fully stripped: he is a coward who took himself for courageous, but he deliberately tortured his wife and he deserted his cause when he had his back against the wall. He is a coward from every point of view. Inez is not pursued in the same way; she creates her own hell because she is more lucid than the others and recognizes her sadism and her maliciousness. All three have caused suffering and all three are in bad faith: their punishment is well deserved.

The infernal nature of their situation is multiplied by the sexual factor. "Hell is—other people!" also refers to the unsatisfied search by each for a partner. Since they are shut up together, no workable combination among them seems possible. Inez desires Estelle who despises lesbians and has eyes only for Garcin—not for himself but because he is a man ("Any man would do. . . . As I happen to be here, you want me"). Estelle hesitates for a brief moment; she is flattered that Inez finds her desirable and if Garcin does not look at her, there is at least someone for whom she is attractive. More than most people, Estelle has a tremendous need to view herself through another; she is too superficial to know herself from within—she exists only to the extent that others think of her ("When I can't see myself I begin to wonder if I really and truly exist"). But having Inez admire her does not suffice for long; with a glance at Garcin, she finally says "I wish he'd notice me too." With that, the potential link between the women is broken and the ring continues. For Estelle, there is only one truth— the truth of her body—and all the rest, including considerations of morality, carry no weight: "Coward or hero, it's all one—provided he kisses well."

Unfortunately for Estelle, Garcin is too preoccupied with his own life to pay attention to her. What he seeks is the solitude and calm that introspection requires. Thus, at the outset of their "life" together, an implicit pact is agreed on by Inez and him: she will leave him alone and he will yield Estelle to her. But later on, when this arrangement fails to work and he attempts to take vengeance on Inez for tormenting him, Garcin takes Estelle in his arms and prepares to give in to his desire for this beautiful woman who clearly longs for him. Yet once again, the *other* is there. Inez hounds them sarcastically until Garcin lets go of Estelle. He realizes it is Inez and not Estelle he must convince of his courage ("It's you who matter; you who hate me. If you'll have faith in me I'm saved").

As for Inez, she is mesmerized by Estelle. She wants to possess her at all costs; this passion renders her vulnerable—in fact, it is her only weakness, for in all other ways, she is by far the strongest of the three. Only on the level of sexuality do Garcin and Estelle succeed in thwarting her. The three characters of the play pursue one another endlessly and never catch up. The *Other* is there, inhibiting, a judgmental consciousness, an interfering presence. In this exitless Second Empire drawing room, the Other is in the way.

Hell

But in the famous phrase, "Hell is—other people," the notion of the Other is only half the equation; the second half is the idea of hell. Sartre's metaphor works so well because it leads in several directions at the same time. The primary level of interpretation is literal: the Other tracks me, freezes me, reduces me to the status of object— and misunderstands me into the bargain. Nevertheless, this Other is essential to me and from this paradox stems the fact of torture by the Other, that is, of hell. This negation has all too often been interpreted as Sartre's refusal of the possibility of peaceful coexistence among individuals. But the author has made it clear (in a preface to a recording of *Huis clos*) that he does not deem human relationships impossible:

> But "hell is other people" has always been misunderstood. It has been thought that what I meant by that was that our relations with other people are always poisoned, that they are invariably hellish relations. But what I really mean is something totally different. I mean that if relations with someone else are twisted, vitiated, then that other person can only be hell. Why? Because other people are basically the most important means we have in ourselves for our own knowledge of ourselves. When we think about ourselves, when we try to know ourselves, basically we use the knowledge of us which other people already have. We judge ourselves with the means other people have and have given us for judging ourselves. Into whatever I say about myself someone else's judgement always enters. Into whatever I feel within myself someone else's judgement always enters. Which means that if my relations are bad, I am situating myself in a total dependence on someone else. And then I am indeed in hell. And there are a vast number of people in the world who are in hell because they are too dependent on the judgement of other people. But that does not at all mean that one cannot have relations with other people. It simply brings out the capital importance of all other people for each one of us.[4]

In support of Sartre's argument, let us remember that the characters in *No Exit* are not, after all, heroes. Estelle, Garcin, and Inez constitute each other's hell precisely because all three are of bad faith. The nature of their relationships is but the reflection of those they all had with others while they were alive. It is perfectly normal that this negative quality does not change after their life, in hell. For persons of good faith this state of things in no way applies: for them, the Other is still an obstacle but not an insurmountable one on the scale of a hell.

The presence in hell of all three is justified by their respective guilt. (In the context of *No Exit,* neither guilt nor hell are notions linked to Christianity.) Sartre's hell is a place for metaphoric punishment made striking through the discrepancy between it and traditional concepts of hell in religions and in literature. Nothing recalls the Gehenna of legend: no torturer, no instruments of torture. Instead, three sofas, no windows, a closed door, a bronze statuette, a lamp that cannot be turned off, and beyond, hallways, other rooms, and more hallways and more rooms. This is Sartre's ironic portrayal of his hell; the only link to a "traditional" one is the heat. Yet, by substituting mental and psychological torture for the concept of physical suffering, Sartre created a remarkably efficient hell whose evocative power is fully modern.

The drama that unfolds in this stifling atmosphere focuses on the ways people have of assuming their actions. Estelle has no real awareness of her own life; she suffers because she has been deprived of men and male admiration, but she never takes stock of her life for she is devoid of the power of introspection. Inez, on the other hand, is always lucid, with respect to herself as much as to others. She does not need to search within herself; she already knows who she is and what she has done. But she is wrong to consider herself "damned already," thus accepting a deterministic view of herself through this hypocritical phrase that right-thinking people use to refer to lesbians. For Sartre, Inez is a lesbian because she chooses to be one and not because she was made that way. But if that particular verity is beyond her grasp, she does understand all the rest: to what degree she is malicious and sadistic, and how much she has made others suffer.

It is Garcin who quickly becomes the central character. Not only is he the focal point of the psychological triangle, he is also the object of the discussion of ethics at the play's climax. Garcin wants to know the truth about his life while at the same time doing everything possible to avoid facing this truth. Of course, Inez is delighted to take on the role of torturer, and she plays it well for she understands the weaknesses of people (far too well, as far as Garcin is concerned). It is because Inez is able to understand that Garcin must convince her, and that is why, when the door suddenly and mysteriously opens offering him the possibility of fleeing (but where?), that he does not leave.

Once Garcin states his intention of remaining in the drawing room, Inez accepts to be his prosecutor and gets seriously down to work. She launches into her methodical interrogation of Garcin, obliging him to face up to his past acts and the reasons behind them. He tries to take refuge behind the kind of life he had led—that of a man of action; Inez retorts that his courage had been but a useful myth which vanished the moment when courage would have been most required. Desperately, he proposes that "A man is what he wills himself to be," only to have her trump him with "It's what one does, and nothing else, that shows the stuff one's made of." When the journalist objects in vain that a single act of cowardice does not taint a whole life and that he did not have enough time to carry out his projects, Inez condemns him with a definitive verdict: "One always dies too soon—or too late. And yet one's whole life is complete at that moment, with a line drawn neatly under it, ready for the summing up. You are your life, and nothing else."

The succinct statement "You are your life, and nothing else" serves, alongside "Hell is—other people," to provide the mainspring of Sartre's thought in *No Exit.* For existentialism, in the absence of any human nature, the essence that the individual constructs for himself by means of his own life is precisely equal to that life and depends only on him. It is at this point that the metaphor of hell takes on its full resonance. For Sartre chose to place his characters precisely at the moment when they can no longer evolve, that is after their death. So long as one is alive, one can claim not to have done yet everything one wants to do; for Sartre, the possibility of change is always available and only requires a new, different choice. But once life is over, human essence is fixed once and for all; looking back on it then, its moral impact can perfectly well be weighed. This is Garcin's real hell: his excuses are no longer valid and he is forced at last to confront his painful reality.

At this point, Inez can tell Garcin that judgment of him depends on her and that she judges him harshly: "You're a coward, Garcin, because I wish it." Garcin could consider himself a hero if only Inez thinks of him as one. Unfortunately for him, she does not and thus Garcin is convicted, not of *being* a coward—it's too late for that— but convicted of *having been* a coward. Inez is the strongest of the three characters: it is her eyes that see Garcin, her thought that considers him. She dominates him totally and makes him the object of her imagination, her will. No physical torture could be more effective. Under the circumstances, it is not surprising for Garcin to conclude that "Hell is—other people."

Dramatic Technique

No Exit is remarkably spare, even classical, in its construction: the single set of the drawing room, three characters (plus the Valet), a mere seventy-five minutes of performance time, and an ever increasing intensity of dramatic tension. It required all of that for a work which is basically a philosophic drama to keep its audience breathless, despite a minimum of visible action, despite characters who are not in themselves remarkable, and in the absence of a memorable style.

No Exit requires three characters for the infernal mechanism to work—a fourth would already be superfluous. Sartre introduces them into the drawing room quickly, one after the other, and enables the audience to understand practically from the start where they are, even if it is not immediately clear why. The exposition is handled with equal dispatch so as to lead soon to the confrontation of the three protagonists.

Despite the trend of the French theater of his time toward antirealistic dramaturgy, Sartre uses a number of realistic-naturalistic techniques in *No Exit*. Of course the play itself is based on a nonrealistic convention: the totally antirealistic metaphor of hell. This antirealistic technique of presenting dead people in a drawing room which represents hell is amplified by the various moments when the characters "communicate" with the world of the living. But the rest of the play unfolds in a perfectly traditional manner; against an imaginary and strictly antirealistic background, Sartre uses a basically realistic drawing-room technique. Even in the scenes of contact with the Earth, he does not exploit fully the antirealistic potential by *showing* the action described (though undoubtedly he would not have disposed of the technical and financial resources required even if he had wanted to). Everything unfolds in a realistic manner: the relationships among the three characters, their conversations, their interrogations—even if they are not depicted as psychological "cases." Sartre's language is also close to life; it is a familiar, everyday language, devoid of lyricism. This blend of techniques is unusual and successful. The play is clear and perfectly understandable, the dramatic tension is palpable, and yet the antirealistic convention of hell, which generates the entire work, remains intact right to the end and gives *No Exit* its very special tonality.

One of *No Exit*'s strongest features is its irony. The situation itself is deeply ironic: Garcin, Inez, and Estelle find themselves together forever and yet they are three persons destined not to get along. The image of hell is equally ironic: absence of instruments of torture, its Second Empire look with ugly sofas and bronze, the embryo of a Kafka-like labyrinth. The futility of the sexual merry-go-round is also ironic—and especially at the end when Estelle tries to kill Inez with a paper knife. The bitter laughter of the three followed by Garcin's "Well, well, let's get on with it" underlines the terrible derision of their situation which has become permanent, thus giving a repetitive circularity not only to their suffering but to the very structure of the play.

The play's symbolism is ironic, too. To stress that in their present state, with their lives ended, the characters no longer need the bad faith of the past, that the moment of truth has come, Sartre imagines a light that cannot be turned off and eyelids that cannot blink. It will no longer be possible not to take stock of oneself. The absence of mirrors keeps the characters from seeing themselves without resorting to the others and prevents them from continuing in their self-deception, since there is no mirror to reflect flattering images of themselves and since the others are ready and eager to destroy all illusions. Within this infernal relationship to the others, the most ironic and most important symbol is the massive, ugly bronze statuette. Near the end, Garcin goes to touch it and through it he finally comprehends what it means to be in hell. The bronze is a pure object, the perfect *thing-in-itself* that man can never become but to which others tend to reduce him; it reveals to Garcin—and this is the supreme irony—what his real hell is: under the relentless glance of the other two, he is reified. For them, he is an object and can be nothing else since hell (light, eyelids, absence of mirrors) has deprived him of all subjectivity. Through the intermediary of the bronze statuette, Garcin at last understands his situation, his guilt, his damnation.

Translated and adapted from *Huis clos de Jean-Paul Sartre* (Paris: Lire aujourd'hui, Classiques Hachette, 1975), 22–40.

CHAPTER FOURTEEN

Becoming Sartre: The *War Diaries* of Jean-Paul Sartre

What is one to expect from the posthumous publications of an author who published so extensively during his lifetime? Might we not assume that following Sartre's death in 1980, what remained in his files was either anecdotal or minor, or both? In the past two years, three works have come to light in France: the fascinating *Lettres au Castor* (Sartre's nickname for Simone de Beauvoir, "the Beaver"), soon to appear in English; the *Cahiers pour une morale*, his notebooks for a never-completed treatise on moral philosophy; and the *Carnets de la drôle de guerre*, the diary Sartre kept while a soldier during the "phony war" at the beginning of World War II. In making Sartre's numerous letters to her available, Simone de Beauvoir affords us a look at the dialectics of one of the most extraordinary relationships of our time (and leaves us eagerly awaiting her letters to him). The *Carnets pour une morale* will enthrall only specialists. But the truly great find are these diaries.

Sartre's *War Diaries* is no afterthought to an illustrious career; it is one of his most brilliant books, essential for anyone even vaguely interested in the chief exponent of postwar existentialism. It ranks with *The Words* for its insight into this complex personality—the

158

leading intellectual figure of his era. It is a dazzling work, humorous and philosophic, introspective yet ready to embrace the world, concerned both with daily life a few miles from the front lines and with complex speculations on existence. Written when he was thirty-four, the war diaries provide the most human portrait of Sartre the man, while prefiguring many of his later works.

With all that, the diaries represent only a fragment of what Sartre wrote each day from September 1939 to March 1940. Of the fourteen notebooks he filled during that period, only the five that make up the current volume have been found. The loss of the remaining nine is staggering considering the treasures available here.

This was the *drôle de guerre,* the "phony war," that strange period of waiting after the declaration of war when German and French troops stared at each other from behind their fortifications, the Siegfried and Maginot lines. Sartre was stationed in Alsace, attached to the artillery in the meteorological division in which he had done his military service ten years earlier. The idleness of waiting was hard to take; life had been disrupted and there was time to fill. Sartre filled it with a tremendous burst of activity. Writing early in the morning and late at night during those eight months before the Germans quickly overran France, he produced a million or so words—the fourteen volumes of the diaries, hundreds of letters, and *The Age of Reason,* the novel that was to become the first in the unfinished tetralogy, *Roads to Freedom.*

By the time Hitler invaded Poland, Sartre had acquired an important reputation in Parisian intellectual circles. He had taught philosophy and had published a landmark novel, *Nausea,* and a striking collection of stories, *The Wall,* as well as philosophic treatises and literary criticism. The cognoscenti already conceded that he was the most brilliant mind of his generation. The war was to divide his life. Before it, he engaged in relatively unstructured philosophic inquiry, aligned principally with Husserl, and was essentially aloof from the public concerns of his time; afterward, he developed the basic tenets of his existentialist theories, which were Heideggerian in spirit, and became passionately committed to the political and social issues of the postwar world. It is in *The War Diaries* that we can see Sartre become the Sartre who left his indelible mark on this century.

Sartre decided to keep a diary for a number of reasons. He said he wanted to preserve the testimony of an average soldier, but beyond that the diaries allowed him to explore his own identity and authenticity, to free himself from past influences and to prepare himself for future work, to be alone in the claustrophobia of communal living, "to accentuate the isolation I was in, and the rupture between my past and present lives." Prior to his mobilization, Sartre had gone "fifteen years without looking at myself living"; he was now to observe himself closely and record with humor and sensitivity what was happening within him. He wrote his notebooks with the clear conviction that they would one day be published, and they show it.

Many of Sartre's subsequent philosophic concerns surface here. The pages on the problem of nothingness, more readily comprehensible than *Being and Nothingness,* obviously prepared the way for that treatise. Philosophic speculations on such topics as the "other," authenticity, and bad faith are more compelling than elsewhere because they are accompanied by references to his own behavior. For example, on returning from a ten-day leave in Paris, he notes: "I rather think I was authentic before my leave. Probably because I was alone. In Paris, I was not authentic. At present, I'm no longer anything." Or, in relation to others, he berates himself: "I am social and an actor," and "I am nothing but pride and lucidity." After confiding that "every four or five months, I look at my stomach in a mirror and get unhappy," he proceeds to judge himself existentially for his paunch.

In the diaries, too, are the first traces of the brilliant autobiography *The Words,* of his later studies of Genet and Flaubert, of the future novels and plays and of his struggles with the difficulty of formulating a moral philosophy. The analyses of time and history (and especially his readings of Emil Ludwig's biography of William II), the exploration of his links to his own characters and his dismay at not being a poet make equally engrossing reading. Sartre's literary judgments reveal much about his taste and his mentors. He repeatedly mentions Gide with admiration; as to Malraux, he respects the many insights in *Man's Fate* but denies their influence on him. "I could have written that" he notes apropos a line from Malraux's novel, and he admits to a "brotherly resemblance between Malraux's literary techniques" and his own. For Flaubert, to whom he was to devote more than three thousand pages of biography, Sartre has only contempt and irritation, deeming his style clumsy, disagreeable and pretentious. He clearly prefers Stendhal; a rereading of *The Charterhouse of Parma* elicits great (and unusual) enthusiasm: "Stendhal's natural style, charm and liveliness of imagination can't be matched. That feeling of admiration is rare indeed with me, yet I've experienced it in full measure. And the artistry of the novel!—the unity in its movement!"

Even more captivating than these dense, stimulating, and often stunning pages on philosophy and literature are the many passages in which Sartre talks about himself. Taken together with the broader perspective offered by Simone de Beauvoir's autobiographical writings and *Lettres au Castor,* they compose the most revealing portrait available of the man. The reader is struck first by Sartre's astounding clarity about himself, his perpetual need for self-analysis. If ever there was a prototype of the intellectual's mania for watching himself doing, it lies in these diaries. A soldier among soldiers, he is caught up in the dull military routines of the waiting war; he eats, works, drinks, and talks with his colleagues. But he is equally absorbed by reflections about his past, present, and future. Sartre knows himself to be cut off from people and things: "I feel no solidarity with anything, not even with myself: I don't need anybody or anything." Like his hero Orestes in *The Flies,* Sartre feels himself incapable of commitment to the life around him. (That sense of commitment which was to characterize the last thirty-five years of his life was not to "descend on him"—as it did on Orestes—until he was made a prisoner of war during the collapse of France in June 1940.) "I haven't felt Nausea, I'm not authentic," he writes. But, again like Orestes, he adds: "I have halted on the threshold of the promised lands. But at least I point the way to them and others can go there. I'm a guide, that's my role."

If he derided himself for being cut off, at least he was sufficiently involved with women to make constant references to and reflections on his innumerable mistresses, past and present. He admits that he is bored whenever he is not in love even though he feels that he is "decidedly not cut out for rare emotions." How much we learn about Sartre's works when we learn of "the magical attraction dark, drowning women have for me." (Sartre's women are identified by the translator, Quintin Hoare, in his fine introduction. They are not identified in the original by the editor of the notebooks, Arlette Elkaïm-Sartre, whom Sartre adopted late in life as his daughter.) The friendship of men, Sartre confesses, doesn't interest him and makes him uncomfortable. "In short," he writes in a particularly revealing passage, "there's one half of humanity that hardly exists for me. The other half—well, there's no denying it, the other half is my sole and constant concern. I take pleasure only in the company of women." Four years later, in *No Exit*, Sartre wrote his most famous line, "l'Enfer c'est les autres" ("hell is other people"). In his personal life, it seems, that was true only half the time.

Sartre's concern with fame and honors in *The War Diaries* comes as something of a surprise in a man who refused to be lionized and who turned down everything from the Legion of Honor to the Nobel Prize. He describes his quandary when *Nausea* was proposed for a literary prize: he would have to write letters of application to all the members of the jury. A moral dilemma! He doesn't believe in awards but wouldn't mind having one. "My cynicism thus masks a dubious taste for consecration," he berates himself. What to do? He writes de Beauvoir for advice. Her reply, ever pragmatic, is precisely what he had expected and undoubtedly desired: he should apply; he could always use the money. "So I wrote seventeen letters of application and my hand ached." When the literary heavyweights at Gallimard want to propose him for a doctorate by transforming his treatise on imagination into a thesis, he agrees to the idea (though it never materialized). In the diaries, he notes: "No doubt about it, that's how I like to be treated. Conferring a dignity upon me *against my will*; almost apologizing for it." Just a few years later, he would unmercifully deride such hypocrisy.

Finally, *The War Diaries* provides a particularly perceptive account of the phony war. Although he is not happy to be in the army, Sartre is not eager to see the war end, undoubtedly because those strange uneventful months were a sort of vacation for him, an interruption which afforded him time to think and write. Finding the war not so terrible during this stagnant period, he predicts, with a singular lack of foresight, that it "has a modest little future of destruction and death." It is this failure to see what was still to come that enabled him to write, "it's much easier to live decently and authentically in wartime than in peacetime." Nowhere does one find any hatred or even dislike for the Germans; there are signs of a theoretical distaste for Nazis, but Hitler is mentioned rarely and with no special emphasis. Sartre is more rigorous with respect to his own country: he wonders how the future will judge prewar France but rejects the notion that the period has been a decadent one.

Sartre betrays several astonishing notions in the diaries. He dismisses scientists, doctors, and engineers as inauthentic and self-impressed and their work as boring. Several times he refers to Jews as members of a special classification. There is never any hostility, nor could anyone suggest that the author of *Antisemite and Jew* was remotely antisemitic. Yet it is odd to find Sartre referring to Jews as if they were, to use his philosophic terminology, "a category in itself." He describes a trivial incident when something fell "on the head of a small Jew with glasses." Elsewhere, the phrase "this disputatious, Jewish reason" appears in reference to a friend's powers of argumentation. Or again, there is a childhood memory of his Punch and Judy toy theater for which he purchased, he says, various stock puppet characters: "the Jew, the Gendarme, the Old Woman, Punch." These are jarring uses of stereotypes.

While quibbling, one must mention a few unhappy translations here of Sartre's slang. *Discuter le coup* becomes the ungainly "jawing away," and *foirard,* "funk" rather than "scared." More serious in view of the significance of the word in the Sartrean vocabulary is the rendering of *salaud* as "slob" rather than "bastard" or "swine." But these are minor complaints; the translation is strong, especially in the passages of difficult philosophical discourse, and it is particularly adept at rendering the strength, humor, and brilliance of Sartre's prose. "How can a man be grasped in his entirety?," asks Sartre in the diaries. This posthumous publication represents his clearest, most compelling self-portrait and earns a place among his best writings.

From *The Nation* (April 20, 1985): 470–73.

$$\boxed{\text{G}}$$

INTRODUCTION TO BECKETT

I came across Beckett's work in the mid-1950s when I read *Waiting for Godot* and *Endgame*. I was overwhelmed and I was "hooked." I quickly read the novels already published and since then, I have followed Beckett's work enthusiastically and have seen countless performances. I met Beckett in the late 1960s and, for more than two decades until his death in 1989, we would see each other each time I came to Paris. We would dine in one or another of his favorite, very quiet fish restaurants. He always ordered the same thing: a grilled sole with French fries, and a bottle of white Beaujolais. Conversation would touch on anything except the meaning of his work: writing, publishing, translation, performance aspects of his plays, politics, and even soccer. But there were also moments of silence—like in his plays—with no need to say anything, punctuated by a sip of Irish whiskey, or the lighting of one of his ever-present cigarillos.

Beckett became a main focus of my professional activities. I wrote about his work and I staged a number of Beckett conferences and festivals, in New York and in Paris—some of which lasted for months and attracted wide attention. Following his death, I organized a tribute to him at the Pompidou Center in Paris with the actors who had performed his works in several countries. It was an emotion-packed evening, with hundreds who could not get in watching on a video relay.

Samuel Beckett was one of the loveliest of human beings. He cared about his friends with a genuine solicitude, a remarkable desire to know how the other *really* is, what is happening in his life. He shared in joys and in sorrows; he never forgot what was important for his friend. Shy and retiring in public, Beckett was relaxed and loquacious in private. He laughed easily and enjoyed poking fun at himself. We

INTRODUCTION TO BECKETT

normally spoke English together; his soft Irish lilt gave his gentle voice an additional sweetness. When the conversation would switch to French in the company of a French person, the transition was always effortless and elegant. Like everyone else who ever met Beckett, I was struck by his glance—that blue, deep, direct glance—and by the craggy beauty of his face. His extraordinary looks were still intact the last time I saw him, a few weeks before he died, in the spartan room of the rest home where he spent his last year.

Once, when my son Jeffrey accompanied me to Paris, Beckett wanted to meet him. Jeff was fifteen years old at the time. I briefed him before meeting Beckett at La Coupole: no questions about his work; just listen and shut up. If my admonitions did not put Jeff at ease, Beckett did so right away. Since he knew from me that my son was (like himself) a chess freak, he set out talking chess to him. He managed so well that soon Jeff felt comfortable enough to switch subjects: "I would like to ask you which of your works you prefer?" I wanted to dig a hole and disappear. Beckett, who must have noticed my discomfort, just laughed and replied: "I think that the one I dislike least is *Endgame*."

CHAPTER FIFTEEN

On Samuel Beckett: 1906–1989

"I can't go on. You must go on. I will go on," wrote Samuel Beckett in *The Unnamable,* and until his death in December 1989, at age 83, he managed to go on. His oeuvre, comprising novels, plays, short stories, poems, and criticism written in both French and English over a span of six decades, stands out as the quintessential literary creation of the latter twentieth century in its unrelenting stress on the existential anguish of the human condition, through the constant skepticism of its vision, and the desperate search for a positive commitment to life in a world where optimism is impossible.

It seems paradoxical to apply the word "positive" to a writer so often described as nihilistic. But if paradoxes abound in Beckett (and even in this matter of his quest for the positive within pervasive negativity), his supposed nihilism is merely the quickly selected, superficial label with which some critics tried erroneously to sum up the frequent grimness of his universe without seizing the major parallel theme of man's essential nobility in his indomitable spirit, in his willingness and even his need to "continue." Even when expressed with mordant irony, the attachment to life is fundamental: "Try again. Fail again. Fail better."

167

Pessimism, many would argue, represents no more than the logical philosophical posture in our time. Beckett was certainly a pessimist; he viewed the world as absurd and humanity as bleak: his characters are lame, blind, encased in earth or in huge jars, legless, armless creatures suffering or dying. But Samuel Beckett did not offer up this dismal vision as his realistic portrayal of mankind; he was a profoundly nonrealistic artist and his characters, in their intense plight, must be viewed metaphorically as they persevere in the their quest: quest for self, quest for another, a partner, a mate, and an ever-present search for language, for the words that will finally succeed in expressing the quest and thereby bring it to an end.

Despite the desperation of their situation, Beckett's characters do not commit suicide, tempted though they may be and no matter how much they may talk longingly of "finishing it," "getting it over with." Instead, from the tramps in *Waiting for Godot,* to Winnie, buried up to her neck in *Happy Days,* to the protagonists of *Molloy* and other novels, they cling to every shred of life with fiendish tenacity, and they continue—continue to speak, continue to live. "I can't go on. You must go on. I will go on" are the simple, powerful concluding words of *The Unnamable,* as the limbless protagonist, his motionless head and trunk planted in a large earthen jar, resumes the futile but necessary task of discovering himself—a Sisyphus-like figure (though a parody of any classic notion of the hero) whose commitment to his labor against all odds constitutes extraordinary resiliency, a profound tribute to the human spirit. Thus, when Beckett was awarded the Nobel Prize for literature in 1969, the Swedish Academy cited him "for his writing, which . . . in the destitution of modern man acquires its elevation."

Samuel Beckett's initial (and greatest) success came with his first play, *En attendant Godot (Waiting for Godot),* written in French and staged at the tiny Théâtre de Babylone in Paris on January 5, 1953. Vladimir and Estragon (Didi and Gogo), those pathetic and endearing tramps, gave concrete form to a devastating image of modern man in his anguish and his abandonment. In a deliberately ambiguous setting, they wait . . . they wait for the possible but problematic arrival of one who is to extricate them from their misery: a savior, a Messiah, a god, perhaps God. Throughout their wait, which constitutes the texture and perhaps even the real subject of the play, they talk obsessively in order to create "the impression we exist," talk of committing suicide, of the strange master-and-slave twosome, Pozzo and Lucky, who twice pass through their orbit, talk about nothing and everything in a dislocated dimension of time where "yesterday" is some hazy, remote notion relegated to the distant abyss of memory. Two acts, with the second reflecting the first almost exactly, in order to strengthen it, to reinforce the feeling of forlornness and despair. Two acts, each of which ends without Godot's coming. Only the tree changes: it is bare in the first act and has mysteriously sprouted leaves in the second.

At first, the public was disconcerted by this strange play. It clearly was intended to mean something, but what? Soon though, several leading critics and playwrights rallied to this overwhelming work, and in the great period of Parisian theater experimentation in the early and mid-1950s, *Waiting for Godot* was acclaimed as an avant-garde masterpiece. With great perspicacity, playwright Jean Anouilh wrote that Godot marked a historic date for the theater and described the play as "Pascal's *Pensées* treated by the Fratellini clowns," underlining thereby both Beckett's Pascalian concern for the human condition and the clownishness of his humor. Soon after its humble beginnings, *Godot* had become a modern classic, played in countless countries and—especially—perfectly comprehensible although it had seemed so enigmatic when it premiered. It is undoubtedly the most admired serious play of the second half of the twentieth century.

When *Waiting for Godot* brought him to world attention in 1953, Samuel Beckett, an Irish writer living in France, had recently published two novels written in French, *Molloy* and *Malone meurt (Malone Dies)*, which had quickly established his reputation in very small Parisian intellectual circles; he had earlier published poems, short stories, and novels written in English—works that had gone largely unnoticed in the London literary scene. Until *Godot* brought him international renown, the tall, lean, craggy-faced Beckett was almost totally unknown.

He was born on Friday, April 13, 1906, in the town of Foxrock, near Dublin, into a fairly well-to-do liberal Protestant family. Contrary to popular mythology which would take delight in finding the roots of his peculiarly suffering characters in the author's wretchedly unhappy youth, Beckett's childhood was a happy one, spent with a loving and loved family. His school years were equally positive: he was always an

ON SAMUEL BECKETT: 1906–1989

excellent student as well as a popular one, shining in foreign languages, especially French, club theater productions, participating in various sports and other extracurricular activities.

In later years, Beckett was to turn away from Ireland and react against the Puritanism of Irish Protestantism, but he never turned against his childhood; in fact, the simplicity and happiness of his early years remain in his work as the nostalgic though wholly unsentimental glimmer of the only contentment that ever existed—a paradise necessarily lost forever.

In 1923, he entered Trinity College, Dublin, and graduated four years later with a B.A. in French and Italian. His studies proved so outstanding that he was selected to be *Lecteur d'anglais* at the Ecole Normale Supérieure in Paris, a two-year appointment reserved traditionally for Trinity's best. Beckett spent 1928–1930 at the prestigious school on the rue d'Ulm, whose roster of students during that period included Jean-Paul Sartre, Paul Nizan, and Maurice Merleau-Ponty. But the acquaintance that was to mark his Paris stay most was that of his fellow countryman, then living in Paris, James Joyce.

Despite the considerable discrepancy in their ages (twenty-four years), the two men became friends. Beckett greatly admired the author of *Ulysses,* and their friendship not only confirmed the young man's vocation for writing but also led to a major literary influence. Joyce's explosive and corrosive humor, his experiments with language as well as his indictment of Irish life all marked the young Beckett profoundly. Fittingly, his first published work was on Joyce: an essay entitled "Dante ... Bruno ... Vico ... Joyce" in the collection of texts put out in 1929 by Shakespeare and Company in Paris as a commentary on Joyce's "Work in Progress" (which was to become *Finnegan's Wake*). The bond between the two men endured. In the later 1930s, with Joyce's eyesight failing, Beckett, like many of the master's friends, often read to him or performed some helpful chores— but he was never Joyce's secretary, as legend had it.

Beckett's first poems (and first literary prize also) date from the same period. The parodic poem *Whoroscope,* purporting to be a dramatic monologue in which Descartes meditates on subjects serious and playful, was published in Paris in 1930 and earned its author a prize of ten pounds.

On returning to Ireland, Beckett was appointed as assistant in French at Trinity College and seemed destined to university teaching.

ON SAMUEL BECKETT: 1906–1989

He passed his M.A., gave thought to a doctoral dissertation, and published his *Proust,* a brilliant study (one of the very first in English) that not only enlightens *A la recherche du temps perdu* but presages much of Beckett's own work to come. But by the end of 1931, attracted inexorably by the literary life and strengthened by some financial support from his father, he renounced his budding academic career, lived for a while in London, traveled in France, Italy, and Germany, and finally, in 1937, settled in Paris. His father's death, in 1933, provided him with a small inheritance that sufficed to meet his modest needs.

When World War II broke out in September 1939, Beckett was in Ireland on a visit to his mother; he promptly returned to Paris. The following year, after the fall of France, he joined a Resistance group, even though, as a citizen of a neutral country (the Republic of Ireland), he could have continued to live untroubled under the German occupation. But in 1942, the Gestapo discovered the group and arrested several of its members, including Beckett's friend Alfred Peron. Beckett himself just managed to flee with his companion Suzanne Dumesnil (whom he eventually married), to the unoccupied zone, settling for the remainder of the war in the small town of Roussillon in the lovely Vaucluse area of Provence. There he worked the fields and shared the friendship of the peasants, but his evenings were mainly devoted to a new book: it was in the Vaucluse that Beckett wrote his first epic of derision and anguish, his last major prose fiction in English, the novel *Watt.* It is the initiation into that chaotic world which will subsequently be recognized as typically Beckettian.

On the heels of the liberation, Beckett returned to Paris, where he lived his remaining forty-five years. He resumed his writing, but now his language was French. There are not too many examples of major authors who write in an acquired language; the examples of bilingual writers who create equally in two languages are very few. But the case of Beckett is unique: he manipulated both English and French with a brilliance few others achieve in a single language, and the fact that he himself translated his own writings from one tongue to the other gives his work an unmatched bilingual existence in French and English. Yet his writing in French is qualitatively different from his English oeuvre and attests, initially at least, a conscious need to submit to a greater rigor, to a degree of distanciation in handling a nonnative language.

Beckett's "French period" opened with enormous activity. In 1946 alone, he wrote the novel *Mercier et Camier* (only published a quarter century later), and four short stories, two of which quickly appeared in literary reviews. But neither these, nor the publication of the French translation of the novel *Murphy*, earned him much attention. Nor were these fictions bringing him any money; these were difficult years and Beckett did translations to supplement his now meager income. Whatever the difficulties though, the period from 1947 to 1950 was astoundingly fertile. Within less than three years, Beckett produced his most famous works: the dazzling novel trilogy *Molloy, Malone meurt,* and *L'Innommable (The Unnamable)*; *En attendant Godot* as well as another play, *Eleuthéria* (as yet not performed and unpublished); and the short *Textes pour rien (Texts for Nothing)*.

Writing at this feverish pace was one thing; to have works appear in print quite another. Publisher after publisher turned Beckett down, and if his novels finally appeared, it was thanks mainly to two people: Suzanne Dumesnil, who left no stone unturned, despite Beckett's reluctance in the matter, and knocked at countless doors, and Jerome Lindon, the young publisher of the Editions de Minuit who, miraculously, not only recognized genius, but also had the courage and faith to back up his belief and his enthusiasm at the risk of bankrupting his company. Thus, in 1951, first *Molloy* and then *Malone meurt* were published, followed in 1952 by *En attendant Godot*. *Molloy* reaped a considerable *succès d'estime,* but fame came with the premiere of *Godot* in January 1953.

Beckett's renown spread rapidly, as his novels became available in various languages and his plays were performed in many countries. *Waiting for Godot* triumphed in London in 1955 and opened in the United States in 1956 in Miami *(sic)*, where it was advertised as the "laugh sensation of two continents," and managed to survive that catastrophe to be acclaimed in New York later that same year, on Broadway (again, *sic*).

Despite his success with *Godot*, director Roger Blin could not find a theater in Paris that would put on Beckett's next play, *Fin de partie (Endgame)*. Accordingly, the first performance, in French, took place in London in 1957, followed shortly by a Paris production and a German adaptation in Berlin. By 1958, English language versions were staged both in London (on a double bill with a brand-new *Krapp's Last Tape*, written in English) and in New York.

There followed much more activity of a dramatic nature, including

ON SAMUEL BECKETT: 1906–1989

productions of radio plays by the BBC and by the French ORTF. By the early 1960s, *Godot* was already being given important revivals, while the novels of the trilogy had been widely translated. Beckett's fame had reached worldwide proportions; in 1961, he was a awarded the important International Publishers' Prize.

Unlike the characters of his novels who were great wanderers, Beckett was not a confirmed traveler. He would take vacations, usually off-season, in some not-yet-overrun Mediterranean spot (e.g., Tangiers, Malta); beyond that, his trips in later years were limited mostly to London and Germany, to direct one of his plays or to participate in a production. The rest of his time was divided between his Paris flat and his cottage near the Marne river, an hour away ("my hole in the Marne mud," he called it).

Given this relatively sedentary nature, it is surprising, at least in retrospect, that Beckett came to the United States in 1964, to participate in the shooting in New York of his only film script. It was an unhappy experience for the author. New York, that particularly hot summer, was not to his liking. Although he was surrounded by friends—his publisher Barney Rosset, his editor Richard Seaver, and his director Alan Schneider—he felt very much out of his element. The film's star, Buster Keaton, for whom Beckett had great admiration from the early days, was withdrawn, uncomprehending, and generally suspicious. As for Beckett, he never again wandered so far from Paris.

The movie itself, entitled simply *Film,* turned out to be a significant artistic success. It was hardly conceived to be a commercial success. Concerned with the abstract "search for non-being in flight from extraneous perception" (Beckett's phrase), the twenty-two-minute *Film* ties in with Beckett's other works. As he has done with every literary or theatrical form that he has used, he went straight to the essence of cinema, and set up an artistic convention that introduced the camera as active participant in, rather than merely recorder of, the action. *Film* has won numerous prizes, including one at the Venice Film Festival.

Beckett's first television venture followed right after his cinema experience. *Eh Joe,* written in English in 1965 for the Irish actor Jack MacGowran, was produced on BBC, for German and American television, and on French television with Jean-Louis Barrault and Madeleine Renaud. *Film* and *Eh Joe,* as well as stage works such as *Play* and *Come and Go* from the same period, signaled Beckett's move to an ever greater abstraction in which he concentrated on the essence of the essence. Similarly, the prose texts of the 1960s, such as *Ping, Le Dépeupleur (The Lost Ones)*, and *Lessness,* are highly elliptical and rarefied fragments of murmurs that replace the (relatively) long, compelling monologue of earlier years.

In his last two decades, from the 1970s on, Beckett's plays became again more accessible although he continued to utilize ever more refined dramatic techniques. From the frantic speech of a lone woman's mouth isolated on a blackened stage in *Not I* (1972) to the short, powerfully moving *Rockaby* (1980) Beckett's later stage works, as well as his numerous television pieces, succeeded even more brilliantly than in the past in giving strong, concrete, comprehensible images of the human condition, of loneliness, of perseverance. Less well known than *Godot* and *Endgame,* the last plays are unquestionably among his masterpieces, among the highlights of twentieth-century theater. Most of the late prose texts, however, remain quite hermetic, with the exception of *Compagnie (Company),* a deeply anguished yet fairly accessible retrospective summary. Always the ironist, Beckett entitled his last prose work *Stirrings Still,* and his final poem, a reflection of his lifelong quest for language capable of expressing the reality of life, "*Comment dire?*" ("What is the word?").

In need of medical and nursing care, Beckett lived out his last eighteen months in a modest old age home. Suzanne Dumesnil Beckett, several years his senior, died in the summer of 1989; Samuel Beckett died six months later, on December 22, in his eighty-fourth year. He is buried next to her, beneath a simple black stone, in the Montparnasse cemetery, close to that area of Paris, from La Coupole to the Boulevard Raspail, from Denfert Rochereau to the PLM Hotel on the Boulevard Saint-Jacques, to the Closerie des Lilas, which marked him during half a century, and on which he left an indelible imprint.

Samuel Beckett was on vacation in Tangiers when it was announced that he had been awarded the 1969 Nobel Prize for literature. It was a good refuge, for in Paris he would have been overwhelmed by reporters. Genuinely modest and withdrawn, he did not go to Stockholm to accept the award personally (Jerome Lindon went in his place); but he did not turn it down either, as Sartre had done. To turn it down would have represented a degree of hostility of which Beckett was incapable; as to Sartre's fears that adding "Nobel Prize Laureate" after his name might restrict his liberty, Beckett had no reason to worry about that.

ON SAMUEL BECKETT: 1906–1989

He never used the formula nor did he refer to his Nobel Prize in any way at all. Beckett mythology tends to confuse him with the narrators of the trilogy or with some characters in his dramas, and view him as an introverted recluse. But Beckett was not Molloy, nor any of the other characters. He was, however, a very private person who had the notion—perhaps anachronistic in the second half of the twentieth century—that one's life is one's own, that it does not belong in the public domain, even if one is famous.

It has been estimated that more has been written on Beckett than on any other author during his own lifetime. Books by the hundreds, articles by the thousands have analyzed, deciphered, dissected, suggested. The finest critics of our age have, quite naturally, tried to elucidate his universe. Some are struck particularly by his novels, others by his plays, some by his humor, by his tragic vision, his monologuing narrators, his preoccupation with self-perception, with the quest for language, with the absence of God, the hidden presence of God, and so forth, *ad infinitum*. Beckett himself, in characteristic fashion, said nothing; he was not one of those writers who constantly explain in supplementary texts what they mean in their creative works. Rather, in an oft-quoted 1958 letter to Alan Schneider concerning the meaning of *Endgame* (which Schneider was about to direct in New York), Beckett made it crystal clear that he considered it his job to write works, not to interpret them. Referring to his exegetes, he wrote:

> We have no elucidations to offer of mysteries that are all of their making. My work is a matter of fundamental sounds (no joke intended) made as fully as possible, and I accept responsibility for nothing else. If people want to have headaches among the overtones, let them. And provide their own aspirin. Hamm as stated, and Clov as stated [the principal characters of the play], together as stated, nec tecum nec sine te [not with you nor without you], in such a place, and in such a world, that's all I can manage, more than I could.

This statement, astonishing at once in its simplicity and its complexity, is characteristic of the relationship Beckett entertained with his own work, and with the world in general. Asked once whether "Godot" was God, he replied that if he had intended "God" he would have said so. The answer was neither coy nor evasive; simply, it was what Beckett felt, literally. Only his work could explain his work—it had to speak for itself, be grasped for what it is, despite any complications, any ambiguity, any contradiction. *Tant pis* if there are headaches. He did what he was able to do—write novels, plays, poems—not to explain what they mean or what he intended to say. Beckett is very much an emanation of the twentieth century; at the same time, he stands beyond and above it. His journey has been at once contemporary and timeless; his writing, deeply rooted in the modern idiom, reflects bitingly and comically man's situation at the end of his second millennium and anticipates a world to come.

Thirty-five years ago, Beckett wrote to Barney Rosset: "To write is impossible . . . but not yet impossible enough." It remained possible for him to the very end. Only now can he be silent.

From *The French-American Review* 61, 2 (Winter 1990): 30–39.

CHAPTER SIXTEEN

"Heavenly Father, the Creature Was Bilingual": How Beckett Switched

The quotation in the title comes from Samuel Beckett's 1934 collection of short stories (or novellas) *More Pricks Than Kicks,* and while it is said by the "hero" Belacqua about a nurse and written long before Beckett switched to writing in French, it is prophetic of Beckett's own subsequent development. Beckett had, of course, long studied French language and literature at Trinity College, Dublin, and at the Ecole Normale Supérieure in Paris; he had briefly assumed a post teaching French at Trinity but he had not yet settled to live in France.

By the time Beckett switched to French in the early 1940s with *Premier amour (First Love)* and more importantly, *Mercier et Camier,* he had already written a great deal in English over a fifteen-year period, including essays (on Joyce, Proust), poetry, criticism, translations (some from the Italian, mainly of poetry from the French— Breton, Crevel, Eluard, Apollinaire's *Zone,* Rimbaud's *Bateau ivre),* short stories *(More Pricks Than Kicks)* and the novel *Murphy.* He had also begun to write some poetry directly in French.

The last work of Beckett's English-only period, already written while living in France, was *Watt,* a work about which he was to say later that language (the English language) was "running away" with

177

him. For the following decade approximately, Beckett wrote only in French. After that, that is, beginning with the early 1950s, he would write in both languages, now in one now in the other, and he began the task of translating each of the works into the other language.

The most interesting aspects of Samuel Beckett's plurilingual existence relate directly to his manner of working, to his choice of language for any one work, to the complex and fascinating resonances of this quadruple creation—there are indeed four different levels of linguistic existence in Beckett's work (not counting the changes occasioned by time, by his own development as an artist): (1) works originally written in English; (2) the self-translations of these works into French; (3) works originally written in French; (4) the self-translations of these works into English. One might even add one more dimension—as a fluent speaker of German, Beckett worked closely— very closely—with his German translator, Elmar Tophoven, and frequently corrected the latter's translations. But even without the German, the multilingual nature of Beckett's work is *sui generis*.

On several occasions, Beckett commented on his initial transition from English to French, explaining (though he was not in the habit of explaining much) that the nonnative language obliged him to be more conscious of the functioning of language, of the semiotic field of words (this is not his terminology!). The change to French as of the early 1940s offered him the opportunity to distance himself from his own language and influences, to purify, to renew himself.

There are undoubtedly many reasons for the change rather than a single one. He stated that French "had the right weakening effect" and that "in French, it is easier to write without style,"[1] referring to "style" with the same disdain that Verlaine's expression "tout le reste est littérature" refers to literature. He also said, *inter alia,* that "I just felt like it" and that "For me, it was no longer the same as writing in English. It was more exciting for me," and "more amusing." He even wrote—in deliberately stilted French—of his supposed "pour faire remarquer moi."[2]

Surely there was also a matter of distancing himself from the artifices of the Joycean style to which he had been so attracted and which, by the time of *Watt,* had begun to get in his way. He sought a more denuded, a more direct manner to express himself, better suited for the subjects (if one may use the term) he was attracted to at that time. In *Endgame,* Clov shouts at Hamm: "I use the words you taught me.

If they don't mean anything any more, teach me others. Or [he adds ominously] let me be silent."[3] Erika Ostrovsky, in her essay, "The Silence of Babel" (in the *Beckett* Cahier de l'Herne) wrote of Beckett's "switch": "What he did is comparable to a painter who, having too long cultivated drawing with the right hand, and, having acquired an automatic mastery, a facility that smelled of tradition and success, grabs the crayon with the left hand, uncorrupted by habit, virtuosity or conformism."[4]

Another reason might well be the singular lack of success his writings in English had earned for him in Great Britain. His *Proust, More Pricks Than Kicks,* and other works had brought him no more than a modest reputation within a very small circle. (He was to comment on this sarcastically in *Krapp's Last Tape.*) And even *Murphy* did not change that situation substantially.

Martin Esslin suggested that Beckett chose French as a form of asceticism and self-discipline; yet by the time he did so, Beckett was already fully bilingual, was perfectly at ease in his second language and knew and appreciated French culture. Ann Beer has pointed out that

> unlike almost all other major bilingual writers of the 20th century, Beckett's bilingualism was entirely voluntary. He was not persecuted, for political, economic or religious reasons, as many exiled artists have been. Nor was he born into a minority language like many African and Asian writers—like some European ones too—and thus led towards the use of a dominant colonial tongue.[5]

Several things are immediately noticeable when one compares the first French texts to the earlier English ones: the use of "argot" and popular language in the first French texts, *Premier amour, (First Love)* the short stories, *L'Expulsé, Le Calmant, La Fin (The Expelled, The Calmative, The End)* and of course *Molloy.*

At first there are a number of anglicisms, but these diminish rapidly. The rhythm he imposes on these early French texts may be described as "in the English manner" but they are really more "Beckettian" in manner than "English." The texture of the writing has changed from that of *Murphy.* There is much more restraint, more reserve with respect to the expression of emotion and sentiments which tend to be undercut by irony and vulgairity. There is a clear diminution of the by-now familiar word games and puns, à la Joyce, in his English writings—techniques which may in any case be less feasible in French. Irony and acerbity have taken over.

The production of that first French period of less than ten years is astounding. During it, Beckett produced many of his greatest works, including *En Attendant Godot (Waiting for Godot), Molloy, Malone meurt (Malone dies), L'Innommable (The Unnamable), Fin de partie (Endgame),* and the thirteen *Textes pour rien (Texts for Nothing).* And that is not a complete list. It does not for instance include the recently much-discussed *Eleuthéria,* his first play, which despite all the hype intended to turn into a great publishing venture, is not a major work. But are these works different from, say, *Murphy* and *More Pricks Than Kicks* because they are written in French, or were they conceived in French in order to meet a different problematics of esthetics and of expression? Or was Beckett, in the mid- and late 1940s simply a different artist from the one he had been a decade earlier?

In French, Beckett turned away from depicting the outside world; self-exiled from his own language, he removed himself from his familiar, Irish, points of reference and plunged deliberately into an inner world, into that inner abyss which would become his homeland. The main character, or narrator, deprived of a realistic, physical, social milieu, will become progressively mutilated. Language, too, becomes progressively dismembered, tortured, victimized, alienated. It now begins, in French, to express the impossibility of expressing . . . until its anhiliation . . . ALMOST.

Characters of the earlier prose in English died (Murphy, Belacqua); the French characters do not die, they hang on, despite everything, despite the utter forlornness of their physical possibilities (which had best be viewed metaphorically and not realistically—though one could argue that Beckett was a realist, that everything he pictured can be found in life as we see it around us). They seem obliged to survive, in a sort of fictional pseudo-existence which extends them or perhaps replaces them.

In 1953, having boxed himself into a corner and unable to continue writing, Beckett began to translate the works of this great French period into English as a diversion. This self-translation, this veritable recreation, occupied most of Beckett's energies during the remainder of the 1950s. He did write several dramatic works in English, returning to French in 1960 with *Comment c'est (How It Is)*. At first, Beckett had not projected to translate himself at all, if for no other reason than not to be obliged to reread his finished work. The two early short stories written in French, *The Expelled* and *The End* were translated by Richard Seaver with Beckett's collaboration. *Molloy* was initially translated into English by Patrick Bowles, but Beckett didn't like the translation, redid it himself and finally published it as "Translated from the French by Patrick Bowles in collaboration with the author." Perhaps this experience drove him to go on to translate himself afterwards. Ludovic Janvier, who translated *Watt* into French (many years later—because, again, Beckett didn't want to do it himself—he felt too far removed from it), said "One doesn't translate Beckett, one goads him into translating himself."[6]

When Beckett turned back to English after that intensive, brilliant French period, it may have been for reasons very similar to those that had made him turn to French in the first place, namely, the need to distance himself from "his" language. By the time he began to write *All That Fall* in 1956, French had become fully his language and he resorted to English with the same thirst for freshness that made him use French for the first time for *Premier amour* and *Mercier et Camier*.

English had now become the more removed language for him, artistically speaking, and was therefore more apt to serve his task at hand: to find a way out of the impasse ("Nommer, non, rien n'est nommable; dire, non, rien n'est dicible"; "Name, no, nothing is namable, tell, no, nothing can be told")—an impasse in which first *The Unnamable* and then then *Texts for Nothing* had left him.

Ironically, it was not the short dramatic works in English of the late 1950s that definitively broke the impasse, but rather *How It Is,* written in French in 1960. The floodgates of creativity were once again open (Beckett would have laughed derisively at that image!) and remained so until the end of his life, even though, to be sure, some years proved more difficult than others.

Beckett's linguistic choices do not necessarily involve cultural choices; thus, for instance, Ireland remains a key thematic background element without ever being separable into language of composition. One other element that complicates any neat attempt to categorize Beckett's multilingual work habits is the close, nearly inseparable identification of some works with a single language. *Not I,* for instance, was conceived by Beckett as totally linked to the tonic accent of English. For him, the torrential flow of the Mouth's words is organized above all through rythmic stresses of the language itself; consequently, he labored—and suffered—more with the French version (*Pas moi*) than with most of his other self-translations. And the French version is, on the whole, less satisfying than the original. The same is true for one of his greatest plays, *Rockaby,* structured linguistically around the word "down"—to go down, pull down, sit down, move down, and so on. Since there is no single French equivalent for "down," *Berceuse* loses some of the poetic, incantatory beauty of *Rockaby.* And the powerful summation, "fuck life," becomes the strangely feeble "aux gogues la vie." [7] But these are the exceptions to his extraordinary accomplishments in self-translation.

The process of recreating each work, multilingual in nature, is one of the most remarkable and probably unusual features of Beckett's career. What other writer not only shifts back and forth from one language to another, but also systematically translates nearly everything into the language that was not selected for the original composition! It is no exaggeration to claim that Beckett wrote everything twice; he did not merely translate each piece, he wrote it anew. The effort and anguish involved cannot be overestimated. At one point, Beckett expressed some regrets about the time spent on self-translation over the course of a lifetime, precisely because it required both the time of translation and the creative effort of new writing. But the act of self-translation has given us the full texture of Beckett's oeuvre; each translation is not a superfluous addition but an expansion of the work itself.

In the 1950s, when, the masterpieces of his first French period had left him temporarily in a spiritual cul de sac, the work of translating these numerous works into English proved to be a way out of the dilemma. By coming to terms once again with his own writings in the difficult dynamics of self-translation, he was able to find his voice again. Negation, so clearly spelled out in the title, *Texts for Nothing,* yielded to affirmation once more, *Comment c'est/How It Is.*

The reader never ceases to be amazed at his myriad inventions that provide splendid equivalents in the "other" language—whether they relate to the most profound statements, to puns, or to some of his more spectacular exercises in bilingual onomastics. For Beckett, work-

"HEAVENLY FATHER, THE CREATURE WAS BILINGUAL"

ing multilingually means a number of languages criss-crossing various countries, cities, civilizations, all of which are subsumed by and inseparable from the work that stems from him and from all of them.

Writing of the writer as self-translator, Raymond Federman, stated, "It means a total displacement of language from one culture to another. And yet, at the same time, especially in the case of Beckett, it means never stepping outside of language. In other words, Beckett, in his bilingual work, allows us to listen to the dialogue which he entertains with himself in two languages."[8]

From the 1960s on, once the move to French and the possibility of return to English were established for him, Beckett continued to write now in French, now in English. It was no longer a question of something that he needed to prove to himself. Sometimes the choice of the initial language was dictated by events: a radio work commissioned by BBC *(Embers, Words and Music)* or by French radio, *(Cascando)*, a play requested by a Beckett conference *(Ohio Impromptu)*. In general, but with no real system, beginning with circa 1960, he wrote most of his dramatic works in English (i.e., *Happy Days, Play, Eh Joe, Not I, Footfalls, That Time, Rockaby)* but with important exceptions in French (*Cascando*, the four *Roughs* for radio and theater, *Catastrophe, Quoi où* [*What Where*]). He wrote more of his prose works in French—*Imagination morte imaginez (Imagination Dead Imagine), Ping (Bing), Sans (Lessness), Le Dépeupleur (The Lost Ones), Pour en finir encore (To End Yet Again), Foirades (Fizzles), Mal vu mal dit (Ill Seen Ill Said)*, again with important exceptions: *Company, Worstward Ho,* and *Stirrings Still*—all written in English.

It is difficult to draw any significant conclusions from these choices, except perhaps to note the existence—and the strength—of female characters in the English plays *(Happy Days, Come and Go, Not I, Footfalls, Rockaby)* whereas there are no major female characters in his French plays. As for the prose works, the texture of *Company, Worstward Ho,* and *Stirrings Still* is not significantly different from the late French prose text, *Mal vu mal dit (Ill Seen Ill Said)*. The development of Beckett's work from the 1960s on, towards greater abstraction and concision, towards a greater emphasis on memory and loss, is not limited to one or the other language.

Beckett's last work was written in French. It was a poem, called "Comment dire." He did have time to translate it into English, "What

"HEAVENLY FATHER, THE CREATURE WAS BILINGUAL"

Is the Word?" Since he knew he would not have long to go, is it significant that he wrote it in French? Perhaps. What seems clear is that on approaching the time to be silent at last, Beckett wrote of his most constant concern throughout a lifetime of creation: the impossibility of adequately putting the experience of existence into words.

Lecture delivered at Harvard University, April 1995, based in part on "Samuel Beckett: Working Multi-Lingually," *Centerpoint* 4,2 (Fall 1980): 140–42.

CHAPTER SEVENTEEN

The Concept of Truth in Beckett's Discourse

"For I always say too much or too little, which is a terrible thing for a man with a passion for truth like mine,"[1] says Molloy ironically, and all of Beckett's work, since the beginning, can be seen in terms of a perpetual dialectic of truth/lie, or rather of quest for truth versus the trap of falsehood. In that unhappy but marvelous instant that is our life, the instant of birth "astride of a grave" where the day "gleams an instant" before night once more takes over, to use Pozzo's expression,[2] one thing preoccupies the Beckettian character, and that is the attempt to say himself, the necessity to say himself, the impossibility of saying himself—to say himself, to tell the truth about his own experience, to say how it is in relation to the only thing that can be known, the only thing that is worth saying, his truth, my truth, THE truth. Throughout all the imaginings, all the made-up, interposed, recounted stories, a single element persists; a single element seeks to be clarified; a single element resists the necessity of saying; and it is the only one which matters, it is *I*.

"Where now? Who now? When now?"[3] These three preemptive questions at the beginning of that extraordinary narrative, *The Unnamable*, propel us into the very depth of ourselves. Beckett's novels,

THE CONCEPT OF TRUTH IN BECKETT'S DISCOURSE

short stories, and dramatic works have no other goal than to respond to WHERE, WHEN, WHO? But to answer HERE, NOW, MYSELF is not easy; in fact, it is impossible. The unfolding of the Beckettian discourse is a long interrogation which can neither find a resolution nor stop.

This is a discourse in search of truth, but which remains forever at the level of search: "Name, no nothing is namable, tell, no nothing can be told"[4] . . . such is the double polarity of this Beckettian quest: the need to say, the impossibility of saying. Result: zero . . . with the sole exception of the impossibility of saying. (But is this not a significant exception?) Thus, the quotation from *Texts for Nothing*, "Name, no nothing is namable, tell, no nothing can be told," continues as follows: "What then, I don't know, I shouldn't have begun."

In *The Unnamable*, undoubtedly the cornerstone of the Beckettian edifice, the entire text is situated between the WHERE, WHEN, WHO of the beginning, and the end, which brings to a climax the tension, the anguish, the defeat, the triumph of the impossibility of saying oneself, of saying how it is, of speaking the truth. The final words of *The Unnamable* express all the tension of this necessity/impossibility paradox regarding truth—a paradox ever present in Beckett, and which attests both perpetual failure and a fidelity to the superhuman task—that is to say the essentially human task—which permits us to speak of a heroic attitude in Beckett:

> you must go on, I can't go on, you must go on, I'll go on, you must say words, as long as there are any, until they find me, until they say me, strange pain, strange sin, you must go on, perhaps it's done already, perhaps they have said me already, perhaps they have carried me to the threshold of my story, before the door that opens on my story, that would surprise me, if it opens, it will be I, it will be the silence, where I am, I don't know, I'll never know, in the silence you don't know, you must go on, I can't go on, I'll go on. (179)

If to speak is to speak one's truth, it is at the same time to breathe, to live. The proof of existence is no longer a heartbeat, it is *the word*—the word spoken, thought, written, whatever. I speak (or think or write), therefore I am. What I speak is always myself, that self that I do not manage to say but about which I don't manage to remain silent either. As Beckett writes in one of the *Texts For Nothing*, "I let them have their say, my words not said by me, me that word, that word they say, but say in vain." [5]

If only words could grasp my truth, could say me, I could be silent, disappear . . . "that would be silence" . . . the burning, unquenched desire to have done with it. When I succeed in speaking *my* truth, in telling *my* story, in saying "*I*," I will have earned the right to cease existing. That is what the voice of *Cascando* says: "story . . . if you could finish it . . . you could rest." But there's the rub: the terms are always couched in the conditional. "All false" affirms this same voice in *Cascando* speaking of stories: "don't let go . . . finish it . . . it's the right one . . . I have it . . . this time . . . we're there . . . nearly." [6]

But with this "nearly" all we can do is to begin over. You must go on; I'll go on. To go on: there is the affirmation which finally expresses all the grandeur (if one dares to use that word) and all the misery of the human condition—an affirmation which set us off on the dual path (the paradox continues) of the quest for truth and of the made-up stories that lead us away from that truth, that hide it from us. They are not necessarily lies; they are simply obstacles between me and my truth. These inventions interpose various alter egos which take my place, which I create in order to be me, to hide myself from me. So it is in the trilogy. To wit, the locutor (le *parlant*) in *The Unnamable*:

> All these Murphys, Molloys and Malones do not fool me. They have made me waste my time, suffer for nothing, speak of them when, in order to stop speaking, I should have spoken of me and of me alone. But I just said [adds the ironic, self-critical narrator] I have spoken of me, am speaking of me. I don't care a curse what I just said. It is now I shall speak of me, for the first time. I thought I was right in enlisting these sufferers of my pains. I was wrong. They never suffered my pains, their pains are nothing, compared to mine, a mere tittle of mine, the tittle I thought I could put from me, in order to witness it. (21)

All of these Beckett characters—the Murphys, Molloys, Malones, as well as the Morans, Macmanns, Mahoods, Watts, Knotts, Merciers, Camiers, Worms, and others—are fictions in search of the truth of the scribe/speaker, who succeeds only in making that truth recede. "I shall not say I again," announces the locutor in *The Unnamable*, "ever again, it's too farcical. I shall put in its place, whenever I hear it, the third person, if I think of it" (94).

If the trilogy comes to an end with the exhaustion of the narrator who will nevertheless continue to seek his truth, it had begun with the biting irony of *Molloy*. The two parts of this novel, so different from each other, come together through a single search for truth—Molloy's search. In the first part, Molloy speaks to us, speaks his reality, or rather, tries to speak his reality. He talks of things that have happened; he embroiders his stories; he invents; he contradicts himself; he lies outright. Observations made are immediately contested, immediately undercut: "I could say it but I won't say it, yes, I could say it easily, because it wouldn't be true" (19).

The story eventually explodes, as language itself explodes. "Not to want to say," affirms Molloy, "not to know what you want to say, not to be able to say what you think you want to say, and never to stop saying, or hardly ever, that is the thing to keep in mind, even in the heat of composition" (28). The sentence is ironically insinuating through the biting wit of its wrap-up ("in the heat of composition") but above all thanks to that little "hardly ever," barely noticed . . . a little added phrase which totally deflates the supremely confident affirmation, "and never to stop saying." This process is constantly repeated in the first part. For example: "I was surprised to find myself so soon at freedom once again, if that is what it was" (24); "It was a chainless bicycle, with a free-wheel, if such a bicycle exists" (16); and "A and C [reference to two people Molloy confuses with one another] I never saw again. But perhaps I shall see them again. But shall I be able to recognize them? And am I sure I never saw them again? And what do I mean by seeing and seeing again?" (15).

And, concerning a dog: "Yes, it was an orange pomeranian, the less I think of it the more certain I am. And yet" (12). And then, above all, there is the falsely prophetic tone, as in:

> Yes, night was gathering, but the man was innocent, greatly innocent, he had nothing to fear, though he went in fear, he had nothing to fear, there was nothing they could do to him, or very little. But he can't have known it. I wouldn't know myself, if I thought about it. (10)

Truth, in all this, becomes more and more elusive. There is no way to say something and actually to make it stick, to make it apply. From affirmation, to contention, to annihilation. In *The Unnamable*, the locutor offers a marvelous scatological image of this phenomenon.

THE CONCEPT OF TRUTH IN BECKETT'S DISCOURSE

Accompanied by sound effects! Speaking of the identity of his characters—his invented alter egos—the narrator speculates, all the while interrupting himself, correcting himself: "It is true poor Worm is not to blame for this. That's soon said. But let me complete my views, before I shit on them. For if I am Mahood, I am Worm too, plop. Or If I am not yet Worm, I shall be when I cease to be Mahood, plop" (70). Every observation is immediately invalidated. And it is the same for Molloy, who characterizes himself nevertheless as a man "with a passion for truth."

The principal problem, however, concerns language rather than what can be said by language, by inadequate language, by language which is not up to the task: "My life, my life, now I speak of it as of something over, now as of a joke which still goes on, and it is neither, for at the same time it is over and it goes on and is there any tense for that?" (36). Beyond the image of life situated somewhere between death and a poor joke which goes on and on (undoubtedly God's joke, if he exists, and even if he doesn't exist)—a powerful biting image— we find ourselves face to face with the inability of language to describe, that eternal dilemma of the need to say and of the impossibility of saying: "Name, no nothing is namable, tell no nothing can be told." The French poet Alain Bosquet grasped this dilemma so well in two lines of his *Premier Testament:* "I said 'apple' to the apple/it replied: 'lie' " ("J'ai dit 'pomme' à la pomme;/elle m'a répondu 'mensonge' ").[7] Never will the word "apple" speak the apple's truth; language cannot coincide with what it seeks to name. The distance between the object designated and its verbal sign is unbridgeable; signifier and signified cannot be identical. The quest goes on and on.

Old Molloy elaborates on the same thematics, but with derision: "I speak in the present tense, it is so easy to speak in the present tense, when speaking of the past. It is the mythological present, don't mind it" (26). And when once he catches himself using the expression "to tell the truth," he interrupts himself and, astonished, incredulous, repeats "to tell the truth" as though it were the grossest lie to pretend to tell the truth.

As for the second part of the novel—the report prepared by Moran ("Moran Jacques," he states, as though to reassure us, as though to reassure himself) marks a veritable disintegration: the search for truth, in the beginning so sure of itself with its uncontestable affirmations ("It is midnight; the rain beats against the windows") gives way little by little, becomes impotent and ludicrous, through the questioning, first, of all apparent certitudes, then of fiction itself and of the language through which that fiction is transmitted. The end of *Molloy* is chaotic, nihilistic in the extreme, a huge void into which plunges the pseudo-couple Molloy/Moran as well as the novel itself. The very confident affirmation has become grotesque uncertainty:

> But in the end I understood this language. I understood it, I understood it, all wrong perhaps. That is not what matters. It told me to write the report. Does this mean I am freer now than I was? I do not know. I shall learn. Then I went back into the house and wrote, it is midnight. The rain is beating on the windows. It was not midnight. It was not raining. (176)

Moran's report was nothing but a lie; the truth had remained elsewhere. It vanishes, not only in the negation midnight/not midnight, rain/not rain, but also in the slipping from present to past: "It *is* midnight. The rain *is* beating on the windows. It *was* not midnight. It *was* not raining." Here is the present tense that Molloy terms "mythological," a present tense he suggested we not mind. For in fact this present tense of narration does disappear as it recedes into the past which is supposed to be "really true" and not mythological.

After the trilogy, a period of silence; an examination of possibilities for finding a way out of the impasse. The "I can't go on" triumphs over the "You must go on, I'll go on." When Beckett turns once again to the novel, it will be a novel that is like no other, but which nevertheless remains close to the preceding thematics. The novel is *How It Is* and the title alone already indicates the preoccupation with truth, with the nonmendacious account of lived experience: "How it was I quote before Pim with Pim after Pim how it is three parts I say it as I hear it." [8]

From this beginning of the novel, there is a sliding from one tense to another; the ambiguity of the fiction is underlined and becomes increasingly evident. A sliding (in fact a full-fledged skidding!) occurs in the very nature of the voice as well: "I don't say anymore, I quote on" (16). The voice that tells, questions, answers, lies is no longer that of the narrator/narrating but the exterior incorporeal voice of the narrator/narrated. LOGOS.

The end of *How It Is* presents an interrogation more terrible than anything that had preceded in Beckett's work. A search for truth which is absolute and still unable to say "how it is," but only to show what is false—and it is a lot. Almost everything has been imaginary, without substance. Adventures, companions, joys, sorrows—lies, all lies. The final dialogue counterposes the panting locutor and that authoritative unchallengeable voice which answers "yes," "no," or with silence. Here, the tension is at its highest; the truth of the character himself is at stake.

In the final interrogation of *How It Is*, the anguish is almost unbearable, for it is a whole universe that is collapsing—an implosion of truth into the void of lie/fabling/deception/self-deception:

and this business of a procession no answer this business of a procession yes never any procession no nor any journey no never any Pim no nor any Bom no never anyone no only me no answer only me yes so that was true yes it was true about me yes and what's my name no answer WHAT'S MY NAME screams good

only me in any case yes alone yes in the mud yes the dark yes that holds yes the mud and the dark hold yes nothing to regret there no with my sack no I beg your pardon no no sack either no not even a sack with me no

only me yes alone yes with my voice yes my murmur yes when the panting stops yes all that holds yes panting yes worse and worse no answer WORSE AND WORSE yes flat on my belly yes in the mud yes the dark yes nothing to emend there not the arms spread yes like a cross no answer LIKE A CROSS no answer YES OR NO yes

never crawled no in an amble no right leg right arm push pull ten yards fifteen yards no never stirred no never made to suffer no never suffered no answer NEVER SUFFERED no never abandoned no never was abandoned no so that's life here no answer THAT'S MY LIFE HERE screams good

alone in the mud yes the dark yes sure yes panting yes someone hears me no no one hears me no murmuring sometimes yes when the panting stops yes not at other times no in the mud yes to the mud yes my voice yes mine yes not another's no mine alone yes   sure yes when the panting stops yes on and off yes a few words yes a few scraps yes that no one hears no but less and less no answer LESS AND LESS yes

so things may change no answer end no answer I may choke no answer sink no answer sully the mud no more no answer the dark no answer

trouble the peace no more no answer the silence no answer die no
answer DIE screams I MAY DIE screams I SHALL DIE screams good
(145–47)

On this note of total failure we come full circle; exhausted, the interrogation comes to an end: "good good end at last of part three and last
that's how it is was end of quotation after Pim how it is" (147).

What remains after all this negativity? Not much—less light than
before, no hope, resignation rather than affirmation. The stories were
(once again) lies; there is one single certainty: absolute solitude. As for
the fate awaiting the locutor of *How It Is,* silence. No truth can be
discerned.

The I speaking voice relationship, already so close at the end of
How It Is, becomes still closer in *Not I,* Beckett's most important play
in the past twenty years and one of the key texts of his entire oeuvre.
A mouth speaking unrelentingly and at a dizzying speed during the
twenty or so minutes of performance—anguished, tormented, often
rendered practically unintelligible by its astounding rate of delivery—
pursues a single goal: to express the past, to say how it *had been.* In
its total isolation, the woman's voice coming from this mouth projects
a frenetic discourse which applies equally well to the speaking being
in its desperate search for an "I" and to the very idea of language in
its failed but continued attempt to communicate accurately. Spurred
on by the gestures of resignation from a silent auditor as well as by
answers that we cannot hear, the voice of *Not I,* as so many other of
Beckett's voices, seeks its truth, uses the words at its disposal without
finding it, continues to seek, modifying its story, still not finding:

> what? . . . not that? . . . nothing to do with that? . . . nothing she could
> tell? . . . all right . . . nothing she could tell . . . try something else . . .
> think of something else . . . oh long after . . . sudden flash . . . not that
> either . . . all right . . . Something else again . . . so on . . . hit on it in the
> end . . . think everything keep on long enough [9]

The need to say within the impossibility of saying—truth remains
always beyond reach. This is the Beckettian dilemma par excellence.

To continue to track the abortive search for the truth, which offers
the only possible way of having done with it, through many other
fictions and dramatic works of Beckett would only accumulate exam-

THE CONCEPT OF TRUTH IN BECKETT'S DISCOURSE

ples; the situation of the Beckettian character does not change—the paradox need to say/impossibility of saying remains the same. He can neither say himself, nor can he remain silent; he continues "for to end yet again." *Pour en finir encore.*

Already in *Waiting For Godot,* Pozzo had mirrored Beckett's irony towards that impossible task which is to find truth: "I don't remember exactly what it was, but you may be sure there wasn't a word of truth in it." [10] This is akin to Molloy's ironic lassitude, a cynical Molloy faced with the impossibility of saying. But *he* doesn't get too excited about it any more; after all, one must yield to the obvious:

> For if you set out to mention everything you would never be done, and that's what counts, to be done, to have done. Oh I know, even when you mention only a few of the things there are, you do not get done either. I know, l know. But it's a change of muck. And if all muck is the same muck that doesn't matter, it's good to have a change of muck, to move from one heap to another a little further on, from time to time, fluttering you might say, like a butterfly, as if you were ephemeral. (41)

But what is clear, whether it be in the muck or in the *merde,* is the impossibility of ending it, of saying it while it is not yet ended, of putting the muck heaps together and have them all add up to more than just muck heaps, of having them add up to the depiction of the life lived in them, to the truth of our life.

———

From *Point of Contact,* 1/2 (Summer 1982): 27–33.

CHAPTER EIGHTEEN

The Loneliest Monologues: Beckett's Theater in the 1970s

When *Endgame* was produced in 1955, critics who had considered *Waiting for Godot* the ultimate in minimal theater were startled and quickly proclaimed that Beckett could go no further, that this was as far as theater could go. Beyond lay silence. Of course, a few years later, *Happy Days* made *Endgame* seem like a realistic, fully fleshed play by comparison, and again pronouncements were heard that this, now, was the ultimate frontier of drama. Similarly, *Molloy* appeared as the *ne plus ultra* of fiction . . . but *The Unnamable* was more extreme, *How It Is* even more so, and all appear linear and relatively approachable compared to such later prose texts as *The Lost Ones, Lessness,* and *Ping.* Somehow, Beckett has always managed to push his medium further, whether it be fiction, theater, television, or radio, refining, paring away all conceivable—and even some inconceivable—excess, coming ever closer to pure essence.

The process of perpetual purification is clearly evident in Beckett's most recent dramatic works, those written and staged in the 1970s and published under a typically Beckettian title, characteristic for its concision as well as for its modesty: *Ends and Odds.*[1] It is a spare volume; the eight works that comprise the American edition total 128

194

THE LONELIEST MONOLOGUES

pages while the nine works in the later English edition come to 104 pages.

The five dramatic works that make up "Ends" were all written (in English) and performed during the 1970s. Unlike the "Odds," which are retained in the state of sketches (Beckett terms them "Roughs"), they are consequential plays; one of them, *Not I,* ranks among the most dazzling of Beckett's entire output. Each of the five has but a single character visible (although . . . *but the clouds* . . . does visualize the memory of a second person); four are monologues; and the fifth, *Footfalls,* while boasting two separate voices, might also be construed as a monologue. All five could be thought of—or at least, could be thought of also—as taking place within the confines of the mind. They may well be termed "the loneliest monologues" because never before has the speaking voice in Beckett's theater (or anyone else's, for that matter) been so isolated, so helpless. Within the remarkable thematic consistency of Beckett's entire creative output, these five works not only link thematically to earlier writings, but particularly clear parallels may be drawn to past dramatic pieces such as *Happy Days, Krapp's Last Tape, Play, All That Fall, Eh Joe,* and *Embers.* In each case, the main character (and in *Play* all three characters) is confronted by his or her past in an essentially painful and even tragic confrontation that brings out his or her abandonment.

What is new now is an even more radical technique, a greater sense of abstraction, and a forced focusing of our total attention on a minimal quantity of visible matter: a mere mouth in *Not I;* a head in *That Time;* a woman pacing nine steps, back and forth, in *Footfalls,* with only her feet half-lit in an overall dim lighting pattern; a single male figure in a spare room in *Ghost Trio,* seen in a faint light that Beckett describes as "shades of grey"; and a nondescript penumbral space in . . . *but the clouds.* . . . Nothing to distract the single character in each case from the painful confrontation with memory and with his own reality. In each play, we discern a related probing quality, a perpetual interrogation undertaken either by a light source, a voice, or both—an insistent interrogation that allows the protagonist no respite in the pursuit of the ultimate purpose, that is, the acceptance or the articulation of "how it is." Given the inquisitorial quality of the light source, it is no accident that *That Time* and *Footfalls* were staged both in London (at the Royal Court) and in the United States (at the Arena Stage in Washington and at the Manhattan Theater Club in New

York) on a triple bill with *Play,* that earlier work in which Beckett had described the compelling role of the spotlight as a "solicitation." He had even described the light in *Play* as the "unique inquisitor" and the three characters as its "victims." The same dialectic of being-seen/existing implicit in *Play* is at the basis of Beckett's only cinematographic venture, *Film,* in which the character (played by Buster Keaton) is split in two—the eye or camera lens and the object—the object fleeing from perception, the eye/lens pursuing, perceiving. Beckett states in the work's preface that *Film* illustrates and is explicated by Berkeley's fundamental formula, *esse est percipi,* to be is to be perceived.

Not I is the most stunning dramatically of Beckett's theater pieces in the 1970s. This short bravura piece of pronominal conflict, rejection, isolation, and loneliness will likely be considered as one of Beckett's absolute theatrical masterpieces, along with *Waiting for Godot, Endgame,* and perhaps one or two others. Like so many of Beckett's works, and especially *Krapp's Last Tape, The Unnamable, Play,* and *How It Is,* it is conceived within his typical double polarity of the search for self and the attempts of language to state, to tell, to describe—two poles which fuse into one since it is always through language that the self seeks itself, and it is always language which fails to coincide precisely with the reality sought, leaving the individual vanquished but unyielding in his determination to continue. In *Not I,* the self and the voice are identified in the closest possible manner through the single character, represented on stage simply by a mouth—a mouth that talks relentlessly and at a dizzying pace throughout the twenty minutes of performance, beginning before the play starts, continuing after it has ended, anguished, tormented, often practically unintelligible because of its breakneck delivery. This woman's mouth is the only thing visible on stage, with the exception of a barely distinguishable hooded figure across stage, the Auditor, who listens and makes several mute gestures.[2] In its total isolation in the blackness, the starkly spotlighted red mouth spews forth a frenzied discourse that both reflects on the "person" in her desperate search for self (however difficult it may be to imagine a person around the mouth) and the abstract concept of language saying, seeking, lying, continuing to say, seek, lie.

The substance of what the voice relates is at once linear in its directness and complexly involved, full of resonances and shadings. On its most immediate level, the monologue refers to the life story of a woman now seventy years old, prematurely born and abandoned in early childhood. She has suffered greatly and she suffers still; her existence has always spelled insignificance and emptiness, and her skull reverberates with a constant, terrible buzzing. But, although she had spent most of her life silent, she is now possessed by a steady stream of speech, by a veritable logorrhea, incapable of not speaking, incapable of not trying to tell how it was or, more precisely (as she qualifies), how it has been.

The mouth's voice talks in the third person singular: "she," "her." It is interrupted at times by an interlocutor unheard by us (undoubtedly the faint figure of the Auditor) who seeks—and gets—some rectification in the narration. However, five times the Voice is driven to an anguished denial, culminating in the frenzied cry "what! . . . who? . . . no! . . . she!"[3] The "not I" of the title is never spoken, but clearly the protagonist is being urged to acknowledge that the story she is telling actually concerns herself and not some fictional being. Frantically the Voice rejects all notions of shifting its tale to the first person singular, even though it accepts other changes proposed by the inaudible Auditor. "Vehement refusal to relinquish third person," states Beckett in an explicative note (14). At every refusal, at every "what? . . . who? . . . no! . . . she!," the hooded figure is seen raising its arms, then letting them fall back against the body.

The Voice's unwillingness to identify with the story is sharply punctuated by the irony of that story: the Voice explains that the woman (third person) of its tale heard words, a voice, "steady stream" (18), which she did not recognize as being her own until she "finally had to admit . . . to herself . . . could be none other . . . than her own." Eventually, "she began trying to delude herself . . . it was not hers at all" but at last had "to give up . . . admit hers alone . . . her voice alone" (18–19). Thus, while the Voice explores its dilemma, it does so through the interposition of an imaginary third person in a *construction en abyme,* a microcosm used to keep it from coming to terms with the obvious need to identify with its own story. The fictional character has no choice but to accept its identification with the tale it tells; perhaps the Voice will be forced to accept itself before long, as the paradigm of its own fiction might lead to believe. Near the end of the play, after the last rejection of the first person singular, the Voice adds "no matter" and continues with what might indicate an acceptance of the inevitable: "keep on . . . hit on it in the end" (23).

Ever since *Waiting for Godot,* Beckett's characters have had the habit of telling stories in order to avoid having to use the first person — that all-too-painful coming face to face with their own reality. Vladimir and Estragon, as well as Hamm in *Endgame,* readily resort to this delaying action in order to make time go by; but it is the characters in the novels who really rely on this sort of tactic fully and with extraordinary skill. The novels abound in creatures imagined by the narrators as alter egos; they succeed in holding center stage for a while before being denounced as mere myths and exploding like balloons blown up excessively. Macmann, Mahood, Moran, Worm, Pim, Bom, and so on are all fabrications of the first-person singular voice, that subjective consciousness which invents factitious incarnations the better to avoid itself. The subsequent revelation that these contrived characters are mere fictions generates anguish but does not definitively stifle the creative act which touches on the very essence of life. The paradox of this despair linked to so tenacious a strength is stated most forcibly in the celebrated concluding lines of *The Unnamable:* "you must go on, I can't go on, you must go on, I'll go on, you must say words, as long as there are any, until they find me, until they say me." [4]

Beyond the story told in *Not I* is the telling itself, the compulsion to speak, the inability not to speak, the search for self coupled with the evading of that self. To seek oneself but at all costs not to find oneself. "Can't go on" proclaims the mouth before acquiescing "so on" (21). When the Voice invents, the Auditor seems to correct it and force it to change its story, very much like the frantic dialectic of the concluding pages of *How It Is:* "What? . . . not that? . . . nothing to do with that? . . . all right . . . think of something else . . . not that either? . . . all right . . . something else again . . . so on . . . hit on it in the end" (22). The need to speak paired with the impossibility of speaking: the Beckettian predicament par excellence.

If the spectator can determine that the Voice is desperately avoiding the need to identify itself with its own story, to admit that it is its own story and that it should therefore say "I," he or she can only conjecture as to its reasons for retaining the fiction of the third person. The rejected epiphany could imply one or more of several levels of significance, for instance the refusal to accept one's own reality; the final, unresolved review of a desolate life on the verge of ending; perhaps the dynamics of the psychoanalytic process wherein the patient/Voice struggles against the persevering coaxing of the analyst/Auditor to recognize her own authenticity.

But we are far less concerned with the temptation to decipher than with the direct spell cast by the tension of the dramatic movement itself—a circular movement, as so often in Beckett's works, skirting the central focus of self-revelation (no . . . no! . . . she!), but in smaller and smaller circles which imply impending convergence with that feared central point, self-exposure. The anguish, the desperation of the Voice, its fear and suffering reach us through fragmented, agonized phrases, beyond any need to "understand."

Another link between *Not I* and the mainstream of Beckett's writings concerns the biting irony and cynicism that ties suffering to the notion of guilt. Vague but insistent references to sin and repentance filter down throughout the play: "that notion of punishment . . . for some sin or other . . . or for the lot . . . or no particular reason . . . for its own sake . . . thing she understood perfectly" (16). One is reminded of a dialogue between Vladimir and Estragon: "Suppose we repented./ Repented what?/Oh . . . We wouldn't have to go into details./Our being born?" [5] In *Not I,* guilt is felt in the same manner as in *Waiting for Godot,* intuitively, and punishment seems to be meted out in the same arbitrary way. As to God, the very mention of him provokes the Voice's only laughter: "brought up as she had been to believe . . . with the other waifs . . . in a merciful . . . *(brief laugh)* . . . God . . . *(good laugh)*" (16). We are reminded of Hamm's reference to God: "The bastard! He doesn't exist!" [6] From birth—the first words of the play are "out . . . into this world" (14)—until the present of performance, throughout seventy years of a painful existence, it has all been merely a cruel practical joke. There is, there has been nothing, no substance, no becoming aware, no happiness, no respite, nothing but the constant buzzing in her head, nothing but guilt, torment, and the attempt to describe it all: "something that would tell how it had been . . . how she had lived . . . lived on and on . . . guilty or not" (21). If God exists, He is playing us for fools.

That Time is, spiritually, a companion piece to *Not I,* cut out of the same cloth (as Beckett put it) but inverted, like a glove turned inside out. The visible element this time is a man's head: "Old white face," the stage direction reads, "long flaring white hair as if seen from above outspread" (28). Located ten feet above the stage, the head appears to be floating in nothingness, creating a hypnotic effect on the spectator, for, like the mouth in *Not I,* the head is brightly lit and stands out starkly in the otherwise total darkness. Unlike the mouth, though, the head of *That Time* does not speak; instead, its own voice speaks to it, surrounding it in three distinct pitches—three voices that talk about "that time," three separate times, weaving a fabric of memory out of the crucial moments of the past, each time less perceptibly, a movement of resignation or perhaps exasperation that decreases in insistence. The fifth and last time, the figure makes no more gesture at all.

One voice recalls a childhood experience, a building in ruins in which the protagonist had concealed himself as a child and to which he had returned as an adult, only to find everything changed. The second voice relates his seeking refuge one winter's day in a lifeless museum, surrounded by "portraits of the dead," and the ensuing, sudden coming face to face with himself. The third radiantly recalls an early love, pure, ethereal, total. This third voice, surprisingly, speaks the most lyrical, the sunniest passages Beckett has ever written, more elegiac than the punting scene in *Krapp's Last Tape*—a play with many resemblances to *That Time.* In the recent play, the evocation of former happiness is radiant, with no lurking shadows:

> on the stone together in the sun on the stone at the edge of the little wood and as far as eye could see the wheat turning yellow vowing every now and then you loved each other just a murmur not touching or anything of that nature you one end of the stone she the other long low stone like millstone no looks just there together on the stone in the sun with the little wood behind gazing at the wheat or eyes closed all still no sign of life not a soul abroad no sound (29)

In *Krapp's Last Tape,* the one tape to which Krapp comes back again and again contains the following evocation:

> Sun blazing down, bit of a breeze, water nice and lively. . . . We drifted in among the flags and stuck. The way they went down, sighing, before the stem! *(Pause.)* I lay down across her with my face in her breasts and my hand on her. We lay there without moving. But under us all moved, and moved us, gently up and down, and from side to side.[7]

The text from *Krapp's Last Tape* is as lyrical as the one from *That Time,* but tainted with bitterness, with the impossibility of love. Krapp's lyrical recollection also contains this glimpse of defeat: "I said again I thought it was hopeless and no good going on, and she agreed, without opening her eyes" (22). The idyllic interlude had been destined for failure right from the start; on the other hand, in *That Time* the happy evocation remains entirely intact . . . and proves eventually to be disappointing only in relationship to the present, that is to say, in relationship to the time of the play's action. With or without some reservation, the two texts are rare for Beckett, but prove that he can imagine and portray real tenderness directly, without the usual interference of the deforming prism of his cutting irony. Some of his poems—especially from the 1940s—share a similar mood.

Like Krapp, however, the protagonist of *That Time* is also cynical with respect to his past, beyond any sentimental memory. Krapp had managed to get rid of that ancient penchant for happiness with one cutting comment that destroyed everything: "Just been listening to that stupid bastard I took myself for thirty years ago, hard to believe I was ever as bad as that. Thank God that's all done with anyway" (24). Similarly, the third voice of *That Time* corrects itself through corrosive doubt: "hard to believe harder and harder to believe you ever told anyone you loved them or anyone you" (31). The happy remembrance becomes quasimythical, then disappears altogether, engulfed in a whole ludicrous lifetime.

But it is the second voice that speaks from the deepest recesses. Like the Voice in *Not I,* it evokes the snares of self-identification: "did you ever say I to yourself in your life come on now . . . could you ever say I to yourself in your life" (31); or again, this anguish-ridden memory that describes the flight from self to the point of forgetting the self:

when you started not knowing who you were from Adam trying how that would work for a change not knowing who you were from Adam no notion who it was saying what you were saying whose skull you were clapped up in whose moan had you the way you were was that the time or was that another time there alone with the portraits of the dead black with dirt and antiquity and the dates on the frames in case you might get the century wrong not believing it could be you will they put you out in the rain at closing time (32)

And the same voice is the last one heard in the play, casting the man's entire existence into soon-to-come oblivion: "come and gone come and gone no one come and gone in no time gone in no time" (37). The silent, suspended head, which had done nothing more throughout the play than breathe audibly at times and open and close its eyes occasionally, now smiles (a toothless smile for preference, Beckett specifies) as the light fades and the curtain closes on this man's annihilation, his absorption into nothingness. The smile undoubtedly marks his satisfaction that it's almost finished—the profound aspiration toward nothingness of Beckett's characters since Didi and Gogo, Hamm and Clov.

It is interesting to note the strict organization Beckett has imposed on his play, not merely in the systematic but nonsymetrical alternation of the three voices, but also by using a common structural element for each of the three narratives that speak of the past, namely stones:

VOICE A: . . . that time on the stone the child on the stone where none ever came (34)

VOICE B: on the stone together in the sun on the stone at the edge of the little wood . . . (29)

VOICE C: . . . you found a seat marble slab and sat down to rest and dry off . . . (29)

Each time, the point of reference is a stone on which the man had sat at some moment in his past; it is from the departure point of this nexus of related memories that the three voices reach him, bringing a real interior cohesion to the drama.

In contrast to the single, stark focus of vision in *Not I* and *That Time,* May, the middle-aged but already old-looking woman in *Footfalls* walks incessantly across the stage, nine steps and back again, pausing only rarely before resuming her compulsive path. She talks to her aging, infirm mother whose voice we hear without ever seeing her. The mother may be in the next room or merely in the daughter's mind. May has taken tender care of her to the exclusion of any life of her own; she has not even been outdoors since childhood. May washes her mother, dresses her wounds, gives her injections, prays with her and for her.

Relegated deliberately or by circumstances to the role of support for her mother, May has had no life of her own. She is surprised to learn that she herself is only forty years old; "So little" she asks, to which the Mother's voice answers: "I'm afraid so" (44), undoubtedly underlining thereby the fact that she still has a long time to go in what Beckett has called elsewhere "this . . . thing."[8] The Mother pleads with her daughter to free herself from the tyranny of memory: "Will you never have done? . . . Will you never have done . . . revolving it all? . . . It all . . . In your poor mind . . . It all . . . It all" (44). Then she asks her forgiveness for having brought her into the world—that most unforgivable of all sins in the Beckettian universe. Molloy had put it sarcastically: "My mother. I don't think too harshly of her. I know she did all she could not to have me, except of course the one thing, and if she never succeeded in getting me unstuck, it was fate that earmarked me for less compassionate sewers."[9] The first of the three movements of this brief dramatic work ends on a note of regret. May resumes her pacing as the light fades.

In the second movement, only the Mother's voice can be heard, evoking in rapid strokes May's youth; only the sound of her steps imparts a sense of reality to May. It is her only sign of life, her heartbeat, her breathing. Indeed, her footfall is every bit as regular, as rhythmic as the heart or respiration. The Voice declares that May speaks when she thinks no one can hear her—it is then that she tells how it was: "Still speak? Yes, some nights she does, when she fancies none can hear . . . Tells how it was . . . Tries to tell how it was . . . It all . . . It all" (46).

Now, after a second fade out of lights, begins the third and last movement of *Footfalls*. This time, it is May who speaks, who tries to say how it was, but who does so through the interposition of a third person like the Mouth in *Not I*. She relates a story, which resembles her own but concerns another woman, named Amy (an anagram of May) who herself takes care of her mother. This mother, like May's mother, asks her daughter: "Will you never have done? . . . Will you never have done . . . revolving it all? . . . It all . . . In your poor mind . . . It all . . . It all" (48). The third-person narration fails to resolve Amy's dilemma, just as the third person in *Not I* could not manage to convince the Mouth to identity with its story. The schism continues. The light fades, May disappears, all is darkness, and the play ends.

Hermetic and elusive though *Footfalls* may be in the reading, it is mysteriously powerful in performance. The elusiveness and oppressiveness of memory become painfully tangible in the dreary loneliness of the woman, counterpointed by her constant, rhythmic pacing. Noting that May is no longer there at the end, Billie Whitelaw (who created the role) asked Beckett during rehearsals (Beckett directed *Footfalls* for the original London production) whether May had committed suicide. "No," Beckett replied, "she is simply not there." [10]

Like all Beckett's works written especially for television, *Ghost Trio* contains very precise technical directions. Every shot is carefully prescribed as to duration, distance, angle, and so forth. In other words, Beckett's script includes everything needed for the television production, each element being carefully conceived and described. This is not the work of a television amateur; Beckett has had considerable television experience by now. But then, even his first work for the home screen, *Eh Joe,* was already perfectly calculated and orchestrated from a technical point of view.

The title, *Ghost Trio,* stems from Beethoven's Fifth Piano Trio, entitled "The Ghost," whose Largo serves as musical reinforcement for the play—reinforcement and not background, for the music becomes an integral part of the theatrical entity. The play is divided into three parts, labeled Pre-action, Action, and Reaction. The "trio" consists of the Voice of a woman (whom we do not see), a man who can be seen (but who does not speak), and a child that appears near the end only to disappear again after fifteen or twenty seconds without having spoken a word. The single voice of *Ghost Trio* does not evoke memories, as is the case in so many other dramatic pieces by Beckett; rather, it accompanies and comments on the movements of the camera in an objective, uncommitted manner. For instance, it says things like "the familiar chamber" while the camera shows the room in which the action (if one may use the term) takes place—an austere room with only a door, a window, and a bed. "On the right the indispensable door," says the Voice as it plays the role of guide and commentator on a quick camera pan around the room. "Floor" utters the Voice as we *see* a close-up of a rectangle of the floor, followed by: "Having seen that specimen of floor you have seen it all" (55). And so on, for the wall, the window, the door, the bed. Finally we hear: "Sole sign of life a seated figure" (57) and we see the man, seated. End of Part I, Pre-action.

When at the beginning of Part II (Action) the Voice announces enigmatically and for no apparent reason, "He will now think he hears her" (58), the man seems to hear something at the door, at the window, near the bed. But after inspecting the room a second time, there is still nothing. In the third part (Reaction), the Voice is no longer heard at all. The man sets down on a chair a cassette player which he had held in his hand up to then, takes in the room once again. There is a knock at the door, a little boy dressed in a black slicker appears, shakes his head twice, turns around, and vanishes. The music increases in volume; there is a final close-up; end of play. Throughout the three parts of *Ghost Trio,* the man's behavior is unsettled and indecisive.

Of all Beckett's recent works, this one is the most elliptical, the most ambiguous. The fact that the Voice is limited to being a guide results in the spectator's remaining outside; we never enter the man's consciousness and the best we can do is to guess at the functioning of his memory . . . and with few guideposts at that. Twice the Voice puts us on the track by saying: "He will now think he hears her" (58, 60). This statement, multiplied by the man's perturbed comportment, allows us to imagine a distant but tenacious remembrance of a woman, and to associate the cassette with that remembrance. But in fact, such a possible narrative line is created by us out of the scattered bits and pieces at our disposal. As to the boy, is he another fragment of the man's memory? His son, for instance, or himself as a boy? We have no way of knowing for sure; we remain in a dim landscape and with particularly ambiguous signifiers. Our manner of confronting this text is made all the more complex by the surprising attitude of the Voice at the very beginning of *Ghost Trio.* It addresses us in a very practical, businesslike tone: "Good evening. Mine is a faint voice. Kindly tune accordingly. . . . Good evening. Mine is a faint voice. Kindly tune accordingly. . . . It will not be raised, nor lowered, whatever happens" (55).

Beckett's most recent play, . . . *but the clouds . . . ,* also written for television, is less enigmatic and more recognizably "Beckettian." Like in all the "Ends," we are in the realm of memory and involved with familiar themes: the passage of time, the recollection of an earlier happiness. This review of the past takes the form of a calm reassessment, singularly lacking in the anguish that marked *Not I* and the irony and cynicism typical of earlier bouts with memory, such as *Krapp's Last Tape* and *Eh Joe.* With *That Time, Footfalls, Ghost Trio,* and . . . *but the clouds . . . ,* Beckett seems to have achieved a sense of detachment that allows him to adopt a stance of sympathetic objectivity. The title of the work stems from Yeats's 1927 poem "The Tower," which itself looks backward at the experience of a lifetime. The poem ends on a note of quiet resignation, of things being put into ultimate perspective. In quoting the last lines, Beckett stresses the serene, poetic vision where earlier he had dwelled on the absurd and on suffering: "but the clouds of the sky . . . when the horizon fades . . . or a bird's sleepy cry . . . among the deepening shades" (262).[11] When . . . *but the clouds . . .* was performed for German television, Beckett agreed to include the last fifteen lines of the Yeats poem (in translation, of course) rather than just the last four, on the theory that Yeats was not so well known in Germany. In fact, the inclusion of the last two stanzas of "The Tower" as spoken by the Voice helps all but the most avid reader of Yeats to focus more clearly on the spirit of this final ordering of sensations and thoughts:

> *Now shall I make my soul,*
> *Compelling it to study*
> *In a learned school*
> *Till the wreck of body,*
> *Slow decay of blood,*
> *Testy delirium*
> *Or dull decrepitude,*
> *Or what worse evil come—*
> *The death of friends, or death*
> *Of every brilliant eye*
> *That made a catch in the breath—*
> *Seem but the clouds of the sky*
> *When the horizon fades,*
> *Or a bird's sleepy cry*
> *Among the deepening shades.*

The quiet gravity of this Olympian tone is all the more remarkable for Beckett when we think that these are the last sounds of "Ends," that group of plays that had begun with the most thoroughly frenzied discourse of Beckett's entire theatrical output, the Mouth in *Not I:* "out . . . into this world . . . this world . . . tiny little thing . . . before its time" (14). From the agony of birth, through the fury of life, to the stoic acceptance of death following an ultimate recapitulation—these are the markers of the life cycle as well as of the collective movement of the five dramas of "Ends."

Technically, . . . *but the clouds* . . . is fascinating in its very simplicity. Its components could not be simpler: a single set consisting of a circular spot of light surrounded by impenetrable darkness, one voice (a man's), and three different shots—a long shot of the set, either empty or with the Man entering, pausing, or exiting; a medium shot of the Man, head in arm, apparently lost in reflexion or recollection; a close-up of a Woman's face. These minimal devices are used to narrate a bare minimum of action: a male voice remembers a woman, or, to put it more precisely, remembers remembering a woman and describes *how* and *when* he used to remember her. His description is visualized; he "enters" (that is, enters the field of light), pauses, goes off to change his clothes, reappears, pauses, disappears to the rear into what is called his "sanctum," then reappears and goes through the reverse steps. Within the "sanctum" he tries to remember her, begs her to appear to him. In response to his entreaties, four results might ensue: (1) she might appear and then disappear; (2) she might appear, linger, then disappear; (3) she might appear, speak (and we see the woman mouth the phrase "but the clouds"), then disappear; (4) not appear at all—this latter being by far the most frequent. This recitation of events by the Voice and its visual evocation (which for us takes the shape of the images brought to us by the screen) is checked perpetually, tested, examined for veracity. Finally, as the Woman's face is seen, the Voice speaks the lines from "The Tower." The image shifts finally to the Man in his pensive pose before fading out.

As it had been in his other television plays, Beckett's technical domination of the medium is startling. He attains a brilliant utilization of television sound and image with an economy of means that never ceases to amaze. His directions are minutely precise with respect to each camera angle, the duration of every shot, the volume of sounds. In the German version, *Nur Noch Gewölk,* which Beckett directed himself for Südfunks Stuttgart, he added the precision of his directorial talent to achieve a stunning unity of tone.

If . . . *but the clouds* . . . deals with the thematics of memory, lost love, and youth with a matter-of-factness that avoids both the caustic and self-pity, the familiar theme of writing, of saying how it was reappears also in a less frantic manner. Beckett's characters have always struggled with the paradox of the need to speak and the impossibility of speaking. The lifelong quest of his protagonists is to find a means of describing their own experience ("you must say words, as long as there are any, until they find me, until they say me, strange pain, strange sin").[12] The attempt, however, is doomed to perpetual failure ("I let them say their say, my words not said by me, me that word, that word they say, but say in vain").[13] That frustration gave rise in the past to the most anguished utterances, beginning with that most lapidary sentence in *Texts for Nothing,* "Name, no, nothing is namable, tell, no, nothing can be told, what then, I don't know, I shouldn't have begun."[14] In *Cascando,* the Voice pantingly pursues its story, never catching up with it, never really telling it:

> story . . . if you could finish it . . . you could rest . . . you could sleep . . . not before . . . oh I know . . . the ones I've finished . . . thousands and one . . . all I ever did . . . in my life . . . with my life . . . saying to myself . . . finish this one . . . it's the right one . . . then rest . . . then sleep . . . no more stories . . . no more words . . . and finished it . . . and not the right one . . . couldn't rest . . . straight away another[15]

The narrator of *How It Is* is horror-struck at the end of his delirious monologue that he has not managed to tell his story, has not managed to say "how it is," and the Voice in *Not I* gropes desperately (as we have noted) for the words that would finally allow it to be silent: "what? . . . not that? . . . nothing to do with that? . . . nothing she could tell . . . try something else . . . think of something else . . . not that either . . . all right . . . something else again . . . so on . . . hit on it in the end" (22).

The Voice in . . . *but the clouds* . . . is also concerned with the necessity and the difficulty of telling one's story accurately but there is no torment in its self-questioning. "When I thought of her it was always night," begins the Voice, then corrects itself: "When she appeared it was always night." And, after testing that hypothesis visually, it concludes, simply, "Right" (259). Later, it again tests its own veracity and forces itself to review its own memory (which we see as television image): "Let us now make sure we have got it right" (259), and "Let us now run through it again" (261). Each of these run-throughs, as well as other unannounced ones, are concluded with the same "Right." Clearly, in this very recent piece, the past traps of the writing process are less apparent. The story *can* be told, but it is not "the" story, it is only one of the stories. Still, the fact that Beckett concentrates on what is possible in . . . *but the clouds* . . . rather than

THE LONELIEST MONOLOGUES

on the impossible, together with the serenity of the vision itself, is significant. John Calder, Beckett's publisher in England, speaks of a recent "equanimity reminiscent of Cicero and Goethe . . . a mellow acceptance of the inevitable." [16] The brief quotation from Yeats is indicative of the change in spirit and could well serve as a *mise en abyme* of the tranquillity discernible in the last four dramatic works.

If the mood of most of the "Ends" marks, then, a new departure perhaps, blending enduring thematic material with a new-found resignation, the problematics of the theatricality of these five brief works also mark a departure. From the outset, beginning with *Waiting for Godot* and *Endgame,* Beckett had obviously opted for nonrealistic theatrical conventions; since then, he has pushed his antirealism ever further. Yet, what characterizes the theatricality of most of his works before the seventies is their metaphoric representation of the human condition: Gogo and Didi's wait, their empty setting, and even their tree; the room in which Hamm and Clov endure the ending of their end; the mound of earth in which Winnie is buried up to her hips in Act I of *Happy Days,* and up to her neck in Act II; even the massive funeral urns from which only the three heads emerge in *Play.* These powerful stage images depended on and brought out the metaphoricity of the characters and of their situation. At more or less the same period, we find, corresponding to that theatrical use of metaphor, the recourse to metaphor in the prose texts, for instance in *Molloy, Malone Dies, The Unnamable,* and *How It Is.* But as of the early 1950s, in *Texts for Nothing,* Beckett had set out on the road to abstraction, to a demetaphorization which was to become increasingly dominant. *The Lost Ones* still retains a certain metaphoric framework, but *Imagination Dead Imagine, Lessness, Enough,* and "For to End Yet Again," among others, dispense almost entirely with the metaphoric.

The recent plays are similarly the result of extreme abstraction, of a fragmentation of narrative line, and of a depersonalization of character, which, in the cases of *Not I* and *That Time,* permits a reduction of the visible theatrical material to a mere mouth, a floating head, leaving no so-called realistic element which might give rise to a metaphoric interpretation. And if it remains true that we can still deal metaphorically with the situation of the mouth, for instance—or rather, with the situation of the woman whose mouth we see and whose voice we hear—this transposition to the level of metaphor is entirely attributable to the text and no longer at all to the presence on stage of some identifiable visual element. In Beckett's theater in the 1970s, everything is reduced to the relationships existing between consciousness and the voice, relationships which concern identity, memory, and problems of language, or rather, the metalinguistic functions of language. These thematic materials have always been present in Beckett, but now they are exploited in a rigorously nonfigurative fashion, and the fragmented dramatic action remains interiorized.

Some radio and television plays had already paved the way to abstraction several years ago, notably *Cascando, Words and Music,* and *Eh Joe.* Now, everything focuses on the discourse of a speaking person who speaks himself, of a listening person who is spoken by his voice or by that of another speaking person, or, in the case of *Footfalls,* by a combination of the two. The proof of Beckett's prodigious talent as a dramatist is that he succeeds in rendering theatrical in the best sense of the word—that is, *not* in the sense of a realistic or representational theater—fictional elements that are so tenuous as not even to be imaginable in a nontheatrical text, except in one of Beckett's own nontheatrical texts.

Yet, when speaking of antirealistic theater in relation to Beckett, one refers only to theatrical conventions. Beckett's theater is diametrically opposed to the conventions that form the mainstay of realistic theater, namely the fourth-wall convention so dear to Ibsen and which, *mutatis mutandis,* still dominates a sizable segment of what can be termed traditional theater. His new plays are even more antirealistic than most of today's antirealistic theater, and more antirealistic than his own theater of previous decades. But for all of that, if one leaves aside the matter of theatrical conventions and the aesthetic which determines the way a theater piece presents itself to the spectator, Beckett is in fact a realistic author to the extent that whatever is present on stage, up to and including what is most abstract, retains a direct link with our experience of life, beyond any metaphor. Beckett can be thought of as realistic in the same sense that the word applies to, say, Robbe-Grillet. The three voices emanating from three perspectives of the past that converge on the floating head and devastate it, in *That Time,* are directly recognizable for each of us without our having to try to conjure up a "real" picture of a head isolated in space. This persistence, this obsession of memory is a "real" truth, directly comprehensible, and not merely the metaphor of a reality. In . . . *but the clouds* . . ., the need to remember the woman, the difficulty in remembering her, create a tension of memory that is also true. Similarly, the torrential flow of words of the Mouth in *Not I,* in its multiple stratagems to avoid its own reality at all costs, is but a poetic and dramatic intensification of a phenomenon we recognize readily, even in ourselves if we look carefully.

Beckett's novels have a comparable relationship to reality; they, too, plunge us into a special, bizarre universe which doesn't resemble "our world." Nevertheless, how often do we find some woman seen on a street, some old man glimpsed out of a moving car, who seem to have stepped straight out of some Beckett fiction! These characters from his fiction—often grotesque, painful to contemplate, almost dehumanized—are not merely metaphors of the human condition; they *are* the human condition; they really exist in life, in our lives.

The five "Ends" vary greatly in modulation, but all possess unusual dramatic power. They lead us to the heart of the human experience, of suffering, of memory, of lives insufficiently lived. But the plays are neither strident nor overpowering. They reach us more delicately, through a quiet intensity, a controlled structure, and ever-so-much tenderness, like the most exquisite chamber music. Their imagery has been compared to the stark and moving purity of a Japanese garden, and the image is apt.

They may not be the ultimate monologues, not the ultimate reduction to the very essence of things, but these voices speak to us from the loneliest recesses, vantage points which make it hard to conceive of places still further, still deeper.

While a spirit of resignation has made its way in Beckett's work, the tragic vision has nevertheless tended to turn more somber in recent times, with less obvious humor to serve as antidote. But he continues to defend himself against the label of pessimism; his weltanschauung, he holds, is merely realism. He wrote recently: "If pessimism is a judgment to the effect that ill outweighs good, then I can't be taxed with same, having no desire or competence to judge. I simply happen to have come across more of the one than of the other." [17]

From *October* 6 (Fall 1978): 31–45

CHAPTER NINETEEN

Camus and Beckett: Variations on an Absurd Landscape

It may seem surprising and even far-fetched to evoke the name of Samuel Beckett in reference to Camus, and to suggest that a parallel reading of some of their texts might enlighten us about both. A priori, there is a multitude of elements which seem to set these two writers apart. We associate Camus with World War II and the period immediately following, while we think of Beckett's voice as speaking to us since the 1950s; although both men came to Paris to live and work, we naturally associate Camus with North Africa and—less naturally—Beckett with Ireland (naturally and less naturally because Camus continued to the end to think of North Africa as his land, his mother, and Beckett effectively turned his back on *his* native country and has precious little use for it). Instinctively, we label Camus a sort of classicist, both technically and stylistically on the one hand, and from the point of view of the "pensée de midi," that delicate balance of what one may term "constructive moderation"; the same instinctive classification brands Beckett as a stark experimentalist in novelistic and dramatic technique, as well as—and especially—in his handling of language, whose "pensée" would be a "pensée de minuit" elaborating destructive excesses.

While these Manichean oppositions just sketched out are simplistic

212

and only partially accurate at best, they might well argue against a joint consideration of the two writers.

And yet, a closer look at their works will show that there are valid and even illuminating parallels to be drawn. This is what I propose to do—very modestly, I assure you, because I seek no great proofs nor conclusions; I am not searching for influences, nor will I try to squeeze two discrete voices into a single neat package. Rather, I propose a setting side-by-side of certain aspects, certain texts, to allow us to examine Camus's and Beckett's variations on an absurd landscape, in the hope that they might mutually illuminate each other. And by the way, I shall not begin the comparison by linking them because they were each awarded the Nobel Prize!

Some of the factors that would appear to separate Camus and Beckett are actually important links. We are well aware that, against the absurd background of war-torn Europe at mid-century, of a world dripping with the blood of war and crematoria, incapable of renouncing hatred, aggression, and concentration camps, Albert Camus became a conscience for his generation—a difficult and thankless role which Camus never sought and which he scorned but suddenly found thrust upon him.

By no stretch of the imagination can Beckett be considered the conscience of *his* generation. But rather than continue to dwell on differences, I should like to begin the constructive comparison at this point. Perhaps I should refer first of all to the question of Camus's generation and Beckett's. As I mentioned, we think of them as addressing successive generations, yet they really belong to the same: Beckett was born seven years earlier than Camus (1906 and 1913, respectively) and he began to write several years before Camus. But Camus came to world attention and eventually to world fame long before Beckett, and his death in 1960 limited him definitively to an era that was then ending or, more likely, had already ended.

It is therefore perfectly natural that Camus remains for us the voice of reason speaking to the 1940s and 1950s, the era defined by World War II. We can think of Camus reacting vigorously to his environment, not merely if we refer to Algiers, Tipasa, the Mediterranean, the grayness of Europe, and so on, but even more clearly if we define his environment beyond geographic terms, in terms of the moral, psychological, and philosophic climate of his epoch, a climate of absurd realities, or what I term an absurd landscape.

Viewed in this way, Beckett reacts just as vigorously to his environment—just as vigorously, though not in the same manner, not only because Beckett's approach and concerns are different but because the environment itself is different; that is, insofar as Beckett embodies attitudes of the 1950s, 1960s and 1970s, he reacts to realities that are not those confronting Camus a decade or so earlier and which revolved around fascism, Stalinism, and other political considerations.

Beckett's writings do not reflect the great political stresses of Europe's nightmare (although it must be added parenthetically that if his works remained uncommitted, he himself did not: he played a modest but very real role in a Resistance network, despite the fact that he was a citizen of a neutral country); what they do reflect from his earliest days and with ever increasing consistency is a profound concern, rather, with the desperation of the human condition in general, above and beyond any transitory ideological consideration. Beckett both anticipates and reflects an absurdity even greater than the one Camus confronted: the staggering absurdity of man's fate viewed in an escalatingly dehumanizing apocalyptic epoch.

If Camus's writings crystallized the hopes and anguish of a period that needed to come to terms with its guilt, that struggled desperately to reassert frayed but not yet discarded humanistic values, to rise above the genocide, the monstrous destruction that represented the bitter pinnacle of the long ascending path of scientific progress, Beckett, more than any writer of the past quarter century, has succeeded in holding a mirror (a nonrealistic mirror, to be sure) up to the lot of postatomic man. Whereas Camus, as the conscience of his generation, spoke to his time of ethical values and political options, Beckett speaks to an era in which the notion of "a conscience," a moral repository, is no longer conceivable. For the children of Hiroshima, the absurd has ceased to be negotiable, to be transcendable. For this, our era, Sisyphus can no longer be thought of as "happy." At best we can continue (with Camus) to call attention to his fidelity to his task, to his devotion, to his integrity. Given the dire circumstances, that isn't so bad. But any more than that—"happiness"—would strike us as Pollyannaish.

Beckett's role vis-à-vis this new pessimism (Or is it this new realism? Have the facts changed or merely our lack of illusions in relation to them?) is to portray the anguish and the bleakness of the human condition, and he has done this consistently by creating the most startling and most immediately recognizable metaphors of our fate. Camus's time called for an honorable guide; Beckett's time (although it follows immediately on Camus's) dispenses with guides; it limits itself to recognizing and understanding its own plight—that is how much things have degenerated. The road from Meursault and Sisyphus to Vladimir, Estragon, Hamm, Clov, and the protagonist of *The Unnamable* is the straight, downhill road traveled by Western Civilization in the past forty or fifty years.

The geography or the landscape of each of the two writers is, then, conceived in terms of the absurd, and despite the differences, the absurd landscapes that organize the creativity of both men have striking phenomena in common. To begin with, we find a similar recognition of the absurd as the fundamental relationship binding man to his universe. Consider briefly the end of *The Misunderstanding* and the end of each act of *Waiting for Godot*. The old servant's final "No," his stubborn refusal to help Maria in her extreme distress has been widely viewed as the sign of man's abandonment in this world, in the face of God's silence or absence. I say this knowing full well that Camus claimed that the servant "does not necessarily symbolize fate."[1] But Camus was overly defensive about this play. He went to some pains to apply the richly evocative title only to Jan's failure to come forward and name himself—a passage that strikes me as reducing the play's impact. Since Camus also does admit (I say "admit" because, in his introduction to the American edition of his theater to which I am referring, he tries so hard to underline *The Misunderstanding*'s positive aspect), that "Doubtless, it is a very dismal image of human fate,"[2] the identification of the "No" with an absurd order (or lack of order) of the universe becomes compelling. Maria, like man in general, is alone.

Similarly, Vladimir and Estragon wind up alone at the close of each of the two acts of *Waiting for Godot,* just as we presume them to be alone at the conclusion of infinite acts that might precede or follow the two we witness. When they remain on the bare stage, utterly abandoned, obliged to continue their futile wait for the Godot who will likely never appear, we do not need to resort to analysis to discover the absurd; its vivid metaphor reaches us immediately, viscerally.

As to an interpretation of that absurd, that is another matter entirely, just as with *The Misunderstanding*. In the case of Camus's play, we may feel that the negativity of the "No" makes it the final, hopeless word. Or we can go along with the author's accentuating the positive, when, in the same introduction referred to, he states that the play's pessimism "can be reconciled with a relative optimism as to man. For, after all, it amounts to saying that everything would have been different if the son had said: 'It is I; here is my name.' It amounts to saying that in an unjust or indifferent world man can save himself, and save others, by practicing the most basic sincerity and pronouncing the most appropriate word." [3]

That interpretation is attractive, but perhaps more in line with Camus's other writings than with the spirit of *The Misunderstanding*; however, it is not my purpose to seek definitive readings of either author but rather to point to possible parallels, and we can see similar ambiguities in *Waiting for Godot*. We can contrast Godot's failure to materialize with the possibility (at least not excluded) that he will materialize, someday, perhaps in a potential forty-third act. It's the old "the glass is half empty or half full syndrome." But not all interpretations are so subjective. Just as we might construe Maria as finally left to her own devices (and the better for the realization of it), so can we think of Vladimir and Estragon as escaping a fate worse than deliverance (if one may be allowed that contradictory thought) since the supposed savior, Godot, has repeatedly been related to the notion of being tied down to, bound to, and he may well therefore represent a form of enslavement, spiritual or otherwise, for the price of redemption. In other words, Vladimir and Estragon may be better off not only without Godot, but especially without waiting for him. If only they would leave at the end of Act 2, saying to hell with him at last, determining finally to rely on themselves. Remember that there had been some confusion about the identity of Pozzo earlier; there is textual evidence to support the thesis that he is Godot or like Godot, that the coming of Godot would be submission to a Pozzo-type tyranny just as Lucky is subject to his whim. The attraction of powerful metaphors—like Godot and like the servant—is their evocative strength, even in contradictory directions.

If we now look at how Camus and Beckett, having named the absurd, go about describing it, we will have in capsule form a glimpse of their similarities and their divergences.

For Camus, we turn to the initial chapter in *The Myth of Sisyphus*, significantly called "An Absurd Reasoning." I call the chapter title significant because Camus's stress is, in fact, on the reasoning process. Camus, like Sartre, uses rational means to discover and then to analyze the absurd. Beckett proceeds without method, illogically or absurdly as it were, and he does not analyze. Through images and metaphors, the contact with the absurd is direct. Camus moves rationally, from *A* to *B* to *C* to prove the absurd; Beckett moves chaotically from *X* to *Y* to *Z* to bring the absurd directly into contact with our sensibilities.

Thus Camus states early in "An Absurd Reasoning" that "in a universe suddenly divested of illusions and lights, man feels an alien, a stranger."[4] This phrase, which reflects on Meursault's situation, serves as a point of departure—the recognition of the absurd—and leads to more precise explications:

> the feeling of absurdity does not spring from the mere scrutiny of a fact or an impression but . . . from the comparison between a bare fact and a certain reality, between an action and the world that transcends it. The absurd is essentially a divorce. It lies in neither of the elements compared, it is born of their confrontation.
>
> In this particular case and on the plane of intelligence, I can therefore say that the Absurd is not in man (if such a metaphor could have a meaning) nor in the world, but in their presence together. For the moment it is the only bond uniting them.[5]

These are the verities Caligula discovered in his three days' search for the moon following Drusilla's death: "this world of ours, the scheme of things as they call it, is quite intolerable. That's why I want the moon, or happiness, or eternal life—something, in fact, that may sound crazy, but which isn't of this world."[6] These verities also are the illuminations Meursault has, dimly at first in the courtroom and then with startling clarity during his final night on earth. Consider his explosion against the priest:

> What difference could they make to me, the deaths of others, or a mother's love, or his God; or the way a man decides to live, the fate he thinks he chooses, since one and the same fate was bound to "choose" not only me but thousands of millions of privileged people. All alike would be condemned to die one day; his turn, too, would come like the others'. And what difference could it make if, after being charged with murder, he were executed because he didn't weep at his mother's funeral[7]

In regard to Beckett's manner of confronting the absurd, there is no point in looking for such rational statements, except as transformed through the mordant prism of his devastating parody.

Beckett's representation of man's lot alternates surprisingly between the most despairing cries and images and what is probably the most corrosive humor of our times. Consider Pozzo's last, terrible outcry in *Waiting for Godot,* a microcosm of life's suffering:

> Have you not done tormenting me with your accursed time! It's abominable! When! When! One day, is that not enough for you, one day he went dumb, one day I went blind, one day we'll go deaf, one day we were born, one day we shall die, the same die, the same second, is that not enough for you? They give birth astride of a grave, the light gleams an instant, then it's night once more.[8]

And immediately thereafter, less fiercely but no less anguished, Vladimir reflects on the tenuousness of the human situation:

> Was I sleeping, while the others suffered? Am I sleeping now? Tomorrow, when I wake, or think I do, what shall I say of to-day? That with Estragon my friend, at this place, until the fall of night, I waited for Godot? That Pozzo passed. with his carrier, and that he spoke to us? Probably. But in all that what truth will there be? . . . Down in the hole, lingeringly, the grave-digger puts on the forceps. We have time to grow old. The air is full of our cries. . . . At me too someone is looking, of me too someone is saying, He is sleeping, he knows nothing, let him sleep on. I can't go on![9]

These are agonies at the limit of the bearable, joined by two images clear and hard as diamonds—to give birth "astride the grave" and the forceps being applied by the gravedigger.

These despairing moments are counterpointed by a great deal of humor, some of it farcical stage business (with the hats, boots, pants, etc.), some of it caustic commentary, like this dialogue between Vladimir and Estragon:

> VLADIMIR: Suppose we repented.
> ESTRAGON: Repented what?
> VLADIMIR: Oh. . . . We wouldn't have to go into the details.
> ESTRAGON: Our being born?[10]

The entire movement of Didi and Gogo's dialogue, the rapid banter about nothing that fills up the time of living, makes us uneasy while amusing us. What makes it supportable is that the two tramps poke fun at their own situation: "This is becoming really insignificant," says one; "Not enough"[11] chimes in the other, and Estragon adds his bemused but distressed affirmation, "We always find something, eh Didi, to give us the impression we exist?"[12]

The first half of *Molloy* is perhaps the best example of the absurd midnight vision constantly amended by devastating wit. Molloy describes the abysmal nature of his long existence, but he never takes himself tragically: "But it is only since I have ceased to live that I think of these things and the other things. It is in the tranquility of decomposition that I remember the long confused emotion which was my life, and that I judge it, as it is said that God will judge me, and with no less impertinence. To decompose is to live too."[13] The cause for the universal suffering in Beckett's world is simple and equally universal: it is being born. Accordingly, the sole blame is to give birth, and the thought of his mother is the only one that really disturbs Molloy. There is no more mocking passage in all of Beckett's work than the one in which he holds her responsible for his being, for his suffering:

> My mother. I don't think too harshly of her. I know she did all she could not to have me, except of course the one thing, and if she never succeeded in getting me unstuck, it was fate that ear-marked me for less compassionate sewers. But it was well-meant and that's enough for me. No it is not enough for me, but I give her credit, though she is my mother, for what she tried to do for me. And I forgive her for having jostled me a little in the first months and spoiled the only endurable, just endurable, period of my enormous history. And I also give her credit for not having done it again, thanks to me, or for having stopped in time.[14]

After we acknowledge that both writers recognize the absurd as life's operative factor, we detect in them a similar affirmation of man's resistance and nobility in the face of the absurd. Familiarly recognized in Camus's oeuvre, this affirmation is a theme which may surprise in Beckett's, but which is very much present. Beckett treats this theme in his own way, to be sure; that is, it appears not with Camus's cool,

Olympian analysis, but with the intense parody and anguish typical of Beckett.

For Camus, the first step leading from the acknowledgment of the human predicament to the rebellion that transcends it is the consideration and rejection of suicide. It is an essential step, without which Camus could have gotten nowhere in the development of his thought. Accordingly, he attacked the problem at the very beginning of *The Myth of Sisyphus:* "There is but one truly serious philosophical problem, and that is suicide. Judging whether life is or is not worth living amounts to answering the fundamental question of philosophy." [15] And later he states: "Knowing whether or not one can live *without* appeal is all that interests me." [16] We are all familiar with Camus's pursuit of this argument: that the absurd becomes the creative tension in man, his revolt, his projection into life rather than away from it. Suicide is rejected in favor of revolt: "That revolt gives life its value. Spread out over the whole length of a life, it restores its majesty to that life. To a man devoid of blinders, there is no finer sight than that of the intelligence at grips with a reality that transcends it." [17] That revolt which is the refusal to commit suicide and the positive acceptance of life within the limits imposed by the absurd is analyzed in *The Rebel* and illustrated in *The Plague.* For example, Rieux and Tarrou observe:

> since the order of the world is shaped by death, mightn't it be better for God if we refuse to believe in Him and struggle with all our might against death, without raising our eyes toward the heaven where He sits in silence?
> Tarrou nodded.
> "Yes. But your victories will never be lasting; that's all." Rioux's face darkened.
> "Yes, I know that. But it's no reason for giving up the struggle." [18]

Revolt also generates the more lyrical pages of *Nuptials* and *L'Eté.* Thus, in "Summer in Algiers," Camus says: "I know simply that this sky will last longer than I. And what shall I call eternity except what will continue after my death? . . . But, after all, what negates me in this life is first of all what kills me. Everything that exalts life at the same time increases its absurdity." [19]

And in the well-known meditation on the "Return to Tipasa," he says:

I discovered once more at Tipasa that one must keep intact in oneself a freshness, a cool wellspring of joy, love the day that escapes injustice, and return to combat having won that light. Here I recaptured the former beauty, a young sky, and I measured my luck, realizing at last that in the worst years of our madness the memory of that sky had never left me. This was what in the end had kept me from despairing. I had always known that the ruins of Tipasa were younger than our new constructions or our bomb damage. There the world began over again every day in an ever new light. O light! This is the cry of all the characters of ancient drama brought face to face with their fate. This last resort was ours, too, and I knew it now. In the middle of winter I at last discovered that there was in me an invincible summer.[20]

I suppose that, in the final analysis, Camus's strongest and most moving statement concerning the refusal to yield, the positive posture taken in the face of the absurd is the concluding chapter of *The Myth of Sisyphus*:

All Sisyphus' silent joy is contained therein. His fate belongs to him. His rock is his thing. Likewise, the absurd man, when he contemplates his torment, silences all the idols. In the universe suddenly restored to its silence, the myriad wondering little voices of the earth rise up. Unconscious, secret calls, invitations from all the faces, they are the necessary reverse and price of victory. There is no sun without shadow, and it is essential to know the night. The absurd man says yes and his effort will henceforth be unceasing. If there is a personal fate, there is no higher destiny, or at least there is but one which he concludes is inevitable and despicable. For the rest, he knows himself to be the master of his days. At that subtle moment when man glances backward over his life, Sisyphus returning to his rock, in that slight pivoting he contemplates that series of unrelated actions which becomes his fate, created by him, combined under his memory's eye and soon sealed by his death. Thus, convinced of the wholly human origin of all that is human, a blind man eager to see who knows that the night has no end, he is still on the go. The rock is still rolling.[21]

Camus's essentially positive and hopeful reactions to the absurd are precisely the qualities that, in the period right after World War II, endeared him to the youth of many countries athirst for affirmative responses. *Mutatis mutandis* we also find in Beckett's literary production an unrelenting stress on the existential anguish of the human condition, through the constant skepticism of his vision (which is not usually the case for Camus) and through the desperate search for a positive commitment to life in a world where all optimism is impossible.

Beckett is certainly a pessimist (can one really view the world differently in the second half of the twentieth century?); he views the world as basically absurd and his representations of humanity are bleak indeed. But he does not offer up this dismal vision as his realistic sample of mankind; he is a profoundly nonrealistic artist, and his characters, in their intense plight, must constantly be viewed metaphorically.

On this metaphoric level, one is struck by the astounding perseverance of Beckett's characters. They do not commit suicide—not a single one—tempted though they may be and no matter how much they may talk longingly of "finishing it," of "getting it over with." Instead, they cling to life with a tenacity that is all the more remarkable for the grim context in which it operates. "you must go on, I can't go on, you must go on, I'll go on"[22] are the simple powerful, near-concluding words of *The Unnamable*.

Beckett's striking metaphors, at once precise and capable of universal expansion, express the difficulty of being, of tolerating the degradation of existence; but most of them also symbolize the individual's tenacity, and inexplicable, absurd attachment to life, despite it all.

As Beckett's characters become less recognizably human within a progressively grotesque and parodic milieu, their insistent attachment to expressing their reality becomes an ever-greater act of heroism, of self-affirmation. Each of these forlorn characters continues to do the only thing that distinguished him as a man, the only thing no other creature can do: to say, to speak, to signify. The more dismal his condition, the more remarkable the clinging to life. And cling to life they do. In a universe where the manifestation of life is not a heartbeat but the word, they continue to speak, write, think—continue to be. The perception of self through language is the sign of living, a paradoxical chase after one's own tail: as long as I exist, I have to express that existence, as long as I express it, I exist.

The only way out of the dilemma would be to manage finally to speak one's being, to describe "how it is" in its definitive form. From Molloy's ironic jibes to the anguished interrogations of the narrator of *The Unnamable,* Beckett's heroes (?) long to achieve that deliverance.

But always language is imperfect, incapable of rendering human experience adequately. It is the very nature of words not to coincide with the thing designated.

Given this permanent impasse of language, is the insistence of Beckett's characters to keep on talking a paradigm of their alienation or of their resistance, a negative or a positive manifestation? It may well be both; their positive response (to keep on talking) to a negative situation (language's inability to express) gains relief through contrast. The final words of *The Unnamable*, "I'll go on," acquire their powerful, affirmative connotation from the extremity of the circumstances in which they are uttered. It would be difficult to view Beckett as optimistic, but there is much in his writings that underlines man's strength and will in the face of the bleakness of his plight, in the face of the absurd. His affirmation of life may be etched in tones quite different from Camus's and may be the result of a different dialectic, but it is as strong as anything discernible in Camus.

Resisting the temptation to want everything to fit comfortably into my topic, I must add in all fairness that most of Beckett's very recent works fail to echo that indomitable spirit of man identified with his major works. Most of the texts since about 1965 are almost devoid of humor and their outlook is now fully despairing. For the first time, there is not even the faintest glimmer of hope in the predicament of humanity entrapped in rigidly defined geometric spaces. The titles themselves clearly point to the desperation: *Enough, The Lost Ones, Lessness*. But at least the utter hopelessness remains abstract and therefore less imminent. We have ceased dealing with recognizable people; they no longer "speak to us"; they are faceless, nameless, voiceless. We cannot "feel" for them as we do for, say, Winnie in *Happy Days*, Molloy, or even the narrator in *How It Is*.

Leaving now the major framework of the Camus-Beckett comparison, that is, the one dealing with the absurd per se, I would like to address more specifically the theme of aridity chosen for this symposium. Again, and even more so than in the case of the absurd, one should make no giant claims. The two writers are not cut out of the same cloth, but I believe that in this area too there are some interesting parallels alongside the equally interesting divergences. Camus's carefully elaborate North African sun/sea/wind/blue/yellow configuration opposed to the negative gray/rain/cold of Europe has no full equivalent for Beckett, whose personal geography does not encompass, after all, as does Camus's, Algeria and the entire Mediterranean basin but runs mainly from Ireland and London, to France and Germany. But one can detect in Beckett's work a clear leitmotiv involving a destructive, quasi-infernal parching sun/blinding light/aridity that stands opposed to softer, more humid, and more livable climes.

Camus's celebrated North-African pages tell of his sensual attachment to the world. These have been much discussed and I shall not dwell on them, but suffice it to say that the polarity of happiness and fulfillment includes all the elements of sea/sun/blue sky/heat/wind. Real contentment is associated with a balance of these complementary forces and is epitomized by the act of swimming in the sea, in the Mediterranean, an act of consummation; examples are the passage in *The Stranger* and Rieux and Tarrou's illicit dip during the quarantine in *The Plague*.

But the absence of one of the elements or the excess of another can be destructive, even within the otherwise favorable Mediterranean climate. Thus, the unbearable heat and blinding brilliance of the sun are seen as motivating Meursault's murder of the Arab, the desolation of the desert is an alienating force in *Exile and the Kingdom,* both in "The Adulterous Woman" and "The Renegade," and the plague remains in Oran, cutting the city off from the sea, as long as the wind remains stilled; when the wind returns, the plague recedes and eventually disappears. The European polarity in Camus is clear and consistent: the grey dampness of central Europe in *The Misunderstanding* and of Amsterdam in *The Fall* is the correlative to despair, destruction, insincerity. But the lack of balance, lack of *mesure* in the privileged North-African milieu is also, though differently, nefarious.

Since his first novel *Murphy,* Beckett's works have been devoid of specific geographic location. And yet here too there is a sort of climatic opposition representing two poles each with a value of its own.

Around the positive pole (much the smaller of the two) cluster the happy memories of days gone by. These memories are often tied to a temperate climate and some form of vegetation, as opposed to the other pole, of present horror and desolation, frequently associated with blinding light, aridity, a desert landscape. The characters in *Endgame,* for instance, are in a room surrounded by nothingness, with no scenery, no landscape beyond them, no life, only grayness—a metaphor for destitution and perhaps a more direct image of a postcataclysmic universe. Hamm says pompously but hopefully: "But beyond the hills? Eh? Perhaps it's still green. Eh? Flora! Pomona! Ceres!"[23] Or there is this dialogue between Nell and Nagg, Hamm's dying parents, condemned to their ashcans:

NELL: It was on Lake Como. One April afternoon. Can you believe it?
NAGG: What?
NELL: That we once went out rowing on Lake Como. One April afternoon.
NAGG: We had got engaged the day before.

. . . .

NELL: It was deep, deep. And you could see down to the bottom. So white. So clean.[24]

For Molloy, in his long Odyssey-like quest for a haven, occasional passages through verdant forests are evoked in ecstatic language usually reserved for paradise—or, rather, in the *parody* of ecstatic language, and the like. Perhaps the most tender and lyric recollection in all Beckett's works occurs in *Krapp's Last Tape,* and evokes a gentle summer afternoon on some body of water in the Irish or English countryside:

upper lake, with the punt, bathed off the bank, then pushed out into the stream and drifted. She lay stretched out on the floorboards with her hands under her head and her eyes closed. Sun blaring down, bit of a breeze, water nice and lively. I noticed a scratch on her thigh and asked her how she came by it. Picking gooseberries, she said. I said again I thought it was hopeless and no good going on, and she agreed, without opening her eyes. (Pause.) I asked her to look at me and after a few moments (pause—after a few moments she did, but the eyes just slits, because of the glare. I bent over her to get them in the shadow and they opened. (Pause. Low.) Let me in. (Pause.) We drifted in among the flags and stuck. The way they went down, sighing, before the stem! (Pause.) I lay down across her with my face in her breasts and my hand on her. We lay there without moving. But under us all moved, and moved us, gently, up and down, and from side to side.[25]

The case of Winnie in *Happy Days* is very much in point. Buried in earth in an expanse of scorched grass, with the blazing light of a merciless sun beating constantly down on her, she is caught between the recollections of a former, happy existence in a gentler climate and her present desperate circumstance which tends even to obliterate the past:

> With the sun blazing so much fiercer down, and hourly fiercer, is it not natural things should go on fire never known to do so, in this way I mean, spontaneous like. . . . Shall I myself not melt perhaps in the end, or burn, oh I do not mean necessarily burst into flames, no, just little by little be charred to a black cinder, all this . . . visible flesh. . . . On the other hand, did I ever know a temperate time?[26]

I said that there was more accumulation around the negative pole. The empty, hostile landscape of *Godot* is all the more ambiguous and even ominous for the one contrasting sign, the bare tree that has mysteriously grown leaves in the second act. In *The Lost Ones, Lessness,* and *Ping,* the blinding light, or light/heat encountered earlier in *Happy Days, Play,* and other works as a daemonic, torturing, eliciting element, has become all pervasive, inducing total paralysis; the creatures populating these stories merely take up space, float in the space organized by that light.

Lastly, I would like to sketch out elements for a fruitful comparison of *The Fall* and Beckett's trilogy, especially *Molloy. The Fall* and *Molloy* are both written from an ironic point of view which is usual for Beckett and not so usual for Camus; both are first person singular narratives, told by narrators whose veracity we can reasonably question, for while both make much of their attachment to truth, both are constantly fabulating or lying. Both speak compulsively and are incapable of remaining silent. And both, in a basic way, talk about guilt, the guilt of existing, of having been born. Jean-Baptiste Clamence is the most Beckettian of Camus's characters. I imagine that he would get along admirably with Molloy, whether they got together in Molloy's room, or at the sleazy Amsterdam bar called Mexico City. Furthermore, and of more than passing interest, unlike Camus's other novels or *récits,* which are linear in structure, *The Fall,* like *Molloy* and the entire Beckett trilogy, is structured in patterns of circularity. And *The Fall* poses the problem of its own fictivity as does *Molloy* and as do all Beckett's novels.

One could bring up more. For instance, a substantial comparison could be made on the subject of God. I would suggest that both Camus and Beckett think of God as, at the most, silence and absence and, at the least, nonexistence. They both talk about him, yet do not believe in him and do not want him. And for both, critics have tried at times to detect the essence of Christian thought or a conversion; they are quite wrong, I'm convinced, for they are too much taken in by Biblical references, in *Godot* and *The Fall* particularly—as if to refer to Christ is to believe in him any more than, for example, Sartre can be thought of as believing in Jupiter simply because he is a major character in *The Flies*. But the parallels relating to God between Camus and Beckett would bear further probing.

I hope that these various counterpositions have pointed to the usefulness of considering Camus and Beckett as somewhat related writers without my falling into the trap of going beyond that. Camus's and Beckett's backgrounds and the traditions from which they come are different indeed, and there is an evident dissimilarity in their manner of living. But they do react in analogous ways to the dilemma of the human condition in our time; they are both the descendants of battered rationalism and positivism forced by the realities of an unhappy age to come to terms with the absurd. And no matter how contaminated the word may have become these days, they are both emanations of a humanistic tendency in their approach to the philosophic positions elicited by our age, the overwhelming notion of the absurd.

From *Albert Camus's Literary Milieu: Arid Lands* (Lubbock: Texas Tech Press, 1976), 53–69.

P A R T   T W O

THE NEW NOVEL

In its early years—the 1950s—the New Novel was hailed in French intellectual circles as a brilliant new phenomenon that revitalized the French novel. But later, it elicited increasing irritation: it was attacked as a new terrorism responsible for every possible ailment in all of French fiction; it was termed sterile and boring; it was accused of living too long or of being already dead. Because I brought many of the "new" novelists to New York (mainly Alain Robbe-Grillet, Claude Simon, Nathalie Sarraute, and Robert Pinget), I have been accused by some French critics of defending writers that no one reads and of keeping younger novelists from being known in the United States.

I plead guilty to defending the New Novel. For me, it represented unquestionably a revolution in the world of fiction whose consequences have not yet been exhausted. Its leading proponents have become the classics of late-twentieth-century French literature. And if the New Novel has failed in that it has left no progeny, it has triumphed in that it has left an indelible mark on the writing of fiction. Not every reader wants to enter into its universe. Each one has the right to be bored, to put down the book after a few pages. As for me, I accepted what the New Novel demands of its reader: to place oneself

PART TWO: THE NEW NOVEL

at the center of the narrative, to reconstruct it, to track down the narrator by deciphering the grid of his discourse.

The New Novel was a radical departure from traditional forms of the novel. The familiar trappings of nineteenth-century-type novels were deliberately downgraded and tended to disappear: chronology, cause and effect, linear plot, characters in the usual sense of the word, and often direct dialogue. Readers were confronted with fictions that drew them into their vortex and required their active collaboration. The narrative techniques were multiple, as were the voices speaking to us.

With its early insistence on objective description (giving rise to the labels "realism," "Objective Novel," and "l'école du regard"), with its deliberate restriction to a limited field of narrative vision, with its refusal to probe beneath the surface for supposed psychological depths, the New Novel fashioned a newly perceived reality. Robbe-Grillet laid the theoretical foundation for the new concept of realism that more or less applied also to the universe of the other New Novelists. Rejecting essentialist views of man and a verisimilitudinous function for art, Robbe-Grillet enlists the novel in a radical adventure, the phenomenological concern with the here and now, with *Dasein*, the description of the visible and the refusal of all speculation, metaphysical or otherwise. Fiction, then, will no longer be referential to a preexisting reality; it will create its own reality, will be self-referential. As Vivian Mercier noted, "The greatest realism may consist in constantly reminding the reader that he is reading a 'made-up' story, not observing life." [1]

Thanks to the attention paid to contemporary writing in American universities, the French New Novel thrived on American campuses. Not only have practically all French titles been published in American translations, but also American scholars have produced a number of significant critical studies. Since 1960, the leading French "new" novelists have come ever more frequently to the United States to lecture, take part in conferences, and teach in universities. I am proud that at New York University, we were in the lead and that we organized a landmark conference, "Three Decades of the French New Novel" in 1982, with a stellar cast of participants.

CHAPTER TWENTY

The Image of Creation in the Works of
Claude Simon

In Claude Simon's novel *The Battle of Pharsalus,* the allusion
to Poussin's "The Blind Orion Walking towards Light of the Rising
Sun" is one of the numerous cohesive links of that very dense text in
which each word, each theme refers back to other words, to other
themes forming associations that are at times softly rhythmical, at
times jagged, contingent, surprising by their energy as much as by
their vector. In his essay "La Bataille de la Phrase" (The Battle of the
Sentence),[1] Jean Ricardou examined the explicit and implicit possibilities of text generation and organization of a number of terms in
Claude Simon's novel, including the reference to Poussin's canvas. By
giving its name to Simon's next book, this painting attains the summit
of the hierarchy of production within this novel—the starting point of
the narrator narrating his own quest through writing itself, as well
as the final destination to the extent that *Orion aveugle* "reaches a
destination." It is the alpha and omega of a movement of exploration
and invention.

Orion aveugle (Blind Orion) was published separately (in 1970),
before *Les Corps conducteurs* (*Conducting Bodies,* 1971) in the Albert
Skira collection entitled "Les Sentiers de la création" ("The Paths of

Creation"). Subsequently, the text of *Orion aveugle* was incorporated in *Conducting Bodies*[2] —which represents in fact more than the first third plus the last few pages of *Conducting Bodies*. But *Orion aveugle* deserves attention in its own right, as well as the book that incorporates it, because it contains two essential elements not present in the later volume: the photographic reproduction of works of art and simple objects around which the book is organized (that is, the very image of conducting bodies), as well as an important preface by Claude Simon which is a description of his method of working and of his esthetics.

Since *The Wind* and *The Flanders Road* and especially in the more recent novels, *Histoire* and *The Battle of Pharsalus*, Simon's work has been in search of the image of creation—considering the relationships between image and creation as a function of ever more varied possibilities—leading up to *Conducting Bodies,* that book in which Simon's theme of the literary work creating itself out of writing itself is expressed perfectly and totally through the images. More than in earlier works, the mode of association and text generation is pictorial rather than thematic or linguistic, proceeding through the juxtaposition of paintings, objects, and so on (reproduced within the book *Orion aveugle*) as well as remembered scenes which unfold as frozen stills or in slow motion.

In an interview about *The Flanders Road*, Simon had said that he was seeking a "purely sensory architecture." It is his most recent novel that fully answers this quest, the "sense" in question being, naturally, the visual. The constantly evolving series of images evoked by the consciousness of the narrator of *Conducting Bodies* leads to the fragmentation of the world, to the annihilation of the present which fuses with various pasts—a tendency already evident in the earlier novels but which stands out more sharply here. Concerning these preceding novels, one could already speak in terms of "collage"; but it is with respect to *Conducting Bodies* that the collage technique comes into full bloom thanks to subtle resonances and to echoes which, in a constant back and forth movement, relate to the slowly revealed surfaces of these bodies whose exterior they make up. Yet this exterior is not presented to us in its supposedly "normal" aspect but rather "flattened out," stretched out in time so as to suggest a veritable simultaneity. The view of the world is nevertheless realistic—which is not the case for Robbe-Grillet, for instance—not a traditional and supposedly objective realism, of course, but a subjective realism in the manner of cubism. The constant fragmentation of the image marks *Conducting Bodies* as a cubist novel. In fact, the label "cubist novel" applies perfectly and it is probably one of the rare novels for which this is the case.

Until this point for Simon, the associative links that led to exterior or interior chaos (or both) consisted essentially, in *The Flanders Road* or *Histoire,* for instance, of words or sentences floating among different levels of time and space. In *Conducting Bodies,* on the other hand, it is the *bodies* which conduct—these bodies that are paintings, signs, advertising posters, pages of newspapers, and many others, but also the *body* of the character: a body in a moral and physical crisis, a body ill in New York, which itself becomes a conducting and generating body.

In this book, starting from the blank page, the author seeks the multiple possibilities of writing that imposes itself on his own authorial intentions. Simon accepts a rule for his game: to allow writing and thought to follow their own path starting from paintings, objects, lived or remembered images. That is how Simon chose to respond to the initial challenge of the Skira collection. For him, as he states in the preface, the paths of creation cannot be anything other than "the very development of writing."[3] From this point of view, the privileged role given to Poussin's painting is not only that of launching the dazzling free association of images that form a rich inner landscape; it also serves as objective correlative of the situation of the writer.

Without referring to the mythic context that the character of Orion has above and beyond the painting, Simon seems to recognize in the figure of the blind giant the counterpart to himself, wandering, pen in hand—as he depicts himself in his own drawing that illustrates the preface of *Orion aveugle*—in search of the book that is being written. Thus, the path on which we glimpse Orion *is* the path of creation and Orion, advancing painstakingly toward the rising sun (guided by the "small" character standing on his shoulder? propelled by an instinctive heliotropism that wins out over his blindness?), resembles the author seeking through the act of creation what Simon has called this "infinitely richer thing than what I had set out to do."[4] Orion's persistent journey must lead him to the sunrise that will be his libera-

THE IMAGE OF CREATION IN THE WORKS OF CLAUDE SIMON

tion; Simon's journey, starting from "some initial images," also leads to a sort of clarification—the meaning of the total structure revealing itself only at the conclusion of the creative experience.

And yet, at the end of *Conducting Bodies,* we have reached no "conclusion." The voyage on which Simon has taken us can have "no other end point than the exhaustion of the voyager"—this voyager who, exhausted as much by the New York summer as by his dizzy spell, finally manages to get back to his hotel only to collapse in his room. The landscape of the book being "inexhaustible," the narrator must affix a final period at some arbitrary moment of the narration. Similarly, Orion will never really manage to reach the sunset which remains always elsewhere, beyond the mysterious border of the receding horizon:

> There is every indication, however, that he will never reach his goal, since as the sun rises higher and higher in the sky, the stars outlining the giant's body are gradually growing paler and dimmer, and the fabulous silhouette, motionlessly advancing in great strides, will thus slowly fade and eventually disappear altogether in the dawn sky.[5]

Simon's small labyrinthine drawing in the preface graphically shows the author's intention; the narrative thread wanders aimlessly, turning back on itself, crisscrossing, describing a formless surface rather than defining the simple, linear trajectory between a beginning and an end. Thus, the narration never attains a true omega, Orion continues on his path, and the final period is not so far removed from the start. Nothing is resolved for the speaker-voyager. His crisis continues; his pain continues; his memories continue to haunt him. The book ends without concluding—and that is perhaps why the last page is not numbered. Like the more recent novels, and especially like *Histoire* and *The Battle of Pharsalus, Conducting Bodies* does not attempt to relate but to signify through the attempt to relate, the discovery of "the world in and through writing."

Starting with the giant groping his way on his journey in a luxuriantly green landscape and heading towards a horizon where the rising sun is already transforming the blue of the sky into incandescence,[6] the narration rebounds, using the most diverse links, evoking other paintings, imagining scenes, sensations, and conversations—all connected by the single creative spontaneity of the author, the speaker. In

Histoire, the generating objects are postcards that refer back to real and imaginary objects—a springboard for chain reactions within an inner space. In the new book, Simon uses this technique even more overtly. The conducting images which command the meanderings of the imagination of the speaker no longer need to refer back to far-away cities; in *Conducting Bodies* they are simply *there* because Simon decided to use them for reasons he does not reveal to us and perhaps does not clearly know himself. Each of the elements selected by him exists in and for itself, independently: works by Poussin, Robert Rauschenberg, Louise Nevelson, and others; a telephone, a cigar box cover, photographs, an anatomic chart, engravings—in short, objects of different worth or even of no value. Simon neither analyzes nor judges them; he intertwines them through analogy, contrast, or association. The combinations created by these disparate elements often resemble each other without ever being completely alike, somewhat like the light sculptures of Nicolas Schöffer in which several variables combine to project luminous movements which fuse and refuse into one another in a continuum of colors and forms, constantly changing and renewing themselves without repeating. Thus we are frequently introduced into an airplane flying over a great river that traces its path in a tropical landscape (undoubtedly the Amazon), but we find ourselves in a very different atmosphere if we get there through Poussin's *Blind Orion* or through the sea of lights of Times Square at dusk.

Claude Simon practices another form of artistic expression, besides the one for which he is famous, that gives an additional insight into his writing. He creates complex and fascinating collages wherein he brings together and juxtaposes objects, reproductions of paintings, and newspaper and magazine clippings. With a certain degree of premeditation, Claude Simon makes these diverse "bodies" interact on a large screen. The mosaic that forms itself on the ever less empty space of the screen functions in the same manner as the novel *Conducting Bodies:* the very texture of the work is a function of all the generators in their interaction, and the "subject" (if one can use the term) is its own creation—the screen which fills up progressively, becoming finally the finished collage, the novel that is directed at its own writing and writes itself through the reading of it.

The constant and often surprising transpositions which organize *Conducting Bodies,* functioning by means of pictorial elements, are the logical extension of Simon's celebrated frequent use of the present

THE IMAGE OF CREATION IN THE WORKS OF CLAUDE SIMON

participle. They not only destroy the temporal narrative chronology by substituting simultaneity in the same way as does the present participial construction, but also deny any coherence of plastic contiguity in favor of free coming and going among associative elements. Since Simon is dealing in images, he deliberately uses literary techniques comparable to film techniques that lend themselves to the manipulation of images: the dissolve which gently brings together two disparate images; rapid cutting which achieves the same result but radically and suddenly; the zoom effect which permits showing an object in its entirety at first, then converging on a single detail before again returning to the whole image of the start (which is no longer the same, however, since the detail, having been singled out by the zoom lens, tends to assume a greater role henceforth); slow motion and freeze which allow for the same alternation in time that the zoom permits in space by going either from a scene in motion to a frozen moment of that movement to return eventually to the movement itself, or on the contrary, from a freeze to movement and back to the freeze. If the dissolve and the quick cut are useful for the type of transition often translated by the present participle, the freeze succeeds in removing from its time frame and its normal plastic context a single element which henceforth will be isolated, deprived of its usual relationship with the whole—that is the role of the present participle as Simon uses it. Witness this example from *Conducting Bodies*:

A man with a bald head and a long beard, his torso sheathed in a cuirass, with a short peplum beginning at the waist beneath it, is standing on the beach. He has removed his helmet from his head and is holding it in the crook of his arm, with his rigid index finger pointing in the direction of a crucifix, which he is holding up toward the green sky with his other hand. On the right a number of half-naked men and women are joining hands, bowing their heads or touching one knee to the ground. Several of them are still partially hidden by the luxuriant vegetation, with large, sharply outlined leaves or thin, bristling, spiky ones, topped by lofty palms with slating trunks.[7]

This completely immobilized and descriptive scene links up with several images and movements encountered earlier. The above quotation is followed immediately by the sentence: "At this moment, the

THE IMAGE OF CREATION IN THE WORKS OF CLAUDE SIMON

black in white overalls comes out of the shop once again, folding another brown cardboard box flat."[8] Immobility yields to movement, but to a movement of an entirely different nature, linked it would seem by the two hands with which the one holds a crucifix and the other a cardboard box.

The alternation continues with different connections:

> The cross that the steel-gauntled hand of the old warrior is displaying to the savages is surrounded by divergent rays of light, like a sunburst, in an absinthe-colored sky. The cruciform shadow of the airplane glides swiftly across a velvety, or rather, a fuzzy surface, of an almost uniform green, with only a few splashes of a darker green or pale yellowish highlights here and there. The contours of the cross undergo imperceptible distortions as it passes over hillocks choked with dense, luxuriant vegetation[9]

The association begins anew, born out of the frozen scene which itself was imagined after a lithograph, "Christopher Columbus builds a fortress," and couples this time not with the black man leaving a store in New York but with an aerial view of the Amazon—linked first of all and especially by the warrior's cross which "becomes" the shadow in the form of a cross projected on the land by a plane flying at low altitude, and reinforced finally by the landscape transferred from the lithograph to the banks of the Amazon.

Other transitions are more cerebral. An engraving from the illustrated supplement of the *Petit Journal* of 1893, depicting "The Explosion of Vaillant's bomb in the Chamber of Deputies" transforms itself into a conference of Latin American writers where the speech of a young radical delegate (quoted in Spanish and translated by an interpreter) creates a sensation comparable to a bomb because he attacks all forms of literature which remain removed from the social and political problems of oppressed peoples.

Often, throughout the pages of *Conducting Bodies,* the speaker's memory returns insistently to this conference, recalling above all the boredom of its polemical speeches, its consecutive translations, and its righteous resolutions, each word relentlessly discussed and analyzed, as if it could change anything. The resulting doctrine of the writer's engagement and responsibility (close to Sartre's "What Is Literature?")

THE IMAGE OF CREATION IN THE WORKS OF CLAUDE SIMON

implies a concept of writing far removed from the one that Simon's novel embodies: the speaker remains an observer; he feels estranged by the debate, by the political definition required of the conference's participants.

One of the most interesting—and certainly one of the most abstract—creative articulations is one, covering dozens of pages, organized around rectangles. It is no longer an element of a painting or some aspect of an object which serves as conductor, but rather a geometric shape which radiates towards other similar shapes in purely abstract associations, linking elements which have no other connections than their rectangularity. Thus, cigar boxes stacked in a store connect with the checkerboard pattern of a newspaper page made up of black and white rectangles advertising films, which then connects with the enormous rectangles made up of little rectangles of New York's glass skyscrapers, and then with the very small black paper rectangles pasted between the wide-open thighs of girls photographed on the covers of pornographic magazines in the windows of specialized stores around Times Square, connecting in turn with the rectangle of sunlight highlighting on the background of another rectangle—a door frame—a woman whom the speaker stares at while she looks at him with equal intensity. Colors are another abstract feature often associated with these rectangles—mainly yellow, as had already been the case with *The Battle of Pharsalus*. This ordering of diverse elements in a very rapid staccato movement is an astonishing technical success, a real tour de force.

The final transition which puts an end to the whirlwind mental inventory of *Conducting Bodies* is associated with one of the anatomical charts that illustrate the book. On the final page, Simon evokes "the thin membrane of the retina on which the images of the world fall, gliding across it and replacing each other one by one."[10] This is precisely the process that Simon has used throughout this narrative which thus ends with its own genesis. His sight regained, Orion, the artist, the creator, the author, registers as if on an eye's retina the multiple impressions of the very complex external and internal reality. It is with words that the writer translates these impressions—these words which are the result of what he terms "the formless magma of more or less muddled impressions" which exist before any articulation of it in language. Claude Simon's works—and especially *Conducting*

THE IMAGE OF CREATION IN THE WORKS OF CLAUDE SIMON

Bodies—create themselves as he is writing them. Not only does this most recent book take shape before us, but it demonstrates the process of creation by enabling us to follow the artist's eye, his artistic sensibility as it organizes and integrates that substance of the external world in order to turn it into images of creation, to turn it into fiction.

Translated from "L' image de la création chez Claude Simon" in *Nouveau roman: Hier, aujourd'hui, II* (Paris: 10/18, 1972), 61–71.

CHAPTER TWENTY-ONE

The Inquisitory by Robert Pinget

When *The Inquisitory* was published in France in 1962, it received the esteemed *Prix des Critiques* and marked Robert Pinget's accession to the front ranks of "new novel" authors, alongside Alain Robbe-Grillet, Michel Butor, and Nathalie Sarraute. Pinget's fictional world, like that of his French contemporaries, has a highly original consistency, *sui generis,* marked by a baroque, mythical inner geography and history.

The Inquisitory is a long, rambling monologue. Perhaps it would be more accurate to call it a directed monologue for it is formed of a series of answers given by an old servant to an unnamed, all-powerful, policelike interrogator who, presumably in order to find out information about a man's disappearance, forces the old man to talk about his employers, their household, their village, and their province. And yet, as one becomes immersed in the novel, one begins to realize that the servant's replies are not always related to the questions. Through his evocation of myriad incidents involving a veritable miasma of people, streets, and towns, the reader starts to suspect that the servant is telling only part of the truth, perhaps because he is forgetful or perhaps because he deliberately wishes to mislead. The old man is deaf;

240

THE INQUISITORY *BY ROBERT PINGET*

the questions are therefore put to him in writing, and they are necessarily brief. But since he is not mute, his answers often go on at great length, dwelling on details and eliciting impatient messages to "cut it short." The meandering, disordered quality of the discourse is underlined by the absence of all punctuation other than occasional commas, and by a total lack of any real narrative.

At first the picture painted by the servant recreates a fairly prosaic panorama of provincial life. But gradually, behind the innocuous facade emerges a swarm of vices—ranging from theft to orgies, incest, necrophilia, and murder—which have corroded the very fabric of an apparently self-sufficient universe. The old man insists that he has no involvement with the nefarious goings-on, but as his own tragic existence reveals itself in bits and pieces, his complicity becomes a matter of increasing conjecture for the reader. Gradually, too, the perverted provincial microcosm takes on the aspect of life itself in its pointlessness and anguish.

Significantly, the beginning of the "inquisitory" is missing. We can only assume what the cross-examiner is seeking; it is clear, moreover, that the servant doesn't quite know either, and in his disorientation, he becomes a victim. At such times he revolts:

> it's my turn to ask you what are you trying to find out what are you trying to get out of me, I only know bits and pieces I don't know the truth never shall and we'll die not knowing and all the people like you who are mad to find out other people's secrets they'll die first they'll wear themselves out, they don't know how to ask questions though they know how to plant the answers and that's not the way to ask.[1]

But no explanation is forthcoming; like life, the torrent of words continues without ever reaching a conclusion, until the servant cannot go on because he is too exhausted.

The Inquisitory is, beyond the literal and metaphoric levels, a novel about the writing of a novel. In essence, the old man dictates his story, prodded by questions which may be his own. In this sense, Pinget's work focuses on the impossibility of writing. Despite the multitude of details—or rather because of it—the overall picture constantly shifts, and no solid texture is allowed to develop out of uncertainty. The reality so carefully constructed in its minute components explodes in its totality. By accumulating countless characters, streets, and place names, Pinget causes them all to lose meaning as they blend into an overwhelming mass. Ionesco destroyed the concept of personality in *The Bald Soprano* through the device of an entire family whose every member for generations was called Bobby Watson; Pinget achieves the same effect by referring to endless characters, all of whom have different names but who are otherwise indistinguishable. The proper nouns are strangely disturbing, sometimes humorous, more often with ominous overtones; but the translator, Donald Watson, who has brilliantly rendered this difficult work, was forced to leave the fabulous names in French. This was unavoidable; nevertheless it does keep the non-French-speaking reader from fully seizing Pinget's bizarre, unsettling atmosphere. The reader is disconcerted, too, by the many verbal mistakes the old man makes; the title itself is significantly representative of his odd slips.

The Inquisitory is, in fact, a disturbing, bewildering book. But its very confusion dazzles rather than dazes; it creates a compulsive effect on the reader. Once caught in Pinget's maze, one will not want to put it down until one has heard the old servant out.

From *Saturday Review* (February 11, 1967): 41, 54.

CHAPTER TWENTY-TWO

The Park by Philippe Sollers

Over the course of the past decade, Philippe Sollers, now thirty-four years old, has become a major figure in French literary circles. Surprisingly, until the present translation of *The Park,* issued by the enterprising new publishing house, Red Dust, Sollers was totally unknown in the United States. As editor of the avant-garde review *Tel Quel,* he heads a group of particularly talented young writers predominantly concerned with new perspectives of criticism. Along with critics such as Roland Barthes, Lucien Goldmann, Michel Foucault, Serge Doubrovsky, and Georges Poulet, Sollers has helped shape current French criticism into a stimulating, creative form of literary expression.

Philippe Sollers was just past twenty-one when his first novel, *Une curieuse solitude* (A Strange Solitude), earned him considerable renown as a precocious writer in a classic vein with keen psychological insight and a fine sense of poetry. But with *The Park* (which won the coveted Prix Médicis in 1961) and his more recent novels *Drame* (Drama) in 1965 and *Nombres* (Numbers) in 1968, Sollers turned to a much more innovative concept of fiction that has established him as one of the most original novelists in contemporary France.

243

THE PARK BY PHILIPPE SOLLERS

The Park is not easy; it requires of its readers very careful attention to the author's often labyrinthine narrative and a willingness to accept an apparently plotless work. Accordingly, Sollers has failed to reach a broad public, but has been acclaimed by serious commentators on French letters, ranging from the old conservative François Mauriac to today's vanguard.

The principal reward for the patient and willing reader lies in the brilliance of style, beautifully preserved in A. M. Sheridan Smith's translation. Not that *The Park* is some kind of exercise in stylistic showmanship. It is rather a difficult stylistic convention, which becomes both the fabric and the texture of the work, at once *what* Sollers writes and how he writes it. Three pronouns provide the coordinates to orient us along the way (one cannot really speak of characters): *I* is the narrator, observing from his window and his balcony, writing what he observes and *that* he observes, writing that he is writing, imagining and writing that and what he is imagining. *She* is a woman across the street observed by *I,* perhaps a love remembered, anticipated, or dreamed. *He* is a friend who died in a war, perhaps the woman's lover. *I* and *He* at times fuse into the same person: the person thinking and the person being thought; a child is evoked as a past extension both of *I* and *He.*

There is no denying that this scheme leads to confusion, but the appeal of Sollers's book does not lie in who is who or who did what. The author labeled *The Park* "a novelistic poem," and in fact we can approach it best as poetry—dreamlike, nonrational, following its own imperatives. Viewed from this vantage point, *The Park* is a remarkable feast of subjective imagination, progressing by analogy, by recurrent though ever-shifting themes, and by a lyric *élan* rare among contemporary writers.

The role normally played by the main character is assumed by an orange exercise book in which the narrator writes his observations and his dreams. Or does he only imagine writing? The notebook, which is at once the work to be written and the work we are reading, is at times full of notations in the narrator's handwriting, while at others it appears mostly as white space to be used, a challenge to the artist, much like Mallarmé's obsession with the blank page. Thus, like so many important modern French books, *The Park* is also the novel of the writing of the novel, a self-conscious work in the literal sense of the word. But Sollers becomes excessively involuted in depicting his

THE PARK *BY PHILIPPE SOLLERS*

narrator's relationship to the exercise book and its contents. He abuses the device of parentheses instead of experimenting with typography and layout to denote more clearly the varying levels of consciousness.

The epigraph of the novel is a definition of "park" taken from Rousseau: "A composite of very beautiful and very picturesque spots selected for their appearance from different areas and where everything appears natural except their combination."

What Sollers seeks is precisely that bringing together of striking but disparate elements to create the poetic beauty of strangeness. His quest is more intellectualized and less spontaneous than the surrealist esthetic, but it is akin to the basic nature of the surrealist image as a meeting ground of opposites.

The Park is both more than an experimental novel and less than a totally successful one. For many American readers, however, it will be a revelation of an exciting new French literary personality from whom much can be expected.

From *Saturday Review* (July 25, 1970): 30.

INTRODUCTION TO ROBBE-GRILLET

When he wrote *Project for a Revolution in New York,* New York City was still largely unfamiliar to Alain Robbe-Grillet; this was undoubtedly beneficial for the novel since it is meant to depict a purely mythical city. Since 1972, he has been coming to New York regularly as Visiting Professor in New York University's French Department. For seven weeks, he settles at Washington Square, teaches his courses, and leads a very New York-style life in a city that has become very familiar to him and where he feels completely at ease.

The plan to come to NYU took shape in 1971, at the Cerisy colloquium on the New Novel. I wanted to inaugurate a regular rotation of visiting professors with Robbe-Grillet because I felt certain that he would be an excellent teacher. The dominant role he had played at the Cerisy gathering confirmed me in my feeling: in the incredible frenzy of that colloquium, Robbe-Grillet turned out to be a positive and didactic presence; it was always he who brought the discussion back to its subject when it threatened to get too far afield. He emerged from the ten-day conference as the uncontested theoretician of the New Novel.

I took advantage of a brief truce in the violent battles of the colloquium to invite him to come teach at NYU. At first, he was hesitant; he had never taught before and was worried about doing so, but I succeeded in reassuring him.

Alain Robbe-Grillet arrived in New York by boat in January 1972 to begin his career as professor. Our students were enormously excited at the idea of taking courses with the great man. His courses were fascinating, very carefully prepared, and greatly appreciated by the students. This situation never changed. Each time Robbe-Grillet comes to NYU, his courses are just as rigorously prepared and executed, the term papers submitted to him returned with just as precise and subtle annotations. Robbe-Grillet is a born pedagogue who loves his role as professor—"professor of myself" as he likes to say, takes it seriously, and carries it out with enthusiasm.

CHAPTER TWENTY-THREE

The Man Who Lies: An Interview with Alain Robbe-Grillet

TOM AND HELEN BISHOP: For me, *The Man Who Lies* is a film in the making. A film which creates itself and which the spectator must construct for himself. Do you agree?

ROBBE-GRILLET: Yes. "Must construct for himself. . . ." That depends on what you mean. These are not pieces of a puzzle which the spectator can arrange according to his own taste. There is no image which each viewer finds in himself by giving a particular orientation to the different pieces of the puzzle. I don't think so. They are in the order in which they are supposed to be, if you like. That is already an important thing. The form might appear to be a little disjointed in relation to traditional narration. This is something that I have said before and which I say again: This is an open film, a film in which each viewer must enter and find his own way but nevertheless without moving things about. They are in their proper place, and this place is already a path in a labyrinth at the end of which one must find the minotaur. Each one finds his own way but one cannot displace the walls of the labyrinth.

249

THE MAN WHO LIES

B: If everything is in its place, there are still many different approaches. You propose different ways, don't you? One can follow them or not follow them?

R-G: There are different ways but there is a character who himself is already trying to follow them. There is someone who is already trying to tell his own story and who is moving ahead on a particular path, then he runs into a wall, then he gives up, then he explores another path, etc. Just what did you mean by this participation of the spectator you were talking about at the beginning?

B: I meant that, for instance, in your novels, as well as in other important novels of our period, the reader must also work along with the author to reconstruct the meaning of the novel.

R-G: Yes, that's true.

B: For instance, compared to the novels of Balzac or to the films of the 1940s?

R-G: Yes, that's true for novels. It's also true for films. If I was a little bit reticent when you expressed that idea at the beginning it is because there is a contemporary trend toward "participation," whether it be of the spectator or of chance, in which the work, film, novel, or whatever, only appears to be a series of pieces where one can change the order of reading them or the general arrangement of the pieces. For instance, in modern music there are compositions by Yannis Xenakis and other composers where the musicians group things according to dice and decide on the orientation given the performance of the piece through the numbers given by the dice. The same is true for literature. There was the book of a minor writer of the "New Novel" group whose name is Saporta in which the pages were not numbered and where each reader had to put the pages in the order which he felt to be best. Michel Butor had a similar idea when he wrote his "Faust" libretto in collaboration with Henri Pousseur. The performance is dictated by the reactions of the public.

B: In other words, then, this is not what you were trying to do at all?

R-G: No. In fact I discussed this very subject a few months ago with the Hamburg Opera. The director of the Hamburg Opera brought together three people whom he wanted to have work together and who were perfectly well disposed in principle to collaborate. These three people were the designer Nicolas Schoeffer, the creator of cybernetic sculptures, mobiles, and so on; the composer Pierre Henry; and the novelist-librettist was myself. At the very start of our discussions, we hit on a snag which concerned a very important point, as far as I was concerned. Schoeffer wanted to have the public intervene in the development of the opera—of the work—and I was completely opposed because for me the work is open to the spectator. He must participate in it, must recreate it himself, but recreate it as it is. In other words, not to upset the order of the pages of the book, not to change the orientation of the story line in the opera, and so on. If I stress this point it is because there are now two opposing schools, the one which wants chance or the public to intervene—which are really the same thing—and the other which allows the author full liberty to dispose of the orientation of his works more or less in the classical sense.

B: Would you call that the difference between structured and non-structured works?

R-G: Yes, that is exactly it. As a matter of fact, the result of these works left to chance or to the decisions of the public is often an absence of structure. Whereas, on the contrary, in a film like *The Man Who Lies,* as well as in the book *La Maison de Rendez-vous,* a novel I wrote more or less at the same time, all the parts are carefully arranged to interact exactly the way they are exposed.

B: After that, it is up to the spectator to find the meaning; in other words, you do not impose any meaning.

R-G: Meaning? I'm not sure that's the word. I'm not sure there is one. I don't know if the spectator should find one.

B: In any case, you do not impose any meaning yourself?

R-G: No. There is someone who speaks, there is someone who is trying to speak. In *The Man Who Lies,* that someone is Don Juan, the Don Giovanni of the eighteenth century, who was the first man to have chosen his own word against the word of God. Before Don Juan, God had been the guarantor of truth. Man, in order to be truthful, had to conform to the word of God. Don Juan is the man who affirms that his own word is truth and that there is no other truth than his own word and, even more, that there is no God. From this point of view, *The Man Who Lies* is almost a continuous parody of a certain number of Don Juan myths right down to the commander's handshake, the commander who is the Doctor Muller who appears at the end of the picture. Trintignant crumbling under his handshake is exactly like Don Giovanni when the statue of the Commendatore shakes his hand. From this point of view, the title *The Man Who Lies* is somewhat ironic since, after all, he cannot lie because there is no truth. As there is no God, there is no truth and as there is no truth exterior to Man. Man creates his own truth through his word and that is what my protagonist is all about. He is a man who needs to be believed. If people believe him, he will exist, but he is not at all searching for some truth outside of himself which might have escaped him. He is a man who speaks, a man who fabulates. From the very beginning of the film he appears in an atmosphere which is as unrealistic as possible. He is neatly dressed in a suit and tie in the midst of a forest completely surrounded by the German Army in tattered uniforms. He thinks he is persecuted by these people who really don't seem to be running after him. They seem to be running in the forest after something and he himself seems pursued by something. And at that particular moment he tries to speak. He tries to speak; he tries to prove that he exists. He tries to say who he is and he makes a point of affirming his name. "My name is Boris Varisa," as if he were hanging on desperately to this name until that moment where, ironically, he leans on the gravestone on which the name Boris Varisa is written, as if he were already dead in fact. And of course the three women he finds in this chateau are also taken from the Don Juan legend. He must seduce them, but the seduction is also accomplished with words. This is really the problem of the modern novelist, of the modern filmmaker as opposed to the nineteenth-century novelist whose fiction could fall back on fact. Balzac could always claim that what he said was true. All you have to do is look. That's the way it is in the world. Go look at the printers and you will see that the printers I describe are true to life. They are just like the ones you meet in the street. And when Balzac described journalists or bankers or more or less shady hotel keepers it was always in keeping with the reality he had studied or claimed to have studied objectively. The modern novelist is someone who affirms that there is nothing other than what he says. He is precisely in the position of Don Juan and in the position of Trintignant in this film, a position which in the final analysis—and this brings us back to what you were saying before—is also that of the spectator. The spectator who knows that there is no truth outside of himself and that consequently it is he himself who must invent the film he is watching since this film is nothing without him. It is a film which seems to represent a reality exterior to himself but which is actually nothing other than himself, the spectator.

B: Yes. And in that sense, then, the film is like *La Maison de Rendez-vous* which, as you were saying, dates from the same period. I feel that *La Maison de Rendez-vous* is one of the most important works in your own development. There would seem to be a parallel that could be made between the novel which creates itself through the words of the narrator or narrators who attempt to say, to speak, in *La Maison de Rendez-vous,* and the narrator of the film or rather the protagonist of the film, who is also trying, in different ways, to find his own truth to say what he is.

R-G: That's right, yet a difference which is immediately evident is that the central character of *The Man Who Lies,* that is, Trintignant, has a much higher degree of complexity than the narrators of *La Maison de Rendez-vous.* Narration is much more diffuse in *La Maison de Rendez-vous.* Here, however, there is this character who speaks and who comes to grips only with ghosts. They are ghosts which he creates himself. First of all there is his own double who strangely enough has the face of young Kafka, this character whom he calls Jean and who in fact is himself. There is this particular kind of ambiguity which we find in all tales of the resistance; ambiguity of traitor and hero. He is either a traitor or a hero and the other one is what remains that is the hero or the traitor. But they are more or less the same character and, besides, both have the same voice. In the French version of the film, they are dubbed by the same voice and I hope that the same procedure will be followed in foreign versions. In short, it is like a ghost of himself that pursues him constantly.

B: Which allows you at the end of the film, to underline this identity?

R-G: Yes.

THE MAN WHO LIES

B: It seemed to me that at the end the two identities tended to merge.

R-G: Yes. There is even an overlapping of the two faces and the character played by Trintignant sees himself again pursued by his double and he goes back into the forest where he will again be pursued by the same soldiers and so on; but it is really his double that pursues him and he is himself in pursuit of his double as if he were desperately trying to stick two halves together.

B: What is the function of the other characters?

R-G: The three women are themselves only ghosts which he creates. And the characters that he finds in the café or at the inn are already telling the story. They are also like ghosts. He is very much alone, lost in a labyrinth, in a world of ghosts to which he tries to give a degree of reality because, through his own words, he will create a reality for himself and at the same time for the world. In a certain manner of speaking, the film is his failure since he doesn't manage to do it but at the same time it is a moment of victory, but a victory which always ends in defeat. At the beginning he speaks rather intelligibly, relating almost believable things, but without any conviction. It is a bit weak and then, little by little, as the film develops, what he relates becomes increasingly mad, increasingly hysterical and yet at the same time, he says it with more conviction and with a kind of passion as if it were really becoming true. There is an obvious contradiction here which the spectator feels in the form of a disappointment each time a sequence begins, every time a story takes shape. It is cut sharply by Trintignant, by a splendid movement of his hands.

B: You know, it is strange. You have spoken about your main character in terms of Trintignant, that is, you don't speak about him in terms of Boris but in terms of Trintignant. Is it inconceivable for you to think of the character without referring to the actor who plays him?

R-G: The film was written for Trintignant. I had worked with Trintignant in *Trans-Europe Express,* and I felt like making a film for him, and this film was written entirely for him and almost with him, and at one point when I was having financial problems, Trintignant suddenly became a famous actor and his fee had multiplied by ten. The producer of the film felt that his price had become excessive for this kind

THE MAN WHO LIES

of experimental film and I thought for a while that Trintignant's agent was not going to come to an agreement with my producer. I think that I would have given up on this film and not made it because Trintignant really is the central character.

B: The women in the film don't seem to believe his story either. When a seduction scene begins we believe in it, we expect it, we almost hope for it, but the women don't seem to be involved or believe in it themselves.

R-G: No. They can't believe in it because what he says is incoherent. He claims that he knew Jean very well, this man who was the husband of one of the women and the brother of the other and yet he recognizes no one in the house. All these people who have been there for a long time. He doesn't recognize the old caretaker; he does not recognize the father himself. He asks who he is. He doesn't know the place. It is quite obvious that he has never been there before.

B: Yet something struck me as strange. There was a moment of ambiguity in his relationship to the women, for the women themselves didn't really seem to believe in it. In view of the complicity that exists among the three women, I wondered whether there was not a rejection of the male as well as a rejection of the character himself.

R-G: Yes, you are right, but that introduces a completely different point of view about the film. This story is the story of a man who isn't there. There is someone who has gone and there are three women who live together in a more or less narcissistic or even lesbian manner. It is as if the three of them loved one another through the man who isn't there. With the man gone, they organized their world so well without a man (since there were only old men around) that they actually had an instinctive reaction to exclude him at the moment that he reappears. If you want to consider the plot from a realistic point of view, you can wonder what would happen at the end of the film between the women and the man who came back, since all they can do is to reject him and to continue their game of blind man's bluff; at the same time we have trouble imagining that this man—who was present everywhere through his portraits and his photographs in every room of the chateau could now live there like a real character. These three women can only live with ghosts because they are ghosts themselves.

THE MAN WHO LIES

B: Aren't we now discussing literary allusions other than Don Juan?

R-G: Yes, particularly to Boris Godunov. My main character is called Boris. Boris Godunov was the usurper of a czar who reigned after having assassinated a child that should have been the real czar and he was pursued, psychologically, by the ghost of the czarevitch he had killed and who finally gets the upper hand. Because someone else assumes the role of the czarevitch and succeeds in dethroning him and in taking his place.

B: Did you deliberately look for this dimension and this possible identification of Boris Varisa with Boris Godunov?

R-G: He is clearly a part of it. There is especially an important hallucination scene which is almost copied from Pushkin's scene. It doesn't have to be identifiable in an absolute manner. I think of it rather as an ironic illusion because, naturally, the story of Boris Godunov is quite different since in Pushkin's mind there was a truth. He either was a murderer or he was not, whereas here that isn't the case. He invented the notion that he was the murderer.

B: Have you been particularly fascinated by the character of Boris Godunov?

R-G: Let's say I have been fascinated by the characters of mad kings. Of course there is Boris Godunov but there is also Macbeth. There is Pirandello's Henry IV and there is a whole tradition in the theater of the mad king which is very important now because someone who is mad is someone who does not know the same truth as other people. Someone who is king is a man who by that very fact imposes his truth on other people. The mad king is a character who is very disturbing in a metaphysical way because what he says is true since he is the king and what he says is false since he is mad. There is another famous one, Eric XIV of Strindberg. And all these characters made a great impression on me in my readings. *The Man Who Lies* is full of allusions to mad kings. This king, by the way, Czar Boris, is similar to the one we find in *La Maison de Rendez-vous*. The person who knocks with his cane on the floor above. He is Czar Boris, Boris Godunov. By the way, the allusions to *La Maison to Rendez-vous* are quite numerous in *The Man Who Lies*. And there is Jean, who is naturally an allusion to *The Voyeur*.

B: I found that very surprising.

R-G: And then there are also all the dead heroes whose names are written on the gravestones. They are all the heroes of my novels. There is Matthias, the hero of *The Voyeur*. There is Manneret, the hero of *La Maison de Rendez-vous*, as if this village were entirely inhabited by the characters of my novels.

B: Since you mentioned Pirandello's *Henry IV*, I would like to ask you something which is of particular interest to me. It seems to me that there is a sort of Pirandellian game of reality and truth and of multiple personality in some of your works such as *La Maison de Rendez-vous*, *Trans-Europe Express*, and *The Man Who Lies*. Do you think that you were influenced by Pirandello?

R-G: Yes, I certainly have been but I do think that there is a rather important difference; namely, that the Pirandellian games of truth are psychological games. They are more or less variations on the theme of "right you are if you think you are." That's what Pirandello is all about. Every person has a different view of the situation, everyone lives the same story in a different manner and I think that it takes place in the world whose dimensions are the same as those of my works. Certain works of Pirandello have, in fact, turned out to be very important for me. *Six Characters in Search of an Author*, for instance. There is a direct quotation of Pirandello in *The Man Who Lies*. It is a very difficult quotation to identify for the spectator. When Trintignant wakes up in the maid's room after having spent a fitful night with her and then the father arrives with the caretaker to throw him out, there is something very special about the scene. I don't know if you noticed it but one can constantly hear noises which are not the noises of the scene itself and if you listen carefully you notice that they are the noises of a theater. Moreover, you eventually hear the applause.

B: Yes, you had already used that technique in *La Maison de Rendez-vous*, where applause from the audience in a theater comments on the action going on elsewhere.

R-G: Yes, but this time I really superimposed on the scene, as background sound, a recording made in a real theater and the play that was being performed in this theater—it was the Théâtre de France—was a play by Pirandello. During the whole scene in *The Man Who*

Lies, you hear the reactions of the spectators, you hear the laughter, you hear the noises of the seats, the murmurs of the theater crowd at the Pirandello play, in other words, all the noises at the same time.

B: Let's get back to the three women. Several times during the course of the film these three women play blind man's bluff. Does this represent something akin to what Bruce Morissette calls "an objective correlative," a way of guiding the spectator who may be a little bit lost himself?

R-G: Yes, one might say that but I really did it more for esthetic reasons. I felt like seeing girls blindfolded for esthetic reasons. By the way, I used this technique again in the film I am finishing right now. The theme of the blindfold, of the covered eyes, runs right through this film. One can certainly see an objective correlative but yet it might seem to be overly metaphoric.

B: What role does eroticism have for you in the cinema?

R-G: It plays a very important role for me but less in the more recent films. *Trans-Europe Express* is the only one that enjoyed a long career as an erotic picture. That's probably the reason for its success. Not for me, of course.

B: It is a beautiful film on a very different level.

R-G: Perhaps, but I think it did well because of that. People reacted well to the nude girls in chains. I must say that, for me, eroticism in the cinema is a very important matter. Speaking of myself as a spectator I am very, very often, let's say more than half the time, motivated by erotic reasons when I go to see a film. Perhaps because I am interested in a particular actress or perhaps in some particular type of scene and if I take a very close look at my contacts with the cinema I must acknowledge the truth of what Freud proclaimed a long time ago, namely that contact with a film is under all circumstances an erotic contact. That contact with art in general is more or less always probably an erotic contact but that this is particularly clear in the case of the art of the film, that there is an erotic type of contact with this big screen in front of which we are lost in the crowd of spectators but where we are, in fact, alone. Any close-up of a face on the screen even without any sexual allusion is always erotic and I think that one must not neglect this. That one must see it, show it, say it, and to take

THE MAN WHO LIES

it into consideration as one of the most significant elements of the cinema.

B: I would like to go on with this matter of eroticism in films. There is a subjectivity to the nature of fantasies in your films and I wonder whether it is while writing, a scenario that you deliberately or unconsciously, perhaps, find a vehicle for your particular fantasies.

R-G: Well, you might even ask that question in a more chronological way. Why did I begin to write and why did I begin to make films? I was an agricultural engineer. I had a profession which I found fascinating, which provided me with status and money and suddenly I began to write strange things that no one was interested in at the time. A psychoanalyst or a psychiatrist might be interested in that transformation. There is something in that which is not quite right and in fact I have often wondered whether there is not something in this transformation of an engineer into a writer which might have something to do with the kind of revelation of his sexual peculiarities, to put it in general and delicate terms. This peculiarity which on the one hand sets him apart and on the other hand really moved him to affirm himself with other people in terms of the one who really knows what the truth is. I am convinced that my work as a writer and as a maker of film is very closely linked to my erotic life.

B: Your novels seem to bear that out as much as your films.

R-G: I frankly think this is true for any creative person and when the critics carry on about an erotic invasion in modern art and all that, then that is just bullshit because that is what people write for, that is what people have always written for. When Flaubert began to write it was certainly for erotic reasons. Well, nowadays, people simply say it more openly. They are more aware of it. If anyone had told Lewis Carroll that he wrote for erotic reasons he would have been very upset and very indignant and yet today it is perfectly clear to everyone. If our contemporary period has been so invaded, as people like to say, by this eroticism, it is simply that now artists have realized that there is no longer any reason to camouflage it, that, on the contrary they had to study this eroticism and in all fairness they had to underline it. As far as I am concerned, what is really immoral is to hide behind alibis. For instance, to hide behind a moral alibi even a moralizing alibi, in order to make a film on prostitution or slavery or Nazi sadism. A film which will really seek a public interested not at all in this struggle against the Nazis but in sadism. I think that our era is much more honest in that it does away with these puritanical alibis.

B: Can you tell me about the film that you have just finished? What is it about? What is it called?

R-G: I have just finished shooting, but for me the editing is extremely important and very long and I am still in the midst of it. The film is called *Eden and Afterwards,* and it was shot partly in a studio in Czechoslovakia, on location in Czechoslovakia, and in Tunisia. It is difficult for me to speak about it. I can talk with ease about works once they are finished because I can have a somewhat removed critical point of view about them. Right now I am still in the middle of this one. As far as creating a film while shooting it is concerned, I went further with this one because I refused to write a scenario ahead of time. The producer agreed to let me shoot with a very vague outline for the beginning of the film, for the Czech part. The scenes which were shot then called for other scenes which we shot subsequently, and so on. It was a fascinating experience for me, especially because I had the help of three collaborators who really participated in this film with enthusiasm. The first was the cameraman who shot *The Man Who Lies,* Igor Luther and who, I think, will have a great career as a cameraman. He shot this new film in color whereas *The Man Who Lies* is in black and white. Next, a Tunisian production assistant named Farib Bougdir, who really participated in the process of creation on a day-to-day basis. And for the first time an actress. With Trintignant I'd had a really creative and fascinating collaboration but this had never happened with an actress before. It was Jacques Doniol-Valcroze in *L'Immortelle,* Trintignant in *Trans-Europe Express and The Man Who Lies,* and since this last film has the erotic importance for me that I was talking about a while ago, it was a very new and exciting experience for me to have this creative collaboration with a girl. Her name is Catherine Jourdan and she is an actress you'll hear a good deal more about in the future because she really participated in the film with an intensity that can be called creative and which was a marvelous thing for me.

B: In a film shot without a rigid scenario, does real life tend to play a greater role?

R-G: Let me answer you indirectly by telling you an anecdote that concerns *The Man Who Lies,* and which has to do with the truth of lies. It is a story that interested me a great deal. There were things invented and even deliberately invented to be laughable which became true during and after the film. The film was shot at a time when all scenarios had to be submitted to the Central Committee of the Communist Party of Slovakia. This is again the procedure now, but during the spring of Prague's liberalism, scenarios were free. However, my film was shot before this period of liberalism, and scenarios still had to be submitted to the Central Committee and despite the fact that the Communist Party of Slovakia was full of good will towards me, there were certain details which were considered to be shocking from the point of view of historical accuracy. The first was that there are no longer any Czech aristocratic families who keep domestics and then the Central Committee felt that no son of an aristocrat in a Communist state ever participated in the liberation of his country. That was impossible. And often there were some very precise details. At one point one sees a German officer dressed in a Wehrmacht uniform who reads a newspaper and this newspaper is *Pravda.* Not the Russian *Pravda* in Cyrillic but *Pravda* in Roman letters the organ of the Communist Party of Slovakia, in other words, a Czech newspaper and not a Russian one. The party inspector pointed out to me that *Pravda* did not appear during the occupation—the German occupation—and therefore no German officer could read it. I said, "Okay, let's have him read *Le Monde* if you prefer," but finally I let it stand because I found it extremely amusing that this minor detail was so ambiguous since it was obviously a lie. This German officer can only be a lie since he is reading a newspaper which was not in existence during the war and yet at the same time the word *Pravda* means "truth" in Slovak and in other Slavic languages, thus it is the word truth which is the proof of the lie. That is already quite amusing. The film opened in Bratislava in one of the large movie houses of the city on the very day Soviet troops and their "allies" entered the city and on the poster of *The Man Who Lies*—the title, of course, written in Czech—they had added the name Brezhnev. Brezhnev, "the man who lies," and all the scenes of occupation brought on roars of approval from the many students who went to see the film and, in particular, the scene of the German officer reading *Pravda* because there were East German officers in the city wearing the same uniform, reading *Pravda.* Thus this lie had become

THE MAN WHO LIES

the truth. As to the chateau in which we did the shooting, it is a real chateau in which there was a real baroness who had remained there with a servant who had not left her.

B: I suppose, though, that the baroness and her servant were less beautiful than their counterparts in the film.

R-G: The baroness was about seventy-five years old and her servant was also an old woman and they remained on in this completely dilapidated chateau. When I returned to France and the film was shown, I met a Hungarian nobleman who lives in Paris and who told me that he had been raised in this chateau. He asked me whether I knew the old baroness and I said that I had seen her every day during the shooting and he asked me whether I knew why she was there. I said no, I didn't know. Because it seems that all the Hungarian aristocrats had left Slovakia long ago. They all had palaces in Vienna or things like that and the only one that was left was that old baroness. What was she doing there?

B: She was waiting for her son?

R-G: She was waiting for her brother who had disappeared in 1917 on the Russian front. She has been waiting for him ever since because she is sure that he will come back. And every time someone comes into that chateau where only ghosts enter she thinks that it is her brother coming back.

B: One last question. It seems to me that for some time now you have been attracted more and more by the notion of comic strips. Do you think this is true?

R-G: Yes. You are right to say that I have been attracted by the notion and not by the comic strips themselves because, as a matter of fact, I almost always have been very disappointed by the comic strips I have come across. Comic strips for children are always very disappointing and comic strips supposedly for adults which are more or less erotic are interesting in principle but in practice turn out to be very disappointing. But it is true that the notion of comic strips does interest me. Of course there are some exceptions. There is one that I saw recently which is called *Valentina,* which you must know. There are a lot of things in it which I find fascinating—the mixture of dream and real-

THE MAN WHO LIES

ity—and I have a project for doing a comic strip one day together with a cartoonist.

B: Is it the two-dimensional element of comic strips which attracts you?

R-G: Yes. It certainly is. After all, a comic strip makes no pretense at any depth. It is very interesting from that point of view.

From *Film Festival* (1970): 41–44, 87–89. The interview was made and is signed by "Tom and Helen Bishop." In the text above, the questions are indicated by "B" without specifiying which of the two interviewers was speaking.

CHAPTER TWENTY-FOUR

Robbe-Grillet's Geography

An analysis of numerous texts of Robbe-Grillet brings out a particular and evolving mode of reference to real and imaginary geographic indicators—indicators that are a function of the respective text but that, at the same time, reflect and explain each of these texts. I propose to review certain novels and films according to their geography, that is, to examine the role played within each work by the *place* where the action takes place and to analyze the specific way of using and describing the geographic material.

Readings using this approach show clearly that geography plays a primordial role in Robbe-Grillet and how much geographic references change throughout his literary production. The novels of the 1950s reveal a precise usage of rather specific geographic places. Of course this corresponds to the period of Robbe-Grillet's so-called objective, carefully descriptive and exact writing. As of 1960, that is, in all his films and in *La Maison de Rendez-vous* and *Project for a Revolution in New York,* the geographic referent becomes ever more vague even while the texts point generally to real places, like New York, Hong Kong, Istanbul, Central Europe. At the same time, we know to what degree his novel and film narration becomes deconcretized and is cast more and more into doubt.

264

In his two styles (if one is willing to accept the general notion of two Robbe-Grillet styles, with the second beginning more or less at the time of *In the Labyrinth*) the central function of geography seems evident. The place is perfectly integrated into the work's structure; it does not dominate it, but neither is it arbitrary nor merely added. By that I mean that if, as Jacques Leenhardt has noted,[1] *Jealousy,* for instance, is not a novel of African colonialism—which would imply a novel which gives details of political, sociological, psychological or other aspects of life in a European colony in Africa—it is nevertheless a book in which the colonial framework, the human relationships involved in African colonies, as well as the facts of climate and vegetation (down to the famous banana grove with its carefully aligned banana trees) are not simply "added on," are not gratuitously inserted into the text, but rather are inextricably linked to the narration and form an integral part of the texture of *Jealousy.* Robbe-Grillet could not, I suggest, have chosen to situate his text, say, in Wales. Though not a colonial novel, *Jealousy* cannot do without the colonies.

Similarly, as we shall see, *The Voyeur* requires by its very nature that the action of the novel take place on an island sufficiently far from the mainland to have its own little isolated world, sheltered from what one might term "normal" concerns. And *Project* is obviously not a text "about" New York but it *is* a text which needs New York, or rather, needs a mythological New York which represents one of the summits of popular imagination of our day.

In each case, the geography supports the narration, clarifies it, and in turn is clarified by it, so much so that both geography and narration are necessarily part of the same system.

To start at the beginning, *The Erasers* confronts the reader with a problem of deciphering, forcing him to seek a grid which might enable him to break through the narrative, to decipher the mystery-beyond-the-mystery. The uninitiated reader thus finds himself in front of what seems at first to be a detective story with all the trappings of that well-known genre: a murder, a detective, an enigma, and so on. Yet the reader quickly understands that what is at stake is something other than a crime thriller, that there are personality mix-ups, that the identity of the victim and of the detective seem to coincide, that the same crime has taken place twice, and so on.

The quest for a grid incites the reader quite naturally to pay attention to the geographic facts of the novel, to transpose the situation of Wallas wandering in a city, and to wander like him, trying to find points of reference which might help him get his bearings.

Thus, initially, the reader realizes that he finds himself in an indeterminate city which might be Flemish given its drabness and its canals. He then becomes aware of the city's circularity, its ring road and its veritable maze of main roads. These two aspects of *The Erasers* underline and reveal the circularity of the work itself (the same circularity which was to be the principal direction of movement of Robbe-Grillet's novels and films, as well as of the New Novel in general and the New Theater) as well as the labyrinthine nature of Wallas's quest (the labyrinth being the sign of the interior structure of all Robbe-Grillet's work). Thus, the linearity of the novel yields to a labyrinthine structure within a narrative circularity.

Perhaps the reader does not wish to take notice of the fact that the first place mentioned is the "rue des Arpenteurs" (Street of the Surveyors) or perhaps he is not ready immediately to evoke Kafka and to call to mind the theme of a journey. But there will be other geographic elements within the novel that he will be obliged to confront, whether he wants to or not.

Some time ago, Bruce Morrissette called attention to the Œdipal content of *The Erasers* when he proposed a reading which casts Wallas as Œdipus in the archetypal role of the man who kills his father and seeks his own truth. Morrissette pointed to the Sophocles quotation which the novel bears in epigraph and showed that the very structure of the novel is Sophoclean, that is, the structure of tragedy with five chapters corresponding to the five acts of classical tragedy, preceded by a prologue and followed by an epilogue.

Even the most skeptical reader cannot help recognizing the significance of the "rue de Corinthe" in *The Erasers* since it is precisely on the road to Corinth that Œdipus killed Laius without knowing it. Eventually, we associate metaphorically the unnamed city of *The Erasers* with ancient Thebes (the novel contains the description of a drawing of Thebes in the window of the stationery store) and we link the Œdipal content and the labyrinthine structures to the story of Œdipus in general. Thus the full resonances of *The Erasers* become apparent only through the grid of the geographic indices which enable us to comprehend the texture of the novel in its full complexity.

In *The Voyeur,* Robbe-Grillet's invented geography is even more indispensable to the narrative. Not only does the structure of the novel reflect the island and its location, but Mathias's reactions are determined to a significant degree by the setting. For the plot to function properly, the action must take place in an isolated place—even a very isolated place—where people do not have the same preoccupations as elsewhere and where one really feels cut off from the rest of the world. It is only within this framework that one can understand Mathias's disorientation (even if the island is his birthplace), his real delirium as to the possibility of selling a very considerable number of watches, the lack of concern of the islanders with respect to Jacqueline's death, and the circumstances which prevent Mathias from fleeing after the crime and which force him to spend four additional days on the island during which he must cover his tracks. For these and many other reasons, an island is the ideal setting for *The Voyeur.* Undoubtedly, Robbe-Grillet could have set the novel elsewhere, for instance a secluded village in the Alps in winter, cut off from the world by an avalanche; but having to resort to the contingency of such a solution would probably have seemed ridiculous and would have ill served the need at all times to retain a strict sense of verisimilitude to the objective world. An island is much better suited and the "islandness" of the island becomes an integral part of *The Voyeur*'s structure, which conforms, generally speaking, with the following scheme: mainland ⟶ sea crossing ⟶ island ⟶ sea crossing ⟶ mainland (this final stage being announced but not initiated by the text).

On the island, the geography of the place—and especially the fact of being on an island—determine Mathias's behavior: the inhabitants (very few in number—which is important—on this island far from the mainland) are concentrated in the village where the boat docks and quickly diminish, limited to the fewer and fewer houses around the village and finally disappear completely in the wild spaces of moors and rocks which lend themselves to the crime; the shape of the island in the form of an eight, an eight surrounded by water, a shape which thus reflects itself and gives full strength to the centrifugal forces that pull the focal point to the center of the island, that spot where the two concentric circles making up the eight meet, and which corresponds to the famous hole or blank where the narrative leaves Mathias at the end of the first half and picks him up once more at the start of the second half. Only an island can form this eight; in this way, by situating *The Voyeur* on an island, Robbe-Grillet succeeds in including the geography of the novel in the series of eights (eyes, eyeglasses, pieces of rope, bicycle wheels, movie poster) which are the constant correlatives of this fiction.

The choice of an island is therefore fundamental and allows for a fusion of the narrative with the place implied by it. The center of the island, the hole, organizes the book; we move from the initial anticipation of violence to the repression of its guilty memory, and then to ever more insistent images of violence which give way, following the relief which we do not share, to an obliteration of these same images until memory forces itself on Mathias's consciousness and thus on the narrative. The nature of the island's terrain is also a factor; it allows Mathias to muse with anticipation about the pine trees, the dry shrubs which begin to flame, and Jacqueline/Violette's dress which is set on fire.

At the end of the novel, when Mathias stops wandering around the island while waiting for the ferry, he finally boards the boat having escaped all possible prosecution. He becomes calm once more thanks to the movement of the water which gently rocks the boat and the traveler. The island episode ended, Mathias will resume his mainland habits—habits which we don't know but which may well be different from his bizarre ones during the island interlude.

In *In the Labyrinth,* geography plays a similar role; once again, it is through the precision of the setting that the author spreads doubt and ambiguity. This is what enabled Gérard Genette to refer to "the realistic point of honor of an author who is not a realist but who cannot resign himself to not being one."[2] But there is no basic contradiction in this statement. Indeed, until *In the Labyrinth,* Robbe-Grillet's universe is deliberately divided: the precise realism of descriptions based on precise geographic indications underlines and supports the profound lack of precision of the narration. The contrast between the two can be disconcerting, but it puts into sharp relief the disturbed and vague presence of Wallas, of the husband in *Jealousy,* of Mathias, of the soldier. As to the latter, even if the labyrinthine city "steps out" of the engraving of the battle, it becomes a concrete reality within which the soldier's wanderings stand out with particular clarity.

Renato Barilli pointed out that *In the Labyrinth* was a turning point:

ROBBE-GRILLET'S GEOGRAPHY

The real change begins with *In the Labyrinth*—a two-sided novel suspended between "yesterday" and "today," the last of the narratives conceived from a single vantage point that exists before the narration and conditions it, and the first of the narratives wherein every vantage point becomes a function of the text, capable of being displaced indiscriminately from one character to another.[3]

It is not only the vantage point which changes but the very universe from which this new mobile vantage point operates.

With *Last Year at Marienbad,* the system has changed. Henceforth, the geographic framework will be a reflection of the ambiguous imprecision of the narration rather than its striking contrast. The conflict of contradictory realities is directly helped by a framework which, despite its apparently very realistic surface, is nevertheless the product of fantasy and dream. This "history of a persuasion" takes place in a closed, abstract, fictional, dreamlike, icy universe, which like so many others in the works of Robbe-Grillet, is placed under the sign of the labyrinth. The unreal decor where nothing is clear, where one seems to be in the throes of some spell, is perfectly suited to this narrative which is composed of an alternation of images, memories, false memories, desires, anticipation. The world of *Last Year at Marienbad* is at once distinct and imaginary: drawing rooms, corridors, sharply defined but nonexistent garden paths—that world of Central European spas of days gone by. Like Marienbad which no longer exists, like that "last year" which does not exist and perhaps never existed, the palace and its gardens also do not exist beyond the images projected on the screen.

With *L'Immortelle,* we are again and even more firmly in a mythological, chimerical world. "The Orient seen from Paris, a picture postcard Orient . . . a whole mythological folklore which plays a great role in the imagination of Western society, but which has nothing to do with the Istanbul of the Turks," says Robbe-Grillet. "It is a perfectly imaginary Istanbul, reduced to surfaces, exotic and sexual stereotypes."[4] The disintegration and mythification of realistic geography is now far advanced, almost complete. The Istanbul of *L'Immortelle* prefigures Hong Kong and New York, the Central Europe of *The Man Who Lies,* and the Western Europe and Africa of *Eden and Afterwards.*

At the beginning of *La Maison de Rendez-vous,* Robbe-Grillet clearly states his intention of presenting a geographic place which is completely true while being perfectly false. That is the function of the double Author's note:

> This novel cannot, in any way, be considered as a document about life in the British Territory of Hong Kong. Any resemblance to the latter in setting or situations is merely the effect of chance, objective or not.
>
> Should any reader familiar with Oriental ports suppose that the places described below are not congruent with reality, the author, who has spent most of his life there, suggests that he return for another, closer look: things change fast in such climes.[5]

Thus, right from the outset, we find ourselves in a comic strip Hong Kong that incarnates all the myths that the West assigns to that Chinese and international city: drug traffic, espionage, luxurious brothels, beautiful Eurasian girls, shameful adventures, torture, and so on. "Everyone knows Hong Kong,"[6] says the narrator, and Robbe-Grillet explained that his novel, taking its impetus from this statement, is based on the fact that everyone knows Hong Kong, that it is a well-known and accepted concept which can function as a fixed point of reference. The falseness of this Hong Kong overruns the narration and determines it because here as elsewhere, geography is merely the reflection of the deeper preoccupations of the text. Thus, the comic strip, pop-art aspect of Hong Kong and its inhabitants is the paradigm of the two-dimensional quality of the narrative itself which is at times presented to us like a succession of comic strip panels. This flat and jagged movement gives the narration its particular texture; it is in the absence of physical and textual depth, in the absence of preexisting meaning, that we follow the itinerary of the literary production. This false and theatrical Hong Kong which mirrors the falsity and the theatricality of the interior of the Blue Villa and its performances, leads to ambiguity everywhere and leads the reader to become uncertain with respect to the narrative and the narration. For example: "Doubtless this scene has taken place another evening; or else if it is today, it occurs in any case a little earlier, before Johnson's departure. It is in fact his tall dark silhouette Lady Ava indicates with her eyes, when she adds: 'Now you'll go dance with him one more time.' "[7] And almost immediately afterwards: "Suddenly the setting changes."[8]

The text designates writing in the process of being written, the writer writing, selecting solutions from among the choices available to him. The geography of *La Maison de Rendez-vous*—that is this artificial and mythological Hong Kong—serves as the ideal setting for the contradictory articulations of the narration. The text questions itself from beginning to end within a landscape that is equally subject to questioning because of its unreality, its lack of relief. In this way, the narration becomes hypothetical, thanks to sentences such as: "The scene which then takes place lacks clarity" or again, even more hesitating with the use of the conditional tense of narration: "and almost immediately, she would come back down clutching to her breast a thick, bulging, brown paper envelope which seems to have been stuffed with sand. But what would have become of the dog this time?" [9]

In this comic-book Hong Kong, all is play, all is unreal, at least in part, including the very narrative that designates this unreality. Everything vanishes; what had been affirmed disappears. Even Lady Ava finally admits that she had never been in China, that the Blue Villa is merely a story which had been told to her. Through the false representation of a city elevated to the level of myth, we are at the center of the fictionality of fiction in the midst of the generation of images which transform themselves, link up to one another and come back to themselves thanks to a series of generators (receptions, theatrical performances, a ring, a Chinese illustrated magazine, etc.) which form a part of this city, of this mythic geography.

A similar phenomenon of comic-strip geography can be seen in *Trans-Europe Express* and in *The Man Who Lies*. In both, we are plunged into a two-dimensional, parodic setting of drug trafficking in the first and of resistance to the Germans in World War II in the second. This comic-strip geography serves as background to contradictory actions, comparable to the attempt to reproduce the hesitations of the creative process in *La Maison de Rendez-vous*. But this time it is film which is used, in its own way, to come back to the problems of narration, of the narrative which does not manage to speak itself.

In *Trans-Europe Express,* the elements of mythological geography are, first of all the train—the setting par excellence since Hitchcock for stories of intrigue and espionage and in our day, for stories of drugs—and the city of Antwerp, whose shady aspects of mystery, prostitution, and crooks is stressed by Robbe-Grillet. The film shows us a real train, the real North railway station in Paris, and the real streets of the Flemish city in order to frame the real Alain and Catherine Robbe-Grillet, the actor Jean-Louis Trintignant, and the film's producer, thus giving them an initial dimension of reality which then dissolves in a series of ambiguities that contest the data of the film. Antwerp becomes a double city, with a "right" side and a "wrong" one.

"Nothing is more fantastic . . . than precision," wrote Robbe-Grillet in his essay "From Realism to Reality." [10] That is precisely the function of the geographical setting in *Trans-Europe Express* and *The Man Who Lies*. Starting from this real train, the fantasies of the story begin to detach themselves and the story becomes all the more hallucinating since it has its starting point in precision. Robbe-Grillet uses real Slovak streets and villages and the Tatra mountains to introduce us to a stereotypical Central Europe which we don't even have to know in order to "recognize." This real-yet-imaginary Czechoslovakia becomes the springboard for Boris's inventions, for his fantasizing about chases, resistance, and heroism. The game of blind man's bluff played by the three young women serves as an objective correlative of the trial and error meanderings of the narrative (as well as the sign of the erotic relationships among the characters). Just as Boris's narration does not correspond to the images shown, the precision of the setting does not match the lack of precision of the narrative.

No work of Robbe-Grillet uses its geography with more imagination and a more precise purpose than *Project for a Revolution in New York*. As in *La Maison de Rendez-vous*, it is again in a fake city—a fake New York, a New York of myths and comic strip images—that unfolds this plot, nonlinear in movement, circular in external and labyrinthine in internal structure. Again, beyond the plot heavily laden with action (deliberately *too* heavily), the real object of scrutiny is fiction itself.

This New York City is completely phony. On the one hand, there is the mythology of New York as the capital of crime and lechery (a mythology dear to the French and spread with delectation by the French press), a metropolis replete with murder, rape, sadistic attacks, where the subway is a world apart, an underground no man's land. On the other hand, this New York is an imposture since it is presented by means of intentionally falsified components, Parisian elements imported to Manhattan and which strike a false note there . . . on purpose: "It never occurred to me to try to find out things about New

York," said Robbe-Grillet at the Cerisy Colloquium in 1971. "Starting with a short and long ago experience of New York, something began to take shape without my having to bother about impossibilities or technical mistakes." [11] Very clearly, Robbe-Grillet's New York subway resembles the Paris métro, with its doors that passengers open with brass handles and its endless corridors bearing dozens of copies of the same poster, side by side. Apartment buildings, with non-New York numberings like "7 *bis*" ("7 A"), are equipped with *minuteries,* that fiendish invention which makes the life of Americans in Paris miserable and which, by its frugal intention, might well be considered anti-American. The key holes in Robbe-Grillet's apartment doors are very convenient for voyeurs but do not exist in the United States, and the apartments themselves invariably feature "French windows." As to the very Parisian alternating sound emitted by the fire engines, this is a particularly amusing imaginary detail for anyone ever terrified by the frequent shrieking of New York firefighter sirens.

Of course, it is perfectly reasonable to have a fake New York serve as the setting for fake revolutions carried out by fake revolutionaries. One could imagine variants of the title: "New York for a Project of Revolution" or "New York for a Revolution of Project." It is against the background of the very idea of the modern metropolis as it exists in the popular imagination of Europeans that we find these masked characters who play at being one another while playing at revolution. It should be noted that if Robbe-Grillet is having a lot of fun, it is not at our expense—he does not make fun of the reader. He accepts us as accomplices, gives us the rules of the game, and invites us to join him in it. One of the most important keys which give us access to the particular movement of the narration can be found in the geography, in the stress of the falsification of New York. Since we are dealing with a stylization of the city that is as two-dimensional as the panels of a comic strip, it is easier for us to accept the flatness of the narrative as well as its constant turning back on itself.

This turning back on itself and this complexity of the narrative are reproduced on the level of the city. Robbe-Grillet presents a falsified, mythological New York and the text designates this imposture:

> One other thing: you mention West Greenwich or the Madison subway station—any American would say 'the West Village' or 'Madison Avenue' "

This time I must say you're the one who's exaggerating! Especially since no one has ever claimed that the narrative was being made by an American. Don't forget that it is always foreigners who prepare the revolution.[12]

Thus, near the end of the novel, the novelist designates his grid and states clearly that it is not about the real New York but about one (like the text itself) by a non-American. New York designates its own fictitiousness; the story does the same, refusing all attempts to signify or to tell a history—for it tells so many and such contradictory ones that none is left with any credibility. The fiction is aware at all times of its own fictitiousness, aware of being nothing other than a narrative element, without any privileged point of view.

If the torturer can say to the girl he is torturing, "Try to invent details that will be exact and meaningful," this injunction mirrors within the particular logic of the text (or rather the *a*logic, as one says amoral) the depiction of a New York that is invented and arranged precisely so as to become in a "meaningful" way the parody of the archetypal great modern city.

Structurally speaking, *Eden and Afterwards* is Robbe-Grillet's most complex film. Conceived of in a series of sequences, *Eden* requires what André Gardies calls a horizontal reading beyond the cyclical reading: "In that way, the particular movement of the film becomes evident: through their cyclical reappearance, the themes give birth to the fiction and structure it, whereas the connotations introduce a horizontal reading. The film is constantly nourished by this double movement." [13]

As in his other films and novels, geography plays an essential role in *Eden and Afterwards*. We start from precise and stylized places: the café, the cinema, the factory, the university, Tunisia. These places serve as generators which produce the sequences of the film; for example, the movement of the image changes from the movie house in which we see Violette, to the film she is looking at in which we find the same Violette in Tunisia: "The passage from an apparently European city to Tunisia designates neither a journey nor a length of time, since it occurs in the course of a film." [14]

The importance of the very strong light in this film which links various sequences has been commented on by others. In this respect, the blue and white painting has a privileged place as the principal

ROBBE-GRILLET'S GEOGRAPHY

generator, leading first to a film about Tunisia shown at the Eden Cinema, and then to Tunisia itself—a Tunisia dominated by geometric forms (like the painting), made up entirely of white and blue of a particularly intense luminosity.

Need one add that all the geographic elements are dreamlike and false, just as in the rest of Robbe-Grillet's geography? Café, cinema, factory, even Tunisia: everything is mythified, everything is invention. For the Café Eden is the perfect place for make believe and for theatrics. What the narrator's voice tells of Marie-Eve's behavior serves as analogy: "She pretends to pretend that she is jealous." And then she adds this little sentence which casts what has just been written to another level, once removed, and reflects the subversion of the narrative: "But no one is fooled." [15]

The stylization of the places, the sharp light, the blue and the white, the lack of relief of geometric surfaces render a real geography more abstract and thus correspond to the abstraction of the fundamental structure of *Eden and Afterwards*. Robbe-Grillet has called this "a mobile creation wherein strong architectures, leaving nothing to chance, would still be undermined from within, always in the act of constructing themselves, of organizing themselves, and of falling apart at the same time, in order to leave the field free for new constructions." [16]

At the 1971 New Novel Colloquium in Cerisy, Robbe-Grillet made a statement which relates precisely to these problems of his geography:

Rightly or wrongly, New York is for us the perfect place where there is nothing natural left, everything there is constantly transformed into myth. Thus for me it was a privileged place. And I called it New York. Since I took a rather long time undoubtedly to liquidate certain conflicts with nature, I completely refused to name anything in my first books. The setting of *The Voyeur* was made up of a mixture of islands off Brittany which I knew (since, after all, it is still from experienced sensations that one fabricates something)—let's say Ouessant, Belle-Ile, etc. But I felt the need to disorient the text from Brittany: the characters in the book pay in crowns and not in French Francs. Following the turning point of *In the Labyrinth,* I began to name Hong Kong and now New York. I knew that henceforth it would no longer be a matter of representation and I therefore could name a real city while producing through my own text a perfectly imaginary one.[17]

We can clearly see then Robbe-Grillet's method with respect to these geographic phenomena: first, places precisely described but which remain unnamed and which do not correspond to some particular place; then, real cities and countries, but changed, become legendary, nonrepresentational—a fantasized geography within which the adventure of the narrative unfolds.

Translated from "Géographie de Robbe-Grillet" in *Robbe-Grillet: Colloque de Cerisy,* II (Paris: 10/18, 1976), 52–67.

CHAPTER TWENTY-FIVE

Conversation with Robbe-Grillet

TOM BISHOP: Have you ever been interested in the fragment from a theoretical point of view?

ROBBE-GRILLET: Of course. I distinguish two concepts that are diametrically opposed—*fragmented writing [fragment de l'écriture]* and *writing a fragment [l'écriture du fragment]*. Fragmented writing is very fashionable nowadays. Consider, for instance, Barthes's method when he was asked to do his autobiography. Theoretically, an autobiography is a totality that reconsiders, or attempts to reconsider, the important events of one's life in a chronological or causal sequence; yet Barthes chose to provide fragments. And this is only one example among many. The fragment definitely is accepted as a current style. As far as I'm concerned, my first reaction to this is one of mistrust, because there is a certain facility in this kind of limited presentation. Besides, it is somewhat deceptive. You notice almost right away when reading Barthes (and fragments, in general, such as he has constructed them), that his fragments are not really fragments, but totalities unto themselves. This brings to mind the seventeenth-century genre of the maxim, in which it seemed the whole world, as it were, could be concentrated into a maxim.

277

CONVERSATION WITH ROBBE-GRILLET

TB: The maxim, then, was a total and finite entity, contained within itself?

R-G: It is a total and finite thing and it works as a totality.

TB: And then Barthes, in fact, takes over the same formula, only nowadays it seems a lot less obvious.

R-G: Yes, he takes it over in the cunning way that he does everything. Although I am simplifying the issue, I do remember a heated confrontation with him at the Barthes Colloquium at Cerisy in 1977 about this very notion of the fragment. I had pointed out that, for me, his fragments represented in fact a kind of moralistic hoax. The fragment, when you come down to it, often disguises a hidden spirit of morality, as in the seventeenth century. It contains hidden moral presuppositions because the very idea of stating the totality of anything in a maxim is in fact already a moralistic idea. This is true even of the *Caractères* of La Bruyère; they are little sketches that are solitary worlds in themselves and, in the end, are an image of the larger world in microcosm. All La Bruyère does, in fact, is reproduce in miniature the totality of the world.

TB: Would you agree then that they are short pieces rather than fragments?

R-G: Yes. They are brief images of the totality of the world; this, for me, is not modern. They belong to the category that I call "fragments of writing." What I call on the other hand "fragmented writing" is something that belongs to modernity and is exactly the opposite. You can see it in the contrast between novels like Sartre's *Nausea* and Camus's *The Stranger* and the novels of Balzac. When Balzac describes objects, they are fragments in the sense that we have been discussing, that is to say, in the sense of the past. These objects are limited, like a discourse that is limited, but they are an image of the world. When an object is presented by Balzac, it is linked by its meaning to the totality of the world. His objects are signs of character, of temperament, of social status and so on. They define themselves as symbols of the world. Yes, they are no longer pieces, but synecdoches, and the whole world lies behind them! The screws in the coffin in *The Stranger* or the hand in *Nausea* (when the character speaks of his own hand) are completely different, precisely because here the fragment is marked by

CONVERSATION WITH ROBBE-GRILLET

a break *(coupure)*. It is no longer the synecdoche of any global world, but rather a mark of fragmentation, that is, a sequence of ruptures that prevents the world from becoming a significant whole. In short, the first fragment is transcendent and the second one is not; it is, in fact, antitranscendent. If you prefer, the objects in *Nausea* are contingent, while Balzac's objects are transcendent.

TB: Then we find ourselves with a signifying structure of the fragmentary?

R-G: No, no. Here we have what I call not the "fragment of writing," but "fragmented writing." This is the aspect that interests me, and it is this one that is modern. One can identify the same distinction in painting. When a medieval artist paints a portrait, it is a fragment of the human body. But this portrait is a face; it is the synecdoche of a body that is itself a representation of the world. This portrait then contains the wholeness of a world that is totalized. When Jasper Johns shows us a torso—take, for example, the series that he calls *Torsos*— it is on the contrary, broken. His "portraits" are fragments that cease to signify in terms of a totality and which, as a result, no longer have self-meaning as fragments.

TB: In *L'Absolu littéraire,* the authors, Philippe Lacoue-Labarthe and Jean-Luc Nancy, stress the quality of incompleteness that defines the fragment, and they thus exclude from the realm of the fragment precisely those genres of the seventeenth century, including the *pensée* and the maxim, that are not unfinished in any way but are, on the contrary, very complete. But then Jasper Johns's *Torsos* could in fact be considered as incomplete.

R-G: Personally, I think that I would class the incomplete object on the side of the maxim, because incompleteness can be a ruse of meaning (un piège à sens). When in the eighteenth century a maxim is well rounded and neatly packaged, it clearly and openly shows that it is meaningful and has a total, unquestionable significance. When during the same period one comes across incompleteness, it suggests once again a totality because of its gaping openness. One leaves it as it is, as if indeed afraid to reduce it too drastically. Quite often something incomplete has an even greater all-encompassing effect on me than a well-formed maxim, a greater effect precisely because the piece has been left open so that the ineffable may be included.

CONVERSATION WITH ROBBE-GRILLET

T B : I see incompleteness in a slightly different way. Incompleteness in the sense of something that belongs to a whole, but refuses to be completed. Not a sketch that one would return to, if it were good, in order to complete it, but rather something that cannot be finished.

R - G : Who can't complete it? Give me an example.

T B : Well, let's take an example from your own work. It seems to me in this sense that one might speak of your own idea of the fragment in *La Maison de Rendez-vous,* for example. I tend to think that the definition of "fragment" that would be most valid in relation to your own work is that which cannot be completed.

R - G : Well, let's go a step further. To finish with the examples which I mentioned regarding *The Stranger* and *Nausea,* there is something else that is quite remarkable in these books, and that is the fragmentation that is due to the use of the *passé composé* (present perfect). The *passé simple* (preterit) of the eighteenth and nineteenth centuries is really the verb tense of wholeness, where everything is related and linked chronologically through causal relationships. One of the most curious things about *The Stranger* that makes it such a successful book is precisely the attention that is drawn to fragmentary objects, stripped of meaning and cut off from any relation with the rest of the world, like the screws in the coffin. This is tied to the fact that everything is seen in the first person of the *passé composé,* which in fact serves to prevent the pieces from constituting any continuity or meaning.

T B : It seems to me that this is what you do as well.

R - G : Since the time when these books were written, the whole modern period, the "New Novel" and the new "New Novel" in particular, have leaned in this direction. It is not all by chance that I was able to work with Rauschenberg or with Jasper Johns; it is because all their works are an assemblage of pieces.

T B : Which imply the impossibility of finishing them, not the lack of will, but the lack of desire to finish them.

R - G : The desire to prevent them from being finished. That is to say, a sort of system of aporia as opposed to the function of completion that the reader always tends to seek out. How does one achieve this? Well, by putting together fragments that are incompatible. As long as the

CONVERSATION WITH ROBBE-GRILLET

fragments are compatible among themselves, the gaps can be filled in by the reader. But then the aspiration to incompleteness no longer operates since the reader can introduce his entire metaphysical system into this gap and consequently rearrange the pieces to form a system of completion.

TB: Isn't this already at play in the surrealist image? The putting together of incompatible fragments?

R-G: Yes, it does come into play in the surrealist image, but it is a little different. It is more an appeal to a new sense that has not yet been perceived and of which one will suddenly become aware if two objects are juxtaposed that do not belong together. The shock of seeing them together creates a kind of opening onto potential meaning. My own present experiments, for example, stem from these two tendencies. On the one hand *Nausea* and *The Stranger,* and on the other, surrealism; I recognize this double paternity. And so incompatible fragments may be two versions of a same piece, as when in a story for which one has been given almost all the pieces, there is one piece too many that may be a new version of one of the pieces one has already been given. In this case, the fragment is a fragment in the modern sense; an object that is not in any way a symbol of the totality of the world but which appears itself as impossible to be linked to anything else. It works by virtue of its presence rather than through a meaning. It is very interesting to see that this presence is felt all the more strongly as the meaning is increasingly effaced or minimized.

TB: You have already mentioned Jasper Johns and Rauschenberg. Is this idea of the fragment implicit in the collage?

R-G: No.

TB: What is it then that is special about Rauschenberg and Johns?

R-G: I think that in the case of Jasper Johns it is particularly clear, because he has addressed himself to the human body. There are many paintings of Jasper Johns which are pieces of human bodies and there is even a whole series that contains numerous pieces of a body that might indeed be the same one throughout. Perhaps you recall the series of paintings in which you can see the back of the canvas. On that side, pieces of bodies have been pasted together. One could easily imagine that on the other side of the canvas there is a Renaissance painting of a real body that is completely whole. The pieces that are visible on the canvas could in no way belong to that sort of painting. In the conjunction of the reverse side and the fragment there is something that is very significant, very modern in the full sense of the word. There are many other examples in Jasper Johns's work, even in the large paintings like the American flag. This American flag is made up of a collage of little pieces that create a kind of scattered effect. This, however, is no longer a surrealist collage as we see in the work of Max Ernst. In Ernst, we have the creation of new meaning—the body of a man, the head of a bird and the hands of a frog, for example. This is another type of collage, but these are no longer fragments; it is the reconstitution of an entity that does not exist in nature, but which in fact could.

TB: You have written some texts to accompany pictures, indeed some surrealist paintings too, if I am not mistaken.

R-G: Yes. When I worked with Magritte, for instance, it was his themes that I used. When I worked with Jasper Johns on the catalogue for Beaubourg, I had a strong impression of being inspired creatively by his structures and not just by his themes. Of course I copied some of his themes as well—numbers, pieces, the shoe, etc.

TB: And what about your work with Rauschenberg?

R-G: First I must point out, since Rauschenberg's work is so vast, that it was the period where he was interested in cutouts from magazines—*Paris-Match, Life,* things like that—cutouts that were organized on a page to create a plastic composition. So at that time, the work I was doing with him was inspired and excited by the conjunction of disparate images. He would put together one or another object, for no obvious reason, and their coincidence was presented to me as a given entity. In short, he would work on the cutouts, the ruptures, and my work, on the contrary, was concentrated on working on the meaning. You must realize that this type of work with the fragment and with rupture never works in one direction only. There is the temptation, on the one hand, to fragment global objects in order to cut them off from their meanings, and on the other, to produce meaning by the association of objects displaced from their respective contexts. This is what I think is going on in all my latest novels; there is a kind of *découpage* (cutting up) of the global world and a recomposition of the fragments in order to produce other types of meaning.

TB: That's already obvious in *La Maison de Rendez-vous,* and also in *Recollections of the Golden Triangle.*

R-G: In *La Maison de Rendez-vous,* as in many of my recent films and novels, there is the prop warehouse which is very important to me; it is as if all the fragments had been first cut out and then arranged on display. In *La Maison de Rendez-vous* there's a kind of theater court-yard where all the old stage sets and objects are kept, and these are all the objects of the novel. It's just like the prop warehouse in *Glisse-ments progressifs du plaisir* (The Progressive Slidings of Pleasure), where I filmed a good number of scenes in the enormous warehouse that serves all of French cinema. It's a huge structure where hundreds of brass beds are arranged according to category, along with hundreds of Louis XV chairs, and hundreds of pianos, and so on. The prop warehouse is fragmentation carried to a maximum, since here all the objects that could not exist individually in a given story are on the contrary, multiplied by fifty, a hundred, and more, to open up different possibilities for the producer who will choose one.

TB: When you had finished making *Eden and Afterwards,* is it true that you used the unused pieces of the film to make the movie *N a pris les dés?*

R-G: Not exactly. I included unused pieces, but also some of the same pieces that were then edited differently. When a movie is filmed, one has a certain number of fragments that are generally put together in an order that is decided from the outset. But there is nothing that obliges one to do this. In the experiment with *Eden and Afterwards,* I wanted to work with the two great acausal forms of modern music, seriality and aleatory or chance movement, which stand in complete contrast to the tonal or causal system. The relation between the notes in Bach's scale is hierarchal; there is a tonic, a dominant, a leading note, a subdominant, and so on. This hierarchy is of a causal order as the notes have between them a relation of order. Meanwhile, modern music has experimented with two forms of "disorder." The series breaks all causality and causal effects and the principle of chance movement decrees that the same pieces are played at random and placed in the order in which they appear by chance.

TB: It's an experience of fragmentation.

R-G: It's an experience both of fragmentation and reconstitution, of another meaning made possible by the fragment. First we have the fragment, and then, in addition—contrary to what most people say about films done in this manner—the meaning that is produced through the reorganization of the fragments into a new order which is, nevertheless, a mockery. On the one hand, it recovers only stereotypes, and on the other, it doesn't manage to recover at all the entirety of the fragments that are shown. There is a kind of meaning that runs, for example, in *Eden,* through the speech of the young girl who repeats the anecdote of a possible adventure. If you watch the film carefully, you will see that at any given moment there are fragments in the film that are completely useless and, indeed, troublesome to its development. There's another kind of experiment that was done by Butor in *Faust,* with a chance combination of a certain number of possible fragments. Personally, I once had a project for a film called *Piège à fou rire* (Trap for Wild Laughter). I imagined that the film would very often seem to be in its final state, in nine reels, but the permutations of the reels would have been calculated by the authors. That would have allowed a very great number of possibilities—too many for me, perhaps, because in reality, I like to be in control.

TB: Personally, I can't see you writing a novel that is left entirely to chance.

R-G: Nor even less a film.

TB: It seems to me that randomness is not an essential quality of the fragment.

R-G: No, except in the surrealist fragment or collage. The "cadavres exquis" (exquisite cadavers) of the surrealists were accidents of chance.

TB: Could you explain briefly the nature of the fragment in the collective text you did, *Topology of a Fantom City?*

R-G: Yes, that is another example of the fragment used as generating principle. After I had completed *Project for a Revolution in New York* in 1970, I wrote a long story which is now two novels, *Topology of a Fantom City* and *Recollections of the Golden Triangle.* In this long two-volume story, I chose to use, as a generating principle, images fabricated by producers of images, both painters and photographers.

Among the painters were Delvaux, Magritte, Jasper Johns, and Rauschenberg. Among the photographers, Irina Ionesco and David Hamilton. And I also used as "generators" my own films of that period, *Glissements progressifs du plaisir* and *Le jeu avec le feu* (Playing with Fire). I chose these painters and photographers probably because I recognized in their work a certain number of familiar creative constants that moved me or that related to my own creative work. Some of these creative constants were merely thematic. In the case of David Hamilton, it was purely the young women in bloom that made me decide to use him. Do you remember Stendhal's idea of crystallization? He says that when a passionate feeling has reached its point of maturity, anything one meets will crystallize with it. I wouldn't say "anything" (I don't think even Stendhal said "anything") but there is a moment when one starts picking out elements left and right that feed one's imagination at the time. At that time, these elements were images.

TB: One last question that I must ask you, since you are a novelist. For you, does the fragment have anything to do with the relation between *Snapshots* and your novels? Just because there are short texts in *Snapshots,* should they be considered fragments of novels?

R-G: No. Almost the opposite, I would say. In the collection entitled *Snapshots,* there are some texts that are indeed fine examples of fragmentation—the one called "The Dressmaker's Dummy," for instance. Others, however, like "The Shore," create a kind of continuity.

From *Fragments: Incompletion and Continuity* (New York: New York Literary Forum, 1981), 291–98.

Notes

NOTES TO CHAPTER 1

1. Charles Dullin, "Le mouvement théâtral moderne," *Revue de l'Amérique Latine* (October 1923): 183.

2. See *Les Entretiens d'Helsinki* (Paris: Editions Michel Brient), 1961.

3. Ibid., 13–14. Quoted in Eugène Ionesco, *Notes and Counter Notes* (New York: Grove Press, 1964), 40–41.

4. In "Y a-t-il un nouveau théâtre?" *L'Express* (May 25, 1961): 46.

5. John Palmer, *Studies in the Contemporary Theatre* (Boston: Little Brown, 1927), 11.

NOTES TO CHAPTER 2

1. Guy Dumur, "Théâtre en France 1940–1950; Les Années sombres" in Gilles Quéart, ed., *Encyclopédie du Théâtre contemporain* (Paris: Publications de France, 1955–57), 171–72.

2. *Comœdia*, April 23, 1943. Quoted in Dumur, 177.

3. Jean-Paul Sartre, "Forgers of Myth," in *Sartre on Theater* (New York: Pantheon, 1976), 41.

4. Dumur, 194.

NOTES TO CHAPTER 3

1. Pierre Brisson, *Le Théâtre des années folles* (Geneva: Éditions du milieu du monde, 1943), 34–35. Translation mine.

2. Pierre Brisson, *Au Hasard des soirées* (Paris: Gallimard, 1935), 317. Translation mine.

3. Alfred Mortier, *Quinze ans de théâtre* (Paris: Albert Messein, 1933), 279. Translation mine.

4. Jean Anouilh, *Traveler without Luggage*, in *Seven Plays*, III (New York: Hill and Wang, 1967), 132.

5. Ibid., 131.

6. Ibid., 163.

7. Jean Anouilh, *Mademoiselle Colombe*, in *Five Plays*, II (New York: Hill and Wang, 1959), 239.

NOTES TO CHAPTER 3

8. Jean Anouilh, *Ardèle* in *Five Plays*, II, 156.

9. Jean Anouilh, *The Rehearsal*, in *Five Plays*, I (New York: Hill and Wang, 1959), 216.

10. Ibid., 220.

11. Ibid., 235.

12. Ibid., 200.

13. Jean Anouilh, *Le Rendez-vous de Senlis*, in *Pièces roses* (Paris: Calmann-Lévy, 1942), 140. Translation mine.

14. Ibid., 203.

15. Henri Clouard, *Histoire de la littérature française*, II (Paris: Albin Michel, 1949), 463. Translation mine.

16. S. A. Rhodes, "France and Belgium" in *A History of Modern Drama*, ed. Barrett Clark and George Freedley (New York: Appleton Century, 1947), 296–97.

17. "A Paris et Ailleurs," *Les Nouvelles Littéraires*, 1286 (April 24, 1952): 7.

18. Jean-Paul Sartre, *The Flies*, in *No Exit and Three Other Plays* (New York: Vintage International, 1989), 101.

19. *No Exit*, in *No Exit and Three Other Plays*, 29.

20. Ibid., 45.

21. Richard B. Vowles, "Existentialism and Dramatic Form," *Educational Theatre Journal* (October 1953): 217.

22. *No Exit*, 43.

23. *Morts sans sépultures*, in *Théâtre*, 246. Translation mine.

24. Vowles, 217.

25. "Pirandello et Camus à travers Henri IV et Caligula," *Les Temps modernes*, 61 (November 1950): 952. Translation mine.

26. Albert Camus, *Caligula* (New York: Vintage Books, 1958), 50–51.

27. "Godot ou le sketch des Pensées de Pascal traité par les Fratellini," *Arts*, 400 (February 27–March 5, 1953): 1. Translation mine.

28. Carlos Lynes, Jr., "Adamov or 'le sens littéral' in the Theatre," *Yale French Studies*, 14 (Winter 1954–55): 56.

29. Eugène Ionesco, *The Chairs*, in *Four Plays* (New York: Grove Press, 1958), 132.

30. Ionesco, quoted in "Pirandello vous a-t-il influencé?" *Arts*, 602 (January 16–22, 1957): 2. Translation mine.

31. Germaine Brée, "Georges Neveux: A Theatre of Adventure," *Yale French Studies*, 14 (Winter 1954–55) 67.

32. Statement by Georges Neveux in "Pirandello vous a-t-il influencé?," 2. Translation mine.

33. Ibid.

NOTES TO CHAPTER 4

1. Samuel Beckett, *Waiting for Godot* (New York: Grove Press, 1954), 10, 31–32, 41, 45, 59.

2. Ibid., 57.

3. Peter Handke, "Note on *Offending the Audience* and *Self-Accusation*" in *Kaspar and Other Plays* (New York: Farrar, Straus and Giroux, 1969), ix.

4. Peter Handke, untitled note in ibid., 59

5. Letter to André Gide, dated August 7, 1932, cited in Ronald Hayman, *Theatre and Antitheatre* (New York: Oxford University Press, 1979), 186.

6. Letter to Jean Paulhan, dated September 28, 1932, cited in Hayman.

7. Peter Brook, *The Empty Space* (New York: Atheneum, 1970).

8. Richard Schechner, *Environmental Theater* (New York: Hawthorn Books, 1973), vii.

9. Richard Foreman, "Ontological-Hysteric Manifesto I" in *Plays and Manifestos,* ed. Kate David (New York: New York University Press, 1979), 67.

10. Franz Xaver Krötz, quoted in "Introduction" by Richard Gilman, in *Farmyard* and *Four Plays* (New York: Urizen Books), 8.

NOTES TO CHAPTER 5

1. Henri Clouard, *Histoire de la littérature française,* II (Paris: Albin Michel, 1949), 456. Translation mine.

2. Marie-Jeanne Durry, *L'Univers de Giraudoux* (Paris: Mercure de France, 1961), 18. Translation mine.

3. Giraudoux, *Sodome et Gomorrhe,* in *Théâtre IV* (Paris: Grasset, 1959), 80. Translation mine.

4. Giraudoux, *Tiger at the Gates* (New York: Oxford University Press, 1955), 74.

NOTES TO CHAPTER 6

1. Francis Fergusson, *The Idea of a Theater* (Garden City, N.Y.: Doubleday, 1954), 215.

2. Eric Bentley, *The Playwright as Thinker* (San Diego: Harcourt Brace Jovanovich, 1987), 230.

3. Jacques Guicharnaud, *Modern French Theatre* (New Haven: Yale University Press, 1975), 46–47.

4. In Mauriac's "Bloc Notes" in *Le Figaro Littéraire.*

5. It should be noted that these elements remained constant characteristics in his work throughout his life, giving his diverse artistic endeavors a far greater coherence than is often admitted.

6. "Preface" to *The Eiffel Tower Wedding Party* in *The Infernal Machine and Other Plays* (New York: New Directions, 1963), 154, 156.

7. Ibid., 155. "Parade" in the sense of the small carnival sideshow meant to induce spectators to buy a ticket for the main show.

8. In *L'Express.*

9. Ibid.

NOTES TO CHAPTER 7

1. All quotations from *Antigone* in *Jean Anouilh: Five Plays, III* (New York: Hill and Wang, 1958).

NOTES TO CHAPTER 9

1. Preface to Tom Bishop, ed., *L'Avant-Garde Théâtrale: French Theatre since 1950* (New York: New York University Press, 1975), ix. Translation mine.
2. Ibid., x-xi.

NOTES TO CHAPTER 10

1. Jean Genet, *The Maids and Deathwatch* (New York: Grove Press, 1954), 35. All references to the text are from this edition.
2. Translation mine. "Ces dames—les Bonnes et Madame—déconnent? Comme moi chaque matin devant la glace quand je me rase, ou la nuit quand je m'emmerde, ou dans un bois quand je me crois seul: c'est un conte, c'est-à-dire une forme de récit allégorique qui avait peut-être pour premier but, quand je l'écrivais, de me dégoûter de moi-même en indiquant et en refusant d'indiquer qui j'étais, le but second d'établir une espèce de malaise dans la salle."

NOTES TO CHAPTER 11

1. André Antoine, the founder of the Théâtre Libre in Paris in the last years of the nineteenth century. At the Théâtre Libre, Antoine reacted against the prevailing, vapid forms of theater and revolutionized dramatic performance with a new, realistic esthetic.
2. Jean-Marie Le Pen, the leader of the ultraright Front National party.
3. Jacques Chirac, Mayor of Paris and former Prime Minister, head of the RPR, the neo-Gaullist ruling majority party and Philippe de Villiers, a politician currently gathering political momentum on the right wing of the French political scene.
4. The Theater Festival, held every summer in the southern French city Avignon.
5. Contemporary German playwrights.

NOTES TO CHAPTER 13

1. Jean-Paul Sartre, *Sartre on Theater* (New York: Pantheon, 1976), 198–99.
2. Ibid., 200.
3. *Essays on Existentialism* (New York: Citadel, 1968), 47.
4. *Sartre on Theater*, 199.

NOTES TO CHAPTER 16

1. Comments made to Herbert Blau and Niklaus Gessner, respectively, cited in Richard N. Coe, *Samuel Beckett* (New York: Grove Press, 1968), 14.

2. Cited in Ann Beer, "Beckett's Bilingualism" in *The Cambridge Companion to Beckett,* ed. John Pilling (Cambridge: Cambridge University Press, 1994), 215.

3. Samuel Beckett, *Endgame* (New York: Grove Press, 1958), 44.

4. Erika Ostrovsky, "Le Silence de Babel," in *Cahier de l'Herne: Samuel Beckett,* ed. Tom Bishop and Raymond Federman (Paris: L'Herne, 1976), 208. Translation mine.

5. Beer, 214.

6. Ludovic Janvier, "Au travail avec Beckett," in *Cahier de l'Herne: Samuel Beckett,* 137. Translation mine.

7. Samuel Beckett, *Rockaby* (New York: Grove Press, 1981), 20; *Berceuse* in *Catastrophe et autres dramaticules* (Paris: Editions de Minuit, 1986), 52.

8. Raymond Federman, "The Writer as Self-Translator," in *Beckett Translating/Translating Beckett,* ed. A. W. Friedman, C. Rossman, and D. Sherzer (University Park: Pennsylvania State University Press, 1987), 16.

NOTES TO CHAPTER 17

1. Samuel Beckett, *Molloy* (New York: Grove Press, 1956), 34. Further quotations from this novel will be indicated by page references in the text.

2. Samuel Beckett, *Waiting for Godot* (New York: Grove Press, 1954), 58.

3. Samuel Beckett, *The Unnamable* (New York: Grove Press, 1958), 3. Further quotations from this novel will be indicated by page references in the text.

4. Samuel Beckett, *Texts for Nothing* (New York: Grove Press, 1968), 127.

5. *Texts for Nothing,* 128.

6. Samuel Beckett, *Cascando* in *Cascando and Other Short Dramatic Pieces* (New York: Grove Press, 1970), 9, 15, 18.

7. Alain Bosquet, *Premier Testament* (Paris: Gallimard, 1957), 15. Translation mine.

8. Samuel Beckett, *How It Is* (New York: Grove Press, 1964), 7. Further quotations from this novel will be indicated by page references in the text.

9. Samuel Beckett, *Not I* in *Ends and Odds* (New York: Grove Press, 1976), 22.

10. *Waiting for Godot,* 23.

NOTES TO CHAPTER 18

1. The American edition was published by Grove Press in 1976. It contains four "Ends"—*Not I, That Time,* and *Footfalls,* written for the stage, and *Ghost Trio,* written for television—and four "Odds" entitled simply *Theatre I, Theatre II, Radio I,* and *Radio II.* The English edition, published by Faber and Faber in

NOTES TO CHAPTER 18

1977, contains all the above plus a later television piece, . . . *but the clouds* . . . . The "Odds" were all written in French during the 1960s and published in the original French in the 1970s, either in the review *Minuit* or in the *Cahier de l'Herne* devoted to Beckett: Tom Bishop and Raymond Federman, ed., *Beckett,* (Paris: Edition de l'Herne, 1976). Since the "Odds" were all written in the 1960s, they will not be dealt with in this essay, which concerns itself with Beckett's theater pieces of the 1970s.

2. Both the Paris stage production with Madeleine Renaud and a BBC television production with Billie Whitelaw (who had also acted in the London stage production) dispensed with the Auditor for technical reasons, which were different in each case. The television version, concentrating entirely on a tight close-up of a mouth, undoubtedly could not include the Auditor. His absence, though, is a distinct loss in both cases.

3. Samuel Beckett, *Ends and Odds* (New York: Grove Press), 1976, 15, 18, 21, 22, 23. All further references to *Not I,* as well as to *That Time, Footfalls,* and *Ghost Trio* will be to this edition and will be indicated by page references in the text.

4. Samuel Beckett, *The Unnamable,* in *Three Novels* (New York: Grove Press, 1965), 414.

5. Samuel Beckett, *Waiting for Godot* (New York: Grove Press, 1954), 8.

6. Samuel Beckett, *Endgame* (New York: Grove Press, 1958), 55.

7. Samuel Beckett, *Krapp's Last Tape* (New York: Grove Press, 1960), 22–23. Further quotations from the play will be indicated by page references in the text.

8. *Endgame,* 45.

9. Samuel Beckett, *Molloy,* in *Three Novels,* 18.

10. As related in Michael Davie's "Notebook," in *The Observer Review,* May 2, 1976, 36.

11. References to . . . *but the clouds* . . . are from *The Collected Shorter Plays of Samuel Beckett* (New York: Grove Press, 1984).

12. *The Unnamable,* 414.

13. Samuel Beckett, *Texts for Nothing,* in *Stories and Texts for Nothing* (New York: Grove Press, 1968), 128.

14. Ibid., 127.

15. Samuel Beckett, *Cascando* (New York: Grove Press, n.d.), 9.

16. John Calder, " 'The lively arts': Three Plays by Samuel Beckett on BBC 2, 17 April 1977," *Journal of Beckett Studies,* 2 (Summer 1977): 120.

17. Letter to the author, dated March 20, 1975.

NOTES TO CHAPTER 19

1. Albert Camus, "Author's Preface," in *Caligula and Three Other Plays* (New York: Vintage Books, 1958), vii.

2. Ibid., vii.

3. Ibid.

NOTES TO CHAPTER 20

4. Albert Camus, *The Myth of Sisyphus and Other Essays* (New York: Vintage Books, 1955), 5.

5. Ibid., 22–23.

6. *Caligula*, 8.

7. Albert Camus, *The Stranger* (New York: Vintage Books, 1946), 152.

8. Samuel Beckett, *Waiting for Godot* (New York: Grove Press, 1954), 57.

9. Ibid., 58.

10. Ibid., 8.

11. Ibid., 44.

12. Ibid.

13. Samuel Beckett, *Molloy,* in *Three Novels* (New York: Grove Press, 1965), 25.

14. Ibid., 18–19.

15. *Myth*, 3.

16. Ibid., 45.

17. Ibid., 40–41.

18. Albert Camus, *The Plague* (New York: Vintage Books, 1972), 121.

19. "Summer in Algiers" in *The Myth of Sisyphus and Other Essays,* 112.

20. "Return to Tipasa," in ibid., 144.

21. *Myth*, 91.

22. Samuel Beckett, *The Unnamable* (New York: Grove Press, 1958), 179.

23. Samuel Beckett, *Endgame* (New York: Grove Press, 1958), 39.

24. Ibid., 21.

25. Samuel Beckett, *Krapp's Last Tape* (New York: Grove Press, 1960), 22–23.

26. Samuel Beckett, *Happy Days* (New York: Grove Press, 1961), 38.

NOTES TO INTRODUCTION TO PART II: THE NEW NOVEL

1. Vivian Mercer, *The New Novel* (New York: Farrar, Strauss, and giroux, 1971), 6.

NOTES TO CHAPTER 20

1. In Jean Ricardou, *Pour une théorie du nouveau roman* (Paris: Le Seuil, 1971). *La bataille de la phrase* is an anagram of Simon's title *La Bataille de Pharsale.*

2. Published by Claude Simon's regular publisher, Les Editions de Minuit.

3. All translations of those parts of *Orion aveugle* which do not appear in *Conducting Bodies* are translated by me.

4. The following several quotations are from the preface of *Orion aveugle,* pages unnumbered.

5. Claude Simon, *Conducting Bodies* (New York: Viking, 1974), 187. The image of Orion is "contaminated" by the "Achilles running motionless" of

NOTES TO CHAPTER 21

Valéry's "The Cemetery by the Sea," quoted by Simon in the epigraph to *The Battle of Pharsalus.*

6. In passing, I note a curious phenomenon: after my first reading of *Orion aveugle,* I went to New York's Metropolitan Museum of Art to have a fresh look at the Poussin painting. The reproduction in Simon's book is luminous, with rather strong colors; the original is somber, its colors seem drab; I got an impression of sadness from it.

7. *Conducting Bodies,* 7–8.

8. Ibid., 8.

9. Ibid., 8–9.

10. Ibid., 191.

NOTES TO CHAPTER 21

1. Robert Pinget, *The Inquisitory* (New York: Grove Press, 1966), 249–50.

NOTES TO CHAPTER 24

1. Jacques Leenhardt, *Lecture politique du roman* (Paris: Editions de Minuit, 1973).

2. Gérard Genette, *Figures* (Paris: Le Seuil, 1990). Translation mine.

3. Renato Barilli, in *Nouveau Roman: Hier, aujourd'hui,* I (Paris: 10/18, 1972), 115. Translation mine.

4. Quoted in André Gardies, *Alain Robbe-Grillet* (Paris: Seghers, 1972), 120. Translation mine.

5. Alain Robbe-Grillet, *La Maison de Rendez-vous* (New York: Grove Press, 1966), author's note, unpaginated.

6. Ibid., 2.

7. Ibid., 15.

8. Ibid., 16.

9. Ibid., 22.

10. Alain Robbe-Grillet, *For a New Novel* (New York: Grove Press, 1965), 165.

11. In *Nouveau roman: Hier, aujourd'hui,* II, 166. Translation mine.

12. Alain Robbe-Grillet, *Project for a Revolution in New York* (New York: Grove Press, 1972), 160.

13. Gardies, 91.

14. Ibid., 36.

15. Quoted in ibid., 155.

16. Quoted in ibid., 148.

17. in *Nouveau roman: Hier, aujourd'hui,* II, 166.

Index

Achard, Marcel, 15, 17, 28, 29, 31, 115
Adamov, Arthur, 22, 23, 26, 29, 36–37, 55–57, 58, 73, 89, 117
Akalaitis, JoAnne, 69
Albee, Edward, 23, 37
Anouilh, Jean, 15, 17, 21, 27, 28, 29, 31, 35, 39, 42–49, 55, 61, 62, 73, 74, 75, 91, 92, 95–104, 108, 147, 169
Antoine, André, 19, 25, 107, 134–35
Apollinaire, Guillaume, 15, 20, 26, 90, 177
Aron, Jean-Paul, 1, 3
Aron, Raymond, 143, 144
Arrabal, Fernando, 16, 22, 23, 37
Artaud, Antonin, 29, 33, 56, 66, 67, 107, 108, 128
Audiberti, Jacques, 22, 32, 35, 36

Balzac, Honoré de, 252, 278–79
Barrault, Jean Louis, 1, 30, 31, 33, 34, 35, 37, 39, 40, 85, 105–12, 118, 173
Barsacq, André, 29, 31
Barthes, Roland, 243, 277, 278
Bataille, Nicolas, 37
Baty, Gaston, 26, 30, 107
Beauvoir, Simone de, 32, 141–43, 145, 146, 147, 158, 161, 162
Beckett, Samuel, 12, 13, 14, 16, 17, 22, 23, 25, 29, 37–38, 39, 40, 54–55, 57, 58, 65–66, 67, 71, 73, 75, 94, 96, 108, 109, 111, 117, 121, 130, 165–227
Bellon, Loleh, 15
Benmussa, Simone, 1, 3
Bérard, Christian, 83
Bergman, Ingmar, 19
Bernard, Jean-Jacques, 21
Bernstein, Henri, 27

Bertin, Pierre, 33
Betti, Ugo, 62
Blin, Roger, 37, 109, 172
Bosquet, Alain, 113, 189
Bowles, Patrick, 181
Brasseur, Pierre, 33, 35, 108
Brecht, Bertolt, 32, 39, 88, 119, 120, 142
Brée, Germaine, 58, 84
Breton, André, 177
Breuer, Lee, 69
Brisson, Pierre, 41
Brook, Peter, 12, 67–68
Butor, Michel, 23, 240, 250, 284

Calder, John, 209
Camus, Albert, 11, 23, 28, 32–33, 37, 39, 40, 53–54, 116, 119, 139, 143, 147, 212–27, 278–79, 280
Carné, Marcel, 108
Casarès, Maria, 33
Chaikin, Joseph, 67
Chekov, Anton, 137
Cixous, Hélène, 16
Claudel, Paul, 30, 35, 39, 73, 108, 109, 111
Cocteau, Jean, 15, 20, 22, 26, 27, 28, 29, 31, 39, 42, 62, 73, 74, 86–94, 95, 96, 116
Cohen-Solal, Annie, 142, 145
Copeau, Jacques, 20, 21, 26, 30, 31, 78, 107–8, 147
Craig, Gordon, 20

Dasté, Marie-Hélène, 33
Debussy, Charles, 18
Decroux, Etienne, 107
Delay, Florence, 1, 2, 3

295

Delvaux, Paul, 285
Deutsch, Michel, 16, 69
Dhomme, Sylvain, 37
Diaghilev, Serge, 89, 90
Doniol-Valcroze, Jacques, 260
Doubrovsky, Serge, 243
Dullin, Charles, 16, 26, 28, 30, 31, 35, 39, 41, 107
Dumesnil, Suzanne, 171, 172, 174
Dumur, Guy, 1, 2, 3, 29, 36
Duras, Marguerite, 16, 37, 65, 109, 111
Dürenmatt, Friedrich, 23, 37

Eliot, T. S., 35, 68, 97
Elkaïm-Sartre, Arlette, 161
Ernst, Max, 282
Esslin, Martin, 128, 179

Fabbri, Diego, 62
Federman, Raymond, 183
Fellini, Federico, 19
Feuillère, Edwige, 35, 109
Feydeau, Georges, 35
Filippo, Eduardo de, 62
Foreman, Richard, 12, 69
Foucault, Michel, 243
Fresnay, Pierre, 27
Frisch, Max, 23, 37
Fry, Christopher, 76

Gantillon, Simon, 21, 94
Gardies, André, 274
Gémier, Firmin, 21, 26
Genet, Jean, 12, 16, 17, 22, 23, 28, 32, 36, 39, 58, 61, 65, 75, 94, 96, 109, 123–30, 142, 160
Genette, Gérard, 268
Gide, André, 35, 91, 95, 96, 116, 160
Giraudoux, Jean, 12, 15, 17, 21–22, 25, 27–28, 29, 31, 34, 39, 40, 42, 49, 65, 68, 73, 74, 75–85, 91, 92, 95, 96, 97, 108
Godard, Jean-Luc, 19, 23
Goldmann, Lucien, 243
Grotowski, Jerzy, 12, 13, 40, 67, 68
Grumberg, Jean-Claude, 15
Guicharnaud, Jacques, 87
Guitry, Sacha, 15

Hamilton, David, 285
Handke, Peter, 37, 66, 69
Havel, Vaclav, 23
Hayman, Ronald, 142, 143, 144–45
Heidegger, Martin, 143, 159
Herrand, Marcel, 33
Hoare, Quintin, 161
Hochhuth, Rolf, 120
Honegger, Arthur, 33
Horowitz, Israel, 23
Hughes, Ted, 67
Husserl, Edmund, 143, 159
Husson, Albert, 15

Ionesco, Eugène, 1, 3, 12, 16, 17–18, 19, 21, 22, 23, 25, 29, 36, 37–38, 39, 40, 57–58, 61, 66, 75, 89, 94, 96, 109, 111, 113–21, 242
Ionesco, Irina, 285
Ionesco, Rodika, 2, 3, 119, 121

Janvier, Ludovic, 181,
Jarry, Alfred, 19–20, 25, 26, 40, 90, 116
Jeanson, Francis, 53
Jenkins, Paul, 105
Johns, Jasper, 279, 280–82, 285
Jourdan, Catherine, 260
Jouvet, Louis, 26, 27, 29, 30, 34, 35, 36, 38, 39, 78, 82–83, 85, 107
Joyce, James, 19, 170, 177, 178, 180

Kafka, Franz, 55, 142, 157, 253, 266
Kanters, Robert, 89, 94
Kantor, Tadeusz, 12
Keaton, Buster, 173, 196
Koestler, Arthur, 144
Koltès, Bernard-Marie, 16
Krötz, Franz-Xaver, 69, 70, 137

Lacoue-Labarthe, Philippe, 279
Lavelli, Jorge, 119
Leenhardt, Jacques, 265
Lenormand, Henri-René, 21
Lindon, Jerome, 172, 174
Lugné-Poe, Aurélien, 19–20, 26, 35, 107

Magritte, René, 282, 285
Malaczech, Ruth, 69
Malraux, André, 19, 109, 139, 160

INDEX

Mansour, Joyce, 1, 3
Marceau, Marcel, 33
Martin, Jean, 20
Massine, Léonide, 90
Mauclair, Jacques, 37
Mauriac, François, 87, 115, 249
Mercier, Vivian, 230
Merleau-Ponty, Maurice, 144, 170
Meyerhold, V. E., 20
Miller, Arthur, 62
Minyana, Philippe, 16
Mnouchkine, Ariane, 67
Montherlant, Henri de, 15, 31, 35, 38, 39, 108, 115
Moreno, Marguerite, 34, 83
Morrissette, Bruce, 258, 266
Mostel, Zero, 118
Mrozek, Slowemir, 23, 37

Nerval, Gérard de, 49
Neumann, Fred, 69
Nevelson, Louise, 235
Neveux, Georges, 31, 58–62
Nijinski, Vaslav, 89
Nizan, Paul, 143, 170
Novarina, Valère, 16

Olivier, Laurence, 118
O'Neill, Eugene, 22, 68, 97
Osborne, John, 16–17
Ostrovsky, Erika, 179
Oxenhandler, Neal, 90
Ozeray, Madeleine, 85

Pagnol, Marcel, 15
Palmer, John, 21
Passeur, Stève, 21, 31
Pellerin, Jean-Victor, 21, 94
Peron, Alfred, 171
Philippe, Gérard, 31, 33, 37, 39
Picasso, Pablo, 19, 90, 93
Pichette, Henri, 22, 32, 35–36, 37
Pinget, Robert, 22, 23, 229, 240–42
Pinter, Harold, 23, 37, 66, 71
Pirandello, Luigi, 12, 20–21, 26, 28, 39, 41–63, 73, 98, 113, 128, 139, 256, 257–58
Pitoëff, Georges, 26, 27, 28, 29, 30, 39, 41, 55, 61, 91, 107

Planchon, Roger, 19, 37, 40
Pollock, Jackson, 19
Poulet, Georges, 243
Poussin, Nicolas, 231, 235
Printemps, Yvonne, 27
Proust, Marcel, 19, 139, 171, 177

Rauschenberg, Robert, 235, 280, 281, 282, 285
Renaud, Madeleine, 33, 105, 108–12, 173
Resnais, Alain, 19, 23
Reybaz, André, 35
Reza, Yasmine, 15
Ricardou, Jean, 231
Rice, Elmer, 62
Robbe-Grillet, Alain, 1, 3, 23, 70, 210, 229, 230, 233, 240, 247–85
Robbe-Grillet, Catherine, 2, 272
Romains, Jules, 115
Ronconi, Luca, 67
Rosset, Barney, 173, 176
Rouleau, Raymond, 147
Roussel, Raymond, 20

Salacrou, Armand, 21, 23, 27, 28, 29, 35, 61
Saporta, Marc, 250
Sarment, Jean, 21
Sarraute, Nathalie, 2, 3, 23, 66, 109, 229, 240
Sartre, Jean-Paul, 7, 11, 13, 15, 19, 22, 23, 28, 30–34, 37, 38, 39, 49–53, 59, 65, 68, 73, 80, 91, 93, 95, 96, 97, 116, 120, 139–63, 170, 174, 217, 227, 237, 278–79, 280
Satie, Erik, 90
Schechner, Richard, 67, 68
Schehadé, Georges, 22, 23, 32, 36, 37
Schneider, Alan, 173, 175
Schoeffer, Nicolas, 235, 251
Schönberg, Arnold, 18
Seaver, Richard, 173, 181
Serban, Andrei, 67
Serreau, Jean-Marie, 37
Shaw, George Bernard, 26, 65
Shepard, Sam, 71
Sheridan Smith, A. M., 244
Simon, Claude, 229, 231–39
Sollers, Philippe, 243–45

INDEX

Stanislavsky, Konstantin, 20
Stoppard, Tom, 23, 37
Strauss, Botho, 69, 137
Stravinsky, Igor, 90
Strindberg, August, 256

Tardieu, Jean, 37
Tilly, François, 69, 131–38
Trintignant, Jean-Louis, 252–55, 257, 260, 272
Truffaut, François, 23
Tynan, Kenneth, 118
Tzara, Tristan, 20

Unamuno, Miguel de, 62

Valency, Maurice, 76
Vauthier, Jean, 22, 23, 36, 37, 58

Vilar, Jean, 31, 35, 37, 39, 40, 73
Vildrac, Charles, 16, 21
Vitaly, Georges, 35
Vitrac, Roger, 20

Wallach, Eli, 118
Weiss, Peter, 120
Wenzel, Jean-Paul, 69
Whitelaw, Billie, 204
Wilder, Thornton, 62
Wilson, Robert, 12, 68
Wittgenstein, Ludwig, 69

Xenakis, Yannis, 250

Yeats, W. B., 206, 209

Zimmer, Bernard, 94